MANAGING PUBLIC SECTOR PROJECTS

A Strategic Framework for Success in an Era of Downsized Government

American Society for Public Administration

Book Series on Public Administration & Public Policy

Editor-in-Chief
Evan M. Berman, Ph.D.
National Chengchi University, Taiwan
evanmberman@gmail.com

Mission: Throughout its history, ASPA has sought to be true to its founding principles of promoting scholarship and professionalism within the public service. The ASPA Book Series on Public Administration and Public Policy publishes books that increase national and international interest for public administration and which discuss practical or cutting edge topics in engaging ways of interest to practitioners, policy-makers, and those concerned with bringing scholarship to the practice of public administration.

American Society for Public Administration
Series in Public Administration and Public Policy

MANAGING PUBLIC SECTOR PROJECTS

A Strategic Framework for Success in an Era of Downsized Government

DAVID S. KASSEL

CRC Press
Taylor & Francis Group
Boca Raton   London   New York

CRC Press is an imprint of the
Taylor & Francis Group, an **informa** business

CRC Press
Taylor & Francis Group
6000 Broken Sound Parkway NW, Suite 300
Boca Raton, FL 33487-2742

© 2010 by Taylor and Francis Group, LLC
CRC Press is an imprint of Taylor & Francis Group, an Informa business

No claim to original U.S. Government works

Printed in the United States of America on acid-free paper
10 9 8 7 6 5 4 3 2 1

International Standard Book Number: 978-1-4200-8873-1 (Hardback)

Library of Congress Cataloging-in-Publication Data

Kassel, David S.
  Managing public sector projects : a strategic framework for success in an era of downsized government / David S. Kassel.
      p. cm. -- (American Society for Public Administration book series on public administration & public policy)
  Includes bibliographical references and index.
  ISBN 978-1-4200-8873-1 (hbk. : alk. paper)
  1. Public works--Management. 2. Public contracts--Management. 3. Project management. I. American Society for Public Administration. II. Title. III. Series.

HD3850.K33 2010
352.3'65--dc22   2009045583

Visit the Taylor & Francis Web site at
http://www.taylorandfrancis.com

and the CRC Press Web site at
http://www.crcpress.com

To Julie, Emma, Charlotte, and Simon

Contents

Foreword

There is substantial literature on project management. An overwhelming abundance of books, online courses, software, institutes, and other capacity building resources is available to the project manager. But virtually all of it is oriented to the private sector, and the typical assumption, grounded in the "New Public Management," is that the public sector should simply apply that model. That assumption is a fallacy, and *Managing Public Sector Projects* is more than welcome as a thoughtful examination of project management in an environment that is typically more complex and demanding, requiring a grasp of ethical issues, leadership, the complexity of rules and regulations, the politics of administration, the vagaries of the budget process, and other considerations that are almost never addressed in this context.

David S. Kassel presents a systematic and coherent approach to the management of important projects—important in the sense that citizens depend on the successful completion of public-sector projects for essential services: water supply, sewers, transportation, schools, libraries, ports, space exploration, hospitals, and scores of other elements of government. With the goal of helping the public sector establish the capacity to deliver projects as promised to the citizenry, he lays out a conceptual framework that contains five conditions for successful project management:

1. Adequate planning for proposed projects that will achieve the vision of the planners and project managers, thereby creating public value
2. Selection of qualified team members so that the all-important human resources are in place, providing a firm basis for project management
3. Contracts or agreements that are written to the advantage of public-sector agencies, enabling project managers to do their jobs
4. Monitoring and adjustment of project progress, allowing for midcourse corrections
5. Continued active involvement in the project as implemented, thus extending project management and the valuable insights of project managers beyond the "turnkey" stage

Kassel's extensive use of cases underscores the real-world consequences of poor project management, such as unclear project specifications that open the door for confusion, cutting corners and corruption; vague specifications that lead to major cost overruns; inadequate internal controls that allow for poor quality, and often calamitous failures; and lack of contractual guarantees, or a failure to enforce contract penalties that leave government with substantial liabilities.

But Kassel breaks out of the traditional project management "box." This volume is not only about the management of project systems. It is very much about human resource management systems to the extent that project management is a function of the capacities of people, and those capacities are enabled by qualifications, cohesion, commitment, motivation, and many other intangibles that are typically overlooked by orthodox project management approaches.

Potential readers should also take note of Kassel's emphasis on ethical behavior. He correctly presents integrity and accountability as requisites for public sector project management in a way that the private-sector managers do not as clearly recognize. Transparency is presented as a fundamental value that helps ensure efficient and effective project management, rather than the obstacle that private-sector managers might fear. And since most projects are contracted out to the private sector, Kassel argues for due diligence in selecting those contractors; that is, he is assertive that the politics-as-usual pattern of acceding to the selection of cronies and campaign contributors is counterproductive, unethical, and simply wrong.

Kassel rightly notes that that the public's expectations are so low that there is a "seeming lack of taxpayer shock" about project management failures. And the public sector is often blamed for the failings of its private-sector project contractors. But he also notes that "successful projects abound." They are not as visible as are failures, but they are certainly abundant. Many best practice awards programs are such evidence, as are the public's relatively high levels of satisfaction with highways, transit, water systems, and other basic services.

Under the rubric of project management, then, Kassel is presenting an important and implicit pathway to improved trust in government, one that would minimize the failures and maximize the successes. That is a pathway that the public sector has not been able to follow for decades. Projects that are completed on time and within budget—and that avoid what Kassel terms "the negative outcomes that have become so common in the news"—will not only maintain but will build trust in government. Project successes can help reverse a long trend toward declining confidence in the public sector, and may well encourage the public to reinvest its resources in projects that promote the common good. In other words, the citizenry may be more willing to pay taxes if it has more confidence that the money will be well spent and ethically spent.

Kassel also broadens the dialogue by addressing considerations of equitable risk sharing with partners, both private and not-for-profit. Just as important, he recognizes the need to manage the expectations of stakeholders such as legislators and the public. These subtleties are rarely addressed in the traditional literature.

This is an important volume not only for public sector project management, but for the much broader field of public management—a field that is too often concerned with the "engineering" of the public sector, but without a broad sense of the underlying assumptions of the civic society. This book is very much about the future of government. If it is read carefully and implemented faithfully, government will build capacities that will deliver necessary public services, and the public will enjoy a significantly enhanced return on its investments in government and in its standard of living.

Marc Holzer, Ph.D.

Dean and Board of Governors Professor
and
Executive Director, National Center for Public Performance
School of Public Affairs and Administration
Rutgers University–Campus at Newark

Preface

This book has grown out of my more than 30 years of experience of government and government projects, first as a journalist, later as an analyst with the Massachusetts Legislature and the Massachusetts Office of the Inspector General, and most recently as a consultant. A few things have stood out for me over the years with regard to government and the projects it undertakes. One is the contradiction that appears to exist in the public's mind about government and its proper role. On the one hand, we want smaller government and tend to distrust it as an institution. Yet, we want government to continue to build schools and educate our children, provide for us financially in our old age, explore outer space, keep the peace, and much more.

The second is that politicians and elected officials, perhaps mindful of our distrust of government, have worked steadily to reduce government's roles and responsibilities and to hand many of those functions over to the private sector. Yet, the contradiction remains. We continue to expect and rely on government to do things—to undertake projects, in particular, that are of benefit to us. We don't want too many people in government, but we want competence. We want weapons systems that don't cost too much, and we don't want "bridges to nowhere." Yet, these very problems come up in the news repeatedly—a situation that only serves to reinforce our low opinion of government and the politicians' efforts to further reduce the size and role of government, in a vicious cycle.

While at the Inspector General's Office, I became aware of yet something else—what seemed to be patterns inherent in the management of public projects. For example, many problem-plagued projects appeared to suffer from a lack of advance planning, or from incomplete plans. Many were characterized by the shifting of a disproportionate amount of financial risk from the private contractors to the public agencies involved. I thought that if perhaps public sector managers were to extricate themselves from or avoid dysfunctional management patterns, their projects would be much more successful. Then maybe that vicious cycle could in a small way be reversed. More than a year and a half ago, I put some of these thoughts together in an e-mail in response to a call for book proposals for the American Society for Public Administration's Series on Public Administration and Public Policy. The response to my e-mail from Professor Evan Berman, Editor-in-Chief of the ASPA series, was positive and led to an effort on both of our parts to refine and focus those ideas.

After my formal proposal for this book was accepted and the research and writing process began, I put together an informal advisory board of close to a dozen experts in public projects around the country, who also provided me with much help, information, and advice. Some of those experts were former colleagues of mine at the Inspector General's Office. Others were people who were recommended to me or whom I met in the course of researching the book and who agreed to serve as advisors. This book is the result of that whole process.

What I have tried to do in the book is to present findings and recommendations for successful management of public projects in the form of an easy-to-use framework, with Tips for Success for public sector managers sprinkled throughout. A master list of those tips can be found in Appendix 2 of the book. I have also used more than 30 real-life examples to illustrate relevant concepts. A list of the cases can be found in Appendix 1. Some of these examples are taken from investigations and reviews I was involved in while at the Inspector General's Office. Others, such as the Iraq reconstruction, Belmont Learning Complex, Port of Seattle, and Millennium Dome cases, are based on audit reports, other secondary sources, and interviews.

It is my hope that this book will help public-sector project managers better cope with the adverse environment that currently surrounds them at all levels of government and that it will help them achieve success in undertaking projects that are critical to the functioning of government and society. I hope the book is also of help and interest to students of public administration and public policy, who might someday be managing public projects of their own. I also hope the book is of interest to contractors and consultants who work on public projects and who want a better idea about how those projects are or should be managed from the public agency's perspective. And finally, I hope it is of interest to journalists, regulators, and others who oversee government services and functions, and who are concerned with how government can be made to work better for everyone.

Introduction

In August 2004, the U.S. Agency for International Development issued a job order to Bechtel National, Inc. to construct a 50-bed pediatric facility in the city of Basrah in Iraq. The construction of the hospital was to be part of the overall U.S.-led effort to rebuild the Iraqi infrastructure following the invasion of the country in March 2003. Congress authorized $50 million in funding for the hospital project, which was intended to improve the quality of care and life expectancy for women and children in that war-torn country.

The project, however, continually fell behind schedule. According to the Office of the Special Inspector General for Iraq Reconstruction, the completion date of the hospital had slipped by nearly 270 days as of March 2006, and the projected construction cost had risen from $50 million to a range between $149 and $169 million. The inspector general faulted the management of both USAID and the State Department, which had assumed overall control of the Iraq reconstruction effort through its Chief of Mission in July 2004.[1]

The subject of this book is public sector project management and how it can be done better. In many ways, the story of the construction of the Basrah Children's Hospital can be seen as symbolizing the need for improvement in public sector project management, which seems all too often to fall short of the public's expectations. This is not to say that there have not been notable successes in public sector project management. NASA, while it has had its setbacks, some of them tragic, has still been able to capture the public imagination with projects such as its manned landing on the moon in 1969 and the agency's numerous recent robotic spacecraft probes of the surface of Mars.

On a much smaller and perhaps more mundane scale, successful public projects abound, such as a new public library, which was constructed in Harvard, Massachusetts, where the author of this book happens to live. The library has received almost universal acclaim from the town's residents, not to mention an award from the Massachusetts Historical Commission. The $7.1 million project, which was completed in 2007 on time and within budget, managed to seamlessly match a new brick building to an existing, Queen Anne Victorian-style school building located in the center of town. There is also the successful implementation, discussed in this book, of a new information technology system for the City of Seattle that was completed on time and within budget as well.

Through discussion of more than 30 actual examples from all levels of government, the book offers a strategically oriented framework that is intended to help managers, policy makers, and others draw lessons in managing public sector projects and thereby ensure the completion of those projects successfully. The examples involve projects of varying types and complexity. Some of these examples are of projects that were completed successfully, but most are examples of failures in project management in key strategic areas. The purpose of the book, however, isn't to assign blame in these cases, but to help managers avoid these kinds of managerial mistakes in the future.

This book also discusses public sector project management in a context of current political and historical realities. For more than two decades, governments around the world, but particularly here in the United States, have been undergoing transformations marked by downsizing, privatization, and a reliance on markets. We have witnessed the emergence of the "hollow state," as governments at all levels have increasingly transferred their functions to contractors and consultants, from the construction and operation of municipal sewage treatment plants and prisons to the supervision of nation-building efforts overseas. Governmental employees have gone from being scientists, engineers, technicians, and builders themselves to managers of contracts with scientists, engineers, technicians, and builders. All the while, they have operated in an environment of public disapproval and distrust of government, fueled by calls and actions of politicians to downsize their agencies further.

It has not been an easy environment with which public sector managers have had to cope. Ultimately, the hope of this book is to help public sector project managers deal successfully with this current political environment, achieve success with their projects, and avoid the negative outcomes that have become so common in the news. The Special Inspector General for Iraq Reconstruction and several other reviewers have noted that reconstruction projects throughout that country have been poorly planned, construction in many cases has been shoddy, and much of the billions of dollars in U.S. taxpayer funding for that effort has gone to contractors that have done little work or has simply been unaccounted for.

Day after day, we read and see headlines about public projects right here in America that have been beset by cost overruns, schedule delays, and shoddy workmanship. It may be that the frequency of these headlines has numbed people so much there is a seeming lack of taxpayer shock over the details. There is, for instance:

▪ The Belmont Learning Complex, which was originally conceived as a middle school in Los Angeles and which ballooned into a planned senior high campus, shopping mall, and affordable housing complex before it was officially abandoned. The partially completed facility, moreover, had been knowingly situated on a former oil field and industrial site that was allegedly saturated with hazardous chemical wastes. The scope of the project was later scaled back, and the school was finished under a new name, but with a price tag that had risen by 2008 to more than $400 million.[2]

- A $5 billion federal project to build a new generation of U.S. spy satellites. The Future Imagery Architecture project was killed in 2005, a year after the first satellite was originally to have been delivered. The project was approved despite warnings that the initial cost projection was far too low. By the time the project was killed, cost estimates had run as high as $18 billion.[3]
- Engineering consulting contracts at the Port of Seattle, which grew, without competition, from less than $1 million to $30 million in one case and from $10 million to $120 million in another.[4]
- The Central Artery/Third Harbor Tunnel (Big Dig) project in Boston, whose price tag rose from a projected $2.8 billion to more than $20 billion, including long-term financing costs.[5] The project, while a major feat of engineering and construction, was marred by the collapse of a ceiling panel in 2006 that killed a passenger in a vehicle and by water leaks in portions of the tunnels.[6]

Problematic public sector project management is not confined, of course, just to government in this country. As Bent Flyvbjerg at Oxford University in Great Britain points out, many projects throughout the world are remarkable for the underestimation by planners of their costs and the overestimation of their benefits. Examples of those projects, given by Flyvbjerg, include the Channel tunnel between the UK and France, which came in 80 percent over budget for construction and 140 percent over for financing; Ontario's Pickering nuclear plant; and subways, convention centers, stadiums and other facilities in numerous cities around the world.[7] In Chapter 10, we discuss the UK's Millennium Dome project, whose managers failed to adequately project and track both costs and revenues.

Related to this problem is a wider one that encompasses a lack of planning involving the selection and construction of public projects, and a lack of planning for long-term asset maintenance. Sarah Williams Goldhagen and others describe a growing problem of aging and neglected infrastructure in the United States along with depopulated, boarded up cities, neglected waterfronts, and encroaching brownfields sites, and unsafe school buildings, bridges, dams, and potholed streets.[8] Not only are many public projects poorly planned and executed, but they do not always fulfill the right societal missions and are often not properly maintained once they are built. Many of these problems, of course, are outside the job scope of project managers themselves. The planning and selection of public projects are as much a political process as it is a managerial one. We will limit our discussion in this book as best we can to those planning issues that are within the control of public sector project managers and upper-level managers in public agencies.

Among the questions that naturally flow from all of this is what is it that public sector managers do or don't do that causes their projects to succeed or to fail? What, if any, are the common lessons that can be distilled from the experience, good and bad, that public sector managers have amassed? How can public sector managers ensure that the growing number of contractors they must oversee are accomplishing the work they were assigned efficiently and effectively?

In the private sector, there is a fairly extensive body of literature devoted to achieving success in project management. There is a Project Management Institute and a certification process for project managers. Several textbooks that have been published in the field discuss key project management issues and concepts such as the importance of planning and developing the scope of work, risk assessment and management, critical path management, monitoring progress and controlling costs, and project evaluation. But there is little discussion in this literature of challenges unique to public managers, such as how to distribute project risks equitably in contracts with private and nonprofit-sector partners—or how to manage expectations of legislators and the public rather than of shareholders or private clients in project decision making.

Moreover, the private sector project management literature understandably does not concern itself with competencies specifically required for public sector project managers. Public sector managers, for instance, must be aware of a unique set of ethical issues stemming from their obligation to place the public interest first in the planning and execution of their projects. They must also exercise a delicate leadership balance in attending to the public's demand for close oversight and control of public projects without creating an atmosphere of coercion or distrust among the private sector personnel they oversee. They must deal with the complex rules and regulations that specifically govern projects in the public sector, all the while managing within an often politically hostile environment and downsized staffing conditions alluded to above. And they must often work to maintain their ethical and professional ideals and standards amid strong political pressures to relax or abandon them.

In the face of these pressures, managers in public agencies often seem to neglect adequate planning for their projects and to cede that planning as well as the drafting of key contractual provisions, if not the entire contracts, to private contractors and consultants. In addition, contractors, designers, suppliers, and other project professionals are often procured by public agencies without the aid of robust competition or without any competition at all—sometimes in violation of procurement laws and sometimes as a result of legal exemptions from them. Many of those problematic projects are, in addition, poorly monitored by the public entities involved; and when problems are uncovered, contractual provisions that could have been invoked to deal with them are often ignored. It seems apparent that were public sector managers to extricate themselves from or avoid those dysfunctional management patterns, their projects might be much more successful.

Chapter 1 of this book sets out to define public projects and public sector project management, and offers some preliminary observations on key skills, attributes, and requirements for public sector managers. Chapter 2 introduces a theoretical framework consisting of five strategic elements or managerial steps intended to ensure the success of public projects. In short, the framework calls upon public sector managers to do the following:

1. Undertake adequate planning for the projects they are proposing
2. Select qualified project management team members as well as the best available contractors and consultants to do the work
3. Enact contracts and other agreements for the work that are advantageous to the public sector agencies
4. Monitor projects sufficiently by ensuring adequate information about completion of the work; and adjust the work, resources, and the project plans accordingly
5. Maintain active involvement, if applicable, in the operation and maintenance of the asset or assets created by the project

Each of these framework elements is intended to give public managers tools to ensure that contractors and other agents they employ to complete their projects are doing the work at least to industry and contractual standards. As such, the elements are meant to address a salient challenge in principal/agent relationships, which is the principal's inability to "perfectly and costlessly monitor the agent's action and information."[9]

The remaining chapters of the book (3 through 10) discuss each of the elements of the strategic framework in detail, using real-life examples to illustrate relevant concepts. Chapters 3 through 5 deal with the first element of the strategic framework regarding project planning, with each of those chapters examining the preliminary, intermediate, and final stages of project planning, respectively. Topics of discussion include problem identification, understanding stakeholders and legal requirements, establishing internal control systems, developing project specifications and the project schedule, and refining cost and risk estimates. Chapter 6 discusses factors involved in selecting a qualified and competent project management team, and examines organizational, ethical, and accountability dynamics involved in successful teams.

Chapter 7 considers characteristics of successful procurement systems for contractors and consultants, who have become or increasingly important in the planning and execution of public projects in recent years. Chapter 8 provides tips and recommendations to public sector managers on how to draft contracts with contractors and consultants that are advantageous to the public sector. Much of the discussion concerns the equitable allocation of risk in public contracting. Chapter 9 discusses how to control the production or execution stage of public projects, and focuses on effective strategies for monitoring and controlling a project's schedule, cost, and quality. Finally, Chapter 10 discusses the closeout of the project execution stage and examines long-term operational and maintenance issues that are too often neglected in public sector project management.

The discussion of the concepts in these chapters in conjunction with the illustrative examples is intended to bring the theoretical management framework presented here to life and to enable readers to see for themselves how patterns of management can help ensure successful projects. The stakes in project management are high. Cost overruns, delays, and other failures can have disastrous consequences, not only for a public manager's career, but for the interests of the varied stakeholders of the manager's agency who are directly and indirectly affected by those projects. As one public official put it, managers of public projects will forever be associated with their projects, particularly in smaller municipalities. Far better for those managers and all others involved if those projects are successful.

Endnotes

1. Office of the Special Inspector General for Iraq Reconstruction. 2006. Review of the U.S. Agency for International Development's Management of the Basrah Children's Hospital Project. SIGIR-06-026.
2. Blume, Howard. 2008. Belmont school to reopen with new face, new name. *Los Angeles Times*. August 10, 2008. http://articles.latimes.com/2008/aug/10/local/me-belmont10
3. Taubman, Philip. 2007. In Death of Spy Satellite Program: Lofty Plans and Unrealistic Bids. *The New York Times*. November 11, 2007. http://www.nytimes.com/2007/11/11/washington/11satellite.html?hp#step1
4. Washington State Auditor. 2007. Performance Audit Report: Port of Seattle Construction Management.
5. Murphy, Sean P. Big Dig's Red Ink Engulfs State. *The Boston Globe*. July 17, 2008. http://www.boston.com/news/traffic/bigdig/articles/2008/07/17/big_digs_red_ink_engulfs_state?mode=PF
6. The Big Dig project involved the dismantlement of an elevated expressway section of Interstate 93 through the city of Boston and its replacement by a 3.5-mile tunnel underneath the city. The project also involved the construction of the Ted Williams Tunnel underneath Boston Harbor to connect Interstate-90 (the Massachusetts Turnpike) with Logan International Airport.
7. Flyvbjerg, Bent. 2005. Policy and Planning for Large Infrastructure Projects: Problems, Causes, Cures. World Bank Policy Research Working Paper No. 3781.
8. Goldhagen, Sarah Williams. 2007. American Collapse: Is it already too late for America's infrastructure? *The New Republic*. August 27, 2007. Updated December 25, 2008. http://www.tnr.com/politics/story.html?id=9ead077c-1299-4f58-82d5-f3a91bfe19c4
9. Pratt, John W., and Richard J. Zeckhauser. 1991. *Principals and Agents: The Structure of Business*. Boston: Harvard Business School Press. Pp. 2–3.

Acknowledgments

As with any project, the writing of this book couldn't have been undertaken without a considerable amount of help and cooperation from many people. I would like, first of all, to thank Professor Evan Berman, editor in chief of the American Society for Public Administration (ASPA) book series. With skill and patience, Evan helped me refine my idea for the book and then gently but firmly guided and encouraged me through the entire process. My thanks also to Maura May, Stephanie Morkert, Andrea Demby, and the late Ray O'Connell at CRC Press for their kind patience and help.

I would also like to thank the members of an informal advisory board for the book, who played a number of different roles, from answering my endless inquiries to critiquing selected chapters and sections. The members of the board were F. Daniel Ahern Jr. and Pamela Bloomfield, of Clarus Group; Robert Cerasoli, former Massachusetts inspector general and former inspector general of the City of New Orleans; David L. Cotton, of Cotton & Co., LLC; Peter Jackson, a consultant and former project manager with the U.S. Army Corps of Engineers; Patti M. Jones of CDR Consultants; Robert McGowan of the King County Auditor's Office (Washington State); Paul F. Mlakar of the U.S. Army Engineer Research and Development Center; Guion (Guy) VanRensselaer, Organizational Improvement Specialist for the City of Madison, Wisconsin; Janet Werkman, Esq., of the New Orleans Inspector General's Office; and David Westerling, civil engineer with the New Orleans Inspector General's Office.

Others who provided similar help include the late Roy Moffa and Mary Wilson, who along with Peter Jackson (above), managed the design and construction of the Harvard, MA, library, an example used in this book; Karen Richey and Adam Vodraska of the U.S. Government Accountability Office; Melrose (MA) Mayor Robert J. Dolan and Brigid Alverson, assistant to the mayor; James E. Rooney, Michelle Ho, and Jeanne Sullivan of the Massachusetts Convention Center Authority; Claudia Gross Shader, Bryon Tokunaga, and Paige Packman of the City of Seattle; Claude Lancome of Coast and Harbor Associates, Inc.; Steven Wojtasinski, Esq., of Donovan Hatem, LLP; William Sims Curry, a fellow with the National Contract Management Association; John D. Kassel, Esq., Attorney at Law, LLC; Greg Ceton of the Construction Specifications Institute; Dimitri Theodossiou of Tishman Construction; and Brian O'Donnell of the Massachusetts Attorney General's Office. In addition, I would like to express my appreciation to those anonymous peer reviewers who read over drafts of several chapters and provided invaluable edits, suggestions, and advice for improving them.

Last but not least, I would like to thank my wife, Julie Weigley, for her help with the tables and charts in the book, and for her patience, understanding, and encouragement.

Chapter 1

Introducing Public Sector Project Management

Government builds roads and schools (or at least funds and manages their construction). It funds and manages the construction of submarines and bombers, and missile protection systems. It educates children, provides retirees with Social Security and Medicare, helps care for people with disabilities, regulates consumer products, undertakes manned space flight, fights wars, keeps the peace, protects property, preserves natural landscapes—the list goes on and on.

These myriad projects, programs, and operations are critically important to the functioning of our society, and yet there is much public confusion and disagreement over the proper role of government and its fulfillment of that role. Disagreement may exist in the minds of government administrators and managers themselves. Government's role is changing, and with it, the ways governmental employees must go about doing their jobs. As we discussed in this book's preface, some of this change is due to the replacement of many traditional governmental functions by private sector services and markets.

Coupled with that change is what appears to be simple lack of experience and training in management in the public sector. Public projects, in particular, seem to have become symbolic of the mixed record of government in undertaking the public's business.

Public Sector Project Management— Getting beyond the Confusion

What is it that enters the public's mind when headlines appear about public projects that have overrun their budgets? First of all, there is often confusion—confusion over just who is responsible, for example. While the Department of Defense might be blamed for a cost overrun in the development of a major weapons or satellite system, the actual builder of that system was in all likelihood a private contractor or a consortium of contractors. There is also often confusion over what went wrong. Was the cost overrun due to a schedule delay, and why did the delay occur? Was it the result of a problem in the development of software for the system? Was it due to a lack of proper standards and specifications set by the government agency? Were the agency's expectations realistic? Was the delay the result of a strike by employees of the contractor? This confusion may exist as well in the minds of the managers and administrators directly involved. The answers are likely to be complex.

To begin to sort through questions like these and to bring some clarification to these issues, let's begin with the consideration of a very basic issue about which there is much confusion—the question of what public projects actually are. The objective of this chapter is to begin to address the challenge of public sector project management and how to do it better by first defining the terms "public project" and "public sector project management." The chapter will continue with a discussion of public sector project managers—who they are and what are their skills, attributes, and requirements. It will discuss the changing and ongoing conditions under which public sector project managers currently operate; and it will conclude with a short discussion of ways in which public sector project management can succeed and in which it often fails.

What Are Public Projects?

Some of the activities listed at the start of this chapter could be considered to constitute public projects, while some might not be considered to be such. Yet, just what it is that differentiates public projects from other activities is mired in the confusion we alluded to above. Most people would agree that when government undertakes to build discrete things—such as roads, schools, submarines, and missile protection systems—it is undertaking public sector projects. Nevertheless, other governmental activities that do not involve construction might also fall into that category as well. An agency that undertakes a study or investigation and produces a report has completed a public project. So has a public agency that adopts and implements a strategic plan.[1] On the other hand, when government agencies issue Social Security and Medicare benefits checks, or even when soldiers are engaged in combat, we consider them to be involved in operations, not public projects.

Taking all of those examples into consideration, the following is intended to provide some clarity to the question of what constitutes a public project:

> A public project is a temporary endeavor, undertaken, managed, or overseen by one or more publicly funded organizations to create a unique product of public value.

This definition is based, in part, on the Project Management Institute's (PMI's) definition of a private sector project. The PMI defines a project as "a temporary endeavor undertaken to create a unique product, service, or result."[2]

That temporary and unique nature of projects separates them from an agency's operations, for example, which tend to be ongoing and repetitive. Thus, both a new government office building and a document produced by publicly funded researchers could be considered "products" produced by public projects.

Journalists' Questions

As broad as it is, the PMI definition above of a private sector project still seems somewhat incomplete. It says only *what* a project is and something about *when* (it takes place during a discrete interval of time, i.e., it's temporary). What about other journalists' questions that might be addressed in a comprehensive definition: who, where, and why? It would probably be asking too much of the definition to answer where projects are undertaken since they're undertaken just about everywhere. But in defining "public project," we have broadened the definition above of "private project" to answer the question why public sector projects are undertaken and who undertakes them. First, the "why." James Lewis notes that all projects are undertaken to solve a problem of some kind.[3]

An office building might be constructed because an agency has expanded its operations and its current location has become too small. The project becomes a solution to the problem of a lack of space. A problem doesn't necessarily have to have negative connotation, though. Lewis points out that a problem is basically a goal with obstacles in the way of reaching it. A project therefore can become a way to overcome obstacles and reach the goal. As we will discuss in Chapter 3, the planners of a new public library in the town of Harvard, Massachusetts, faced the problem of a declining lack of space for books in the existing town library. The new library building was the solution to the obstacle created by the cramped space in the old building.

In a public project, there is an added dimension to the "why" question. Unlike private sector projects, public projects are undertaken to serve public purposes or create public value. Public value is a broad concept that pertains to actions that promote the public interest and to stewardship of the common good among many other public characteristics.[4] A product of public value produced by a construction project might be a courthouse, a submarine, a school building, a highway, and so on. The product might also be the delivery of food and medicine to the victims of an earthquake as part of a humanitarian relief project. Or it might be the findings of a publicly funded study on links between a particular chemical and cancer in humans. Thus, the definition above of a public project includes a reference to public value.

The question of who undertakes public projects is not as straightforward a question as it might first appear to be. It could be argued that public projects are undertaken by agencies that are supported in whole or in part with public funds. But that raises the question what are public funds. Clearly, money for projects that comes from tax revenues is public funding. But what about an airport construction project that is funded by an airport commission through fees imposed via a surcharge on tickets? We discuss some of the different aspects of public-project financing below.

Definition of *public project*: A public project is a temporary endeavor, undertaken, managed, or overseen by one or more publicly funded organizations to create a unique product of public value.

There is another important aspect to the "who" question implied in our definition of public projects. As we will discuss throughout this book, much of the planning and execution of public projects is undertaken today by private sector entities—principally contractors and consultants. In some cases, often referred to as "public-private partnerships," public agencies enter into contractual, leasing, or other arrangements with private "partners" to construct and sometimes finance and operate facilities that serve the public. Those facilities can range from water and wastewater systems to prisons to highways. In some of these cases, the private partners or entities take on nearly all design, construction, and management responsibilities for the systems; yet, these systems are still public in some fundamental ways. The public, first of all, continues to pay for them, either indirectly through tax dollars, or directly through user fees, such as highway tolls or water rates. Second, these projects continue to serve public purposes in that the broad public interest or stewardship of the common good is promoted by their operation. As a result, public agencies continue to oversee these facilities or systems, usually in the form of contractual controls that determine which costs can be passed through to taxpayers or ratepayers.[5]

Hence our definition of a public project is that it is a temporary endeavor undertaken, managed, or overseen by one or more publicly funded organizations to create a unique product of public value. There is a class of fully or partially publicly funded projects that are largely undertaken by private entities and which do not serve primarily public purposes. Professional sports stadiums are an example. They are consequently outside the scope of this book.

What Is Public Sector Project Management?

Public sector project management is also a source of much confusion. Where does public sector project management end and private sector project management begin, for instance? One way to begin to clarify that issue is to define public sector project management as

> the application and integration of project planning, selecting agents, enacting agreements, and monitoring and controlling work to achieve a unique public sector project vision.

As will be discussed more thoroughly in Chapter 2, the activities listed in this definition correspond to the elements of this book's strategic framework for successful public sector project management. That framework calls first and foremost for adequate project planning to correctly identify both the problem to be solved and the project's scope of work. Next, the public sector manager must select the best possible agents (e.g., in-house staff, consultants, and contractors) to undertake that work and must enact clear and mutually advantageous agreements with them. The manager must then monitor the work that gets done and make corrections or else change the plan itself.

The Project Vision

As previously noted, the purpose in undertaking projects is to solve problems, and, in the case of public projects, to create public value. But project management could be said to go further than that. Not only do public sector project managers manage projects to solve problems and create public value, they seek, in doing so, to achieve a vision they hold—a vision that can exert a powerful hold over them as well.

"You're not building a middle school," says Robert Dolan, the mayor of Melrose, Massachusetts. "Yeah, you're building it for the kids, but you're building a part of you."

A project vision, as James Lewis notes, "literally paints a picture" in a project manager's or planner's mind of what they hope the project will accomplish.[6] This vision may well change over time, but it is extremely important because it serves as a motivating force in undertaking the project to begin with, and, for successful project managers, in seeing the project through to completion. In a sense, the development of a vision in undertaking a project corresponds to the development of a "vision of success" in strategic planning for public and nonprofit organizations as a whole. Bryson notes that a vision of success describes "how the organization should look when it is working extremely well in relation to its environment and key stakeholders."

Moreover, there is something transcendent about the vision of success for an organization. Bryson maintains that it is intended to "excel, surpass, and go beyond the range of current experience."[7] A vision held of a planned project can similarly be transcendent. Great project managers, such as Robert Moses, who planned and managed the construction of so much of the infrastructure of New York City, use their visions to excel and surpass, although much debate may later take place over the ultimate costs and benefits of those visions. Great projects are nevertheless clearly based on transcendent visions.

This isn't to imply, though, that project managers are the only people involved in projects who hold transcendent visions, or that they are necessarily the originators of those visions. In many cases, the conceptual ideas for public projects come from elsewhere. The project vision may come, for instance, from the top management of an agency, or from legislative sources, or court rulings, or other sources. The project manager is often handed those project visions and told to make them work; but, in each case, the project manager must make the project vision his or her own. And, as we will discuss in Chapter 6, the project manager must communicate that vision to his or her project team and to other stakeholders in the project.

> Definition of *public sector project management*: The application and integration of project planning, selecting agents, enacting agreements, and monitoring and controlling work to achieve a unique public sector project vision.

In public sector project management, achieving the vision successfully also creates public value. In the planning of a new library in the town of Harvard, Roy Moffa, one of the citizen managers of that project, had long held a vision of attaching a new building to an historic, brick school building in the center of the town, and rehabilitating the old building at the same time. He developed his vision in response to two related problems. One, as noted above, was that the existing town library, located less than a quarter mile up the road, was rapidly outgrowing its space. Because of its cramped location, there wasn't an opportunity to expand it. The second problem was that the historic school building was falling into increasingly decrepit condition and needed to be repaired under the terms of a lease between the building's private trustees and the town. Moffa's vision was of a project that would solve both of those problems simultaneously. That vision provided the motivation for Moffa and a handful of other citizen managers to arrange public and private financing for the project over the next several years, and to guide the project firmly and efficiently through design and construction. The project was completed on time and within its budget.

Financing Public Projects

At all levels of government, legislative bodies control the purse strings and make decisions about financing public projects. Congress, state legislatures, and municipalities appropriate funding to public agencies, which, in turn, use that money for public projects.[8] Capital funding for transit projects in the United States, for instance, amounted to $9.6 billion in 2000. This included a mix of federal, state, and local funding as well as funding directly generated from the transit operations, such as directly levied taxes and tolls.[9]

In addition to direct appropriations, governments and other entities finance projects by issuing general obligation bonds, which are backed by their full faith and credit, and tax-exempt revenue bonds, in which the principal and interest are often paid from revenues generated by the projects. Due, in part, to taxpayer revolts in many states in the 1970s and 1980s, laws placed caps on the amount of general obligation debt state or local governments could incur without voter approval.[10] As a result, the use of general obligation bonding has declined in some cases. Alan Altshuler and David Luberoff note that in the case of convention centers, municipalities have cut back on the issuance of general obligation bonds since the 1970s in favor of revenue bonds issued by special authorities.[11] In Chapter 2, we will discuss alternative project financing arrangements under some "public-private partnerships" that similarly allow public agencies to borrow without issuing general obligation bonds, thus circumventing the need for voter approval of the bond issues.

Funding for public projects may also come from a range of tax levies and user taxes, such as the federal gasoline tax, which has fueled the Highway Trust Fund. Creative sources of project financing may include such things as State Infrastructure Banks, which have been set up by a number of states to fund transportation projects. These banks create revolving funds, which make loans of capitalized funds to borrowers, who then pay back the loans with interest. That funding is used by the banks to make new loans. In some cases, the infrastructure banks issue letters of security or loan guarantees to borrowers who, in turn, obtain financing through private sources such as banks or trusts. Borrowers may be both public and private entities, from cities, towns, or regional agencies, to railroads or private toll road builders.[12]

Other alternatives to traditional debt financing of public projects include leasing arrangements, in which public entities lease assets from private sources and make lease payments in lieu of payments of principal and interest on bonds. They also include equity or partnership mechanisms in which private entities provide up-front financing for public projects. These mechanisms are sometimes part of the public-private partnership arrangements referred to above. In addition, government agencies may support direct financing arrangements by providing such things as bond insurance, letters and lines of credit, and governmental guarantees.[13]

Project versus Program and General Management

If a public agency's efforts result in a series of products rather than a unique product, that agency could be considered to be managing a *program*. Trevor Young, in a private sector context, defines a program as

> a collection of interdependent projects managed in a coordinated manner that together will provide the desired business outcomes.[14]

While an office building, a prison, a sewage treatment facility, a highway, or a baseball field in a public park might be considered unique products created by public projects, an agency or organization that manages the construction of several sewage treatment plants may be building them as part of a program. To be considered a program, however, Young maintains that the individual projects must be interdependent. In other words, if any one project is not completed on time, the whole program is put at risk and considerable cost overruns may occur.

By that definition, NASA's several missions to orbit and land spacecraft on Mars together constitute an ongoing agency program, while each individual mission would be considered a project. U.S.-led efforts to restore services and infrastructure in Iraq might also be considered a program made up of a series of individual construction projects. However, the interdependence of the various individual projects does not appear to be as clear in the Iraq case as it does in the NASA case. Nevertheless, in both of these cases, public sector managers must coordinate the efforts of the individual project managers. In many cases, program management gives organizations an opportunity to break down what might have been large and unwieldy projects into smaller interdependent pieces, and to coordinate the management of those pieces as part of a program.

We can further distinguish projects and programs from operations, which tend to have no defined ending point. Some of the activities listed at the start of this chapter, such as providing Social Security and Medicare benefits or caring for the disabled, are operational in nature and are undertaken as part of the agencies' general management. The Social Security Administration processes thousands of claims and distributes benefits on an ongoing basis, as does the Centers for Medicare and Medicaid Services. There is not very much that is unique about these individual claims or benefits, and the activities of processing and distributing them are ongoing and repetitive.

Agency operations undertaken as part of an agency's functional or general management are largely beyond the scope of this book. However, an agency's project management activities tend to have important impacts on its general management activities—if only that they often take resources away from them—and to that extent, we will consider relationships between management in these two areas.

Who Are the Public Sector Project Managers?

Just as challenging as defining public projects and public sector project management is the task of defining the public sector project manager—specifying just who they are, the skills, qualifications, and attributes they must have for their jobs, and what their jobs require them to do. We will also begin here to consider some of the key political, legal, economic, and other conditions that public sector project managers currently face as they do their jobs. As noted in the introduction to this book, much of the public sector project management that gets done in this country seems to fall far short of public expectations. Some of this has to do with the skills, qualifications, and attributes of public sector project managers, but some of it is clearly due to the difficult political, legal, and economic situations they have to deal with.

Types of Public Sector Project Managers

For the purposes of this book, we will consider a public sector project manager to be an individual who is charged with managing public projects on behalf of a project owner. A public project owner is generally a public agency.

It is difficult to be more specific in defining public sector project managers because of the variation in types of public projects that are done and because there are different types of public management structures within which managers operate. Those differing public management structures result in different types of project managers, such as the following:

1. **Public agency project managers.** This category refers to project managers within traditional agencies at the federal, state, and municipal levels of government. These managers exist at various agency levels and they may well supervise other managers for each of a project's major processes, such as procurement, contract management, design and engineering, and construction. In smaller municipalities, administrative agency heads and even elected officials, such as mayors, may become directly involved in overall project management. A hierarchical managerial or accountability structure often prevails in these public agencies in which project managers generally report to divisional or agency heads. As we will discuss in the following chapter, some project owners hire professional project managers from outside their agencies as well. Lines of authority can become quite confusing if several agencies are involved in undertaking individual projects or if contractors or consultants become involved in project management roles. We will discuss those issues more fully in Chapter 6. An example of multiple-agency-driven project management involving the use of contractors as managers is the reconstruction of Iraq. A project management case involving a single management agency, which we will also discuss, is the design and construction of a computer science center at the University of Massachusetts.

2. **Quasi-public agency and public authority managers.** This category refers to managers who work within quasi-public agencies and public authorities, which are nontraditional agencies that are sometimes publicly funded, but can also be funded from sources other than the U.S. Treasury or a state's or municipality's general fund. Some quasi-public agencies and authorities raise money through user fees, for instance, while others are authorized to issue bonds.[15] Often, these agencies are overseen by boards or commissions whose members may or may not receive compensation. In these cases, agency heads themselves are required to report to the boards or commissions, which often have approval authority over funding and other major decisions regarding

projects. The Port of Seattle is an example of a commission-headed agency, which we will discuss. Bureaucratic or hierarchical accountability structures usually prevail within quasi-public agencies themselves, but the relationships between the top administrators of the agencies and the oversight boards or commissions are often legal or political in nature.

3. **Private-citizen managers.** In some cases, private citizens may find themselves managing multi-million-dollar public projects. The construction of a new library in Harvard, Massachusetts, which we have discussed above, is one example. Funding for this project came from the town, from the state via a grant, and from private sources. The project was managed by a handful of town residents who worked with a volunteer building committee to approve key project decisions. The library trustees, who are elected officials, appointed the building committee. The building committee consisted of people with many different sets of relevant skills and expertise. Some were elected officials and members of official town planning and other boards, while others were people with experience in design and construction. In situations like this, managerial accountability structures tend to be nonbureaucratic. Relationships among the citizens, committees, and other stakeholders involved in citizen-led public projects tend to have political, legal, and professional characteristics. It should be noted that all-volunteer management is not always a good idea in undertaking public projects. Even in the Harvard library case, the managers hired a professional owner's project manager, as required by state law for public building projects over $1.5 million in value.

As we will discuss in Chapter 6, public sector project managers assemble project management teams that can consist of public agency engineers, procurement specialists, contract managers, auditors, legal counsel, and others. The project managers may build their teams partly with existing employees in their agencies, partly by recruiting employees from other agencies, and partly from outside of government altogether.

It is important to note that while this book is geared toward public sector project managers, many project-related management decisions—particularly in the preliminary planning stage—are made by people, such as top agency administrators, legislators, or other elected officials, who would not be considered project managers. We will continue to use the term *public sector project manager* in discussing these management decisions; but readers should keep in mind that project managers are not always responsible for all of the decision making on public projects. In the Iraq reconstruction effort, for instance, many different agencies were involved in the preliminary project planning that did get done, and some of the planning decisions were made not only by top administrators in those agencies but by the president himself. In addition, some projects and programs use different managers or management teams during different stages of the projects or programs, e.g., planning versus construction or execution.

The recommendations in this book are intended to be applicable to public projects of all sizes, to multiple projects or programs, and to all decision makers involved in those undertakings. The recommendations are therefore sometimes broad in scope. But we hope they will still prove helpful to readers, given the frequency with which they seem to be disregarded.

Skills, Attributes, and Requirements of Public Sector Project Managers

Whatever the managerial structure in which they work, public sector project managers must possess a wide range of skills and knowledge for their jobs. Those managers must, for instance, have knowledge of the key processes and activities that we have listed in our definition of project management, i.e., project planning, selecting agents, enacting agreements, controlling and monitoring, and enforcing agreements. They must possess a number of general management and interpersonal skills as well. Those include financial and accounting skills and knowledge of procurement rules, contract law, organizational structures, health and safety practices, and information technology. Interpersonal skills include leadership, communication, conflict management, and problem solving.

Clearly, no one manager possesses all of that knowledge and all of those skills. Thus, he or she must have the ability to find people with many of those requisite skills, knowledge, and experience in selecting his or her management teams. It is surprising, as a number of the cases that will be discussed in this book show, how often those important attributes—particularly knowledge and experience—are neglected in hiring people for those teams.

Continuity and Change in Public Sector Project Management

As noted above, public sector project managers, like all employees in government, work in a rapidly changing environment that taxes their skills, knowledge, and experience. The following are some key competencies and considerations of particular relevance to public sector project managers. Some of these considerations are the direct result of the changing environment these managers face, while others have always been of concern and relevance to public sector project management. We have listed some of these issues in Figure 1.1 and have provided more explanation of them below.

Leadership and Managerial Competencies

Public sector managers must combine both leadership and managerial competencies. Managerial competence, as discussed above, involves knowledge of project planning, selecting the best agents, drafting advantageous contracts, evaluating problems, and controlling the project to adhere to schedule, cost, and quality

Competencies needed	Environmental considerations
Managerial: Knowledge of project planning, selecting agents, drafting advantageous contracts, and evaluating and controlling the project work. Financial, accounting, legal, technical, and other knowledge and skills needed.	**Bashing the bureaucracy:** Managing in an environment hostile to public service
Leadership: Ability to motivate management team, maintain open lines of communication, and balance personal involvement with delegation of responsibilities	**"Hollow state":** Dealing with downsized staff and the loss of institutional memory
Ethics: Employing personal integrity in the management and expenditure of public funds, and promoting integrity on the project management team	**Managerial and political pushback:** Managing in an environment sometimes hostile to best contracting practices
Understanding rules and regulations: Understanding applicable legal requirements and how to comply with them while maintaining project performance	**Political ideology:** Managing in an environment marked by ideological pressures

Figure 1.1 Key competencies and considerations for public sector project managers.

constraints. Technical, financial, and other types of knowledge discussed above are needed for this.

Leadership is closely related to managerial competence. It involves the ability to motivate the members of their management team, maintain open lines of communication, and carefully balance the delegation of authority and oversight, particularly with regard to contractors and consultants. If managers delegate too much authority they risk losing control of their projects and potentially subjecting their agencies, and consequently taxpayers, to undue financial risks and higher project costs. If they delegate too little authority, they may lose useful advice and counsel of those with more expertise than they might have in critical areas.

James Rooney, a former assistant project director at the Big Dig project in Boston, expressed a common complaint among critics of that project when he maintained that the project's continuous cost increases and quality control problems were due to "a fundamental structural problem" in which public sector managers delegated too much authority to the private sector design and construction manager (the joint venture of Bechtel/Parsons Brinckerhoff).[16] On the other hand, L. Paul Bremer, the head of the Coalition Provision Authority, the U.S.-led occupational government of Iraq during much of the first year after the invasion, may have been too much of a micro-manager of the Iraq reconstruction effort. Bremer insisted, according to staffers, on approving virtually every decision made by the CPA, including reconstruction decisions. As one staffer maintained, Saddam Hussein had practiced a similar micro-managerial style. "Nothing's changed," the staffer said. "We can't do anything without Bremer's okay."[17]

As a number of experts have noted, public sector project managers must continually look for ways to "stay at the table" during the project planning stages and stay involved during construction without causing undue friction among the major players involved. There is often a temptation in public sector management to let the private contractors take over the project, from planning through construction. This may well be the most serious mistake a public sector manager can make. As the State of Washington Joint Legislative Audit and Review Committee has stated:

> the owner agency's close attention to project and construction management in general, and their day-to-day involvement on the project in particular, was the most critical success factor [in the public construction cases examined by the committee]; no alternative contracting model can substitute for the owner agency's close attention to the project.[18]

Ethics and Internal Controls

Public sector project managers face a different set of ethical issues than do their counterparts in the private sector because they are ultimately accountable to the public in a way that private sector managers are not. From planning through design and construction or execution of public projects, the public interest must be placed first, particularly when it comes to making decisions about the expenditures of funds. In a written response to an interview question about the most important *contractual* protection public jurisdictions can seek in undertaking public projects, Paul Mlakar, a senior research scientist with the U.S. Army Corps of Engineers, responded: "The key may be in the expertise and integrity of the official charged with overseeing the contract!" He added that: "The fundamental canon of a professional engineer is to hold paramount the health, safety, and welfare of the public. The respected managers of public projects similarly do hold paramount the wise expenditure of public funds with which they are entrusted."

One critical way in which public sector project managers accomplish this is by maintaining strong policies and procedures to ensure efficient and effective operations, accurate financial reporting, and compliance with laws and regulations. All too often these policies and procedures, also known as internal controls, are not put in place. *The Guardian* reported that auditors found that the Coalition Provisional Authority failed to keep accounts of hundreds of millions of dollars of cash in its vault intended for reconstruction and other rebuilding projects in Iraq, and was unable to account for money being spent by the interim Iraqi government minis-tries. As of 2007, there was more than $10 billion in questioned and unsupported costs relating to Iraq reconstruction and troop support contracts.[19] We will discuss implementing internal controls on public projects in Chapter 4.

Rules and Regulations

It is worth noting that in recent years, there has been much debate among scholars and academics over the ethical, accountability, and performance implications of legal requirements, particularly procurement rules, in public sector management. Many academics argue that public sector rules have become so complex and burdensome that in seeking to comply with them, managers often have to sacrifice the quality and performance of their projects. Larry Terry maintained that as a result of a "global revolution" in public management during the 1990s, the public bureaucratic system, "with its burdensome rules, controls, controls and procedures [has become seen as] largely responsible for poor government performance."[20] Under the banner of the New Public Management (NPM) movement, governments around the world began experimenting in the 1990s with loosening rules and regulations governing public projects, programs and operations, and with "letting the managers manage."[21]

Terry and others have expressed skepticism of the NPM approach.[22] Terry maintained that

> [i]n their zeal to eliminate rules, regulations, and so-called red tape, advocates of liberation management (a facet of the NPM) failed to rec-ognize the important role that rules and regulations play in strengthen-ing the capacity and integrity of administrative institutions.[23]

Many NPM advocates contend that procurement rules, in particular, are bur-densome because of the time lost in soliciting and evaluating bids. Steven Kelman, for instance, has argued that rules requiring for detailed plans for features and applications in the procurement of computer systems can backfire if the technology fails to work as expected or if the original idea was misconceived.[24]

It is important to note, however, that traditional procurement rules, while cumbersome, were enacted for many good reasons. In Example 5.1 in Chapter 5, we discuss how planners of a computer science building at the University of Massachusetts mistakenly presumed that they would shorten the project's schedule by avoiding the state's then separate designer selection and construction bid pro-cedures required for public building projects. The computer science project never-theless ended up taking 10 months longer than projected for a traditional separate designer selection and construction bid process.

We would argue that compliance with procurement and other rules can help public sector project managers successfully achieve the conditions of this book's strategic management framework for public construction and thereby ensure the success of their projects.

Downsized Government and "the Hollow State"

As the Government Accountability Office and many researchers have noted, government at all levels in this country has undergone significant reductions in staffing since the early 1990s. Downsizing, combined with the related managerial trends of privatization and decentralization, have, in the view of some analysts, resulted in a general rise in governmental mismanagement and fraud and a corresponding decline in morale and productivity.[25] The cutbacks in staff have contributed "to an increasingly hollow state," and have "weakened the capacity of many public agencies" and consequently the capacity of project managers within them.[26] Terry points in particular to a loss in "institutional memory" that has occurred in agencies throughout the federal government due to the departure of "institutional elders—those individuals who possess extensive knowledge, expertise, and valuable information about an organization's history…"[27]

With reduced staff and reduced institutional memory, it is clearly much harder to manage public projects, especially larger and more complex ones. It has become particularly more difficult to manage contractors.

The GAO reported that while federal contracting increased by 11 percent between 1997 and 2001, the size of the federal workforce devoted to managing contracts decreased by 5 percent.[28] This has resulted in weakened government oversight over contractors—a situation that has been especially noticeable in reconstruction projects in Iraq. It has also occurred in other levels of government, notably at the state level, and has affected the management of large domestic public projects, such as the Big Dig in Boston.

Fred Salvucci, who, as Massachusetts transportation secretary in the 1970s and later in the 1980s, is perhaps the individual most closely associated with the conception of the Big Dig, described in a 2006 interview with *CommonWealth* magazine how he and most other key personnel with institutional memory about the project were swept out in a short period of time by the incoming Weld administration in 1991. Salvucci said he had asked to be allowed to stay on the job for six months to manage "the delicate transition from environmental review into basic design."[29] Not only was there no transition, he said, he was gone instantly. Shortly afterward, he noted, the head of the Massachusetts Highway Department, which had direct oversight of the Big Dig was gone, as was the lead Department of Public Works person in charge of the project and five people reporting to him. These personnel decisions shifted the control of the project away from the public managers and toward the contractors. As Salvucci put it:

> The only institutional memory is now Bechtel/Parsons…Bechtel begins with an enormous size advantage in any disagreement with the state, and a competency advantage, and now they have all the institutional memory, and there are no countervailing forces.[30]

Bashing the Bureaucracy

Coupled with reduced staffing, public sector managers have also had to contend with a widespread and ongoing political effort to denigrate public servants of all types. Of course, bashing the bureaucracy has long been part of the political fabric of this country.[31] Mark Goldstein points out that John F. Kennedy, however, ushered in a novel concept that an activist government could be a force for good and for solving problems at home and abroad. His words that the nation would "pay any price, bear any burden, meet any hardship" inspired a generation and gave people entering public service a sense of mission. But it was not to last. Disillusionment over the Vietnam War and Watergate turned the country against government, and most presidents since Kennedy have blasted the bureaucracy (Nixon prior to Watergate), run as Washington outsiders (Carter, Reagan, and Bill Clinton), and campaigned to cut the size of government (Reagan and George W. Bush).[25] The NPM, itself, with its emphasis on downsizing and privatization, was embraced by the Clinton administration and formally implemented by former Vice President Al Gore as part of his National Performance Review.[32]

The impact of all this filtered down to states such as Massachusetts, where incoming Governor William Weld referred to state employees in 1991 as walruses, started a continuing effort to privatize human services, and removed Salvucci and other experienced transportation personnel from the biggest construction project in the state's history.

Managerial and Political Pushback

Thus far, we've seen that public sector project managers must exercise a delicate balance of leadership, all the while placing the public interest first and complying with ever more complex rules as they operate with downsized staffs and are taunted by politicians as mindless bureaucrats. But that's not all they have to contend with. There's the pushback they often face as they attempt to do their jobs ethically. The pushback occurs when others inside and outside their agencies do not share their public-interest impulses or are motivated by political or other impulses that thwart careful planning, selection of the best agents, or other key aspects of successful project management.

William Sims Curry points out, for instance, that while competition in contracting is an important means of ensuring lower pricing and improved quality of services, some contractors lobby elected and appointed officials to pressure contract managers into awarding, extending, or renewing their contracts on sole source bases. In these cases, contract managers can encounter considerable resistance to their efforts to solicit proposals through full and open competition.[33]

Project managers can also encounter resistance to their efforts to maintain basic control over their projects, as Example 1.1 demonstrates.

Example 1.1: Managerial pushback in the design and construction of the University of Massachusetts Computer Science Center

In the design and construction of a computer science center at the University of Massachusetts Amherst, project management staff attempted to enforce a contract requirement with the general contractor that it submit complete design documents for approval before proceeding with any construction work. The project was managed by the Massachusetts Division of Capital Asset Management (DCAM), the state's public construction management agency. A number of the project management staff's recommendations were not accepted by upper-level management at DCAM.

According to the contract requirements, the contractor was required to develop 100 percent complete drawings and specifications (known as "construction documents") for approval. If DCAM required corrections at that stage, the contractor was required to submit revised plans for the agency's approval before starting any construction work.

Project records showed that DCAM project management staff frequently reminded the contractor of its failure to comply with its schedule for submission of construction documents for approval. Three months after the start of the project, DCAM's architectural advisor recommended that the agency reject the contractor's civil/site construction documents, which depicted the overall site plan, including the location of subsurface utilities and details for grading and surface drainage. The architect noted that the provisions for drainage were unworkable and that the planned parking area did not comply with handicapped accessibility requirements. Yet, project records show that the same day that the advisor recommended rejection of the plans, DCAM's top management authorized the contractor to begin site preparation and demolition work. In addition, top DCAM management allowed the contractor to proceed with foundation work before the structural design was complete.[34]

Later, after the building was constructed, DCAM staff found that a drainage problem was causing a pool of water to collect at the south entry of the building. In addition, the project architect working in conjunction with the contractor concluded that grades of parking areas and sidewalks did not comply with state building code requirements for handicapped accessibility.

The Massachusetts Inspector General noted that "given this lack of support from top DCAM management, it is not surprising that DCAM project personnel were unable to maintain effective control over the project."[35]

Political Ideology

As noted above, political impulses can thwart careful planning, selection of the best agents, and other elements of successful public sector project management. As we discuss in Chapter 6, the CPA in Iraq recruited staff based largely on their political party credentials—a clear instance in which political ideology trumped other considerations in the selection of staff of a major public sector project management effort. It is a particularly bad sign for public sector project management if political party affiliations or other aspects of political ideology interfere with such things as project selection the hiring of qualified personnel and project cost estimation. The outcomes in those situations are often approval of unnecessary projects, underestimation of likely costs, and poor project monitoring and control.

How Public Projects Succeed and Fail

Now that we've come up with definitions for public projects and public sector project management and have discussed some critical roles and attributes and considerations applicable to public sector project managers, let's briefly consider some of the key ways in which public projects succeed and fail. These themes will be expanded upon throughout this book.

Barbara Jackson, writing specifically about private sector construction projects, maintains that there are two questions that must be answered in measuring their success. First, she notes, did the project meet the requirements of the owner for aesthetics, function, cost, quality, and time? And second, did the contractor make a fair profit as planned?[36]

Since we are considering public sector projects, it is generally not a consideration of the public sector manager whether any contractors that might have been involved made a fair profit. Yet, as some of the cases we will discuss show, public projects can be placed in jeopardy when contractors are unable to make a profit or have lost money. In general, though, the first question above addresses the key measures of a project's success from the point of view of a public manager.

The Project Management Institute similarly describes a "triple constraint" in project management, which it refers to as project scope, time, and cost. What Jackson refers to as aesthetics, function, and quality appear to be considered by the PMI as part of the project scope. The PMI, in fact, defines project scope as the work that must be performed under the project. The scope of a project may or may not specify that the project must meet certain requirements for aesthetics, function, and quality.[37]

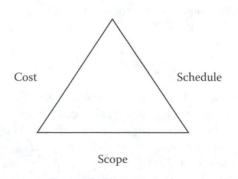

Figure 1.2   The triple constraint in project management.

The three factors of project scope, time or schedule, and cost must be balanced in project management. Successful projects comply with the scope requirements and are delivered on time and within budget. If one of these factors changes, at least one of the other factors is likely to be affected. Figure 1.2 shows that scope, schedule, and cost are ideally balanced in a project, as represented by the equilateral triangle. However, if the schedule is expanded during the project due to some unforeseen problem, this delicate balance is thrown off. Either the cost will have to be increased to accelerate the schedule or the scope will have to be reduced to bring the schedule back to its original length.

John Baniszewski notes that a common saying at NASA in the early 1990s was "Faster, better, cheaper. You can have two out of three."[38] As we will discuss in Chapter 9, many public sector managers become so concerned about meeting a project's cost and schedule goals that they may unduly sacrifice the project's scope and its quality, in particular. In other words, they tend to focus on the faster and cheaper at the expense of the better. Yet, improving the processes that ensure high project quality—i.e., making it better—may ultimately reduce cost and schedule overruns by reducing the amount of rework needed. So, it may actually be possible to have all three—faster, better, and cheaper.

In the next chapter, we will discuss a strategic management framework geared toward processes that ensure high project quality. In subsequent chapters, we will examine individual elements of that framework and discuss cases that illustrate how to avoid project failures involving all three elements of scope, time, and cost.

Endnotes

1. John Bryson (*Strategic Planning for Public and Nonprofit Organizations*, 3rd edition. San Francisco: Jossey-Bass, 2004) defines strategic planning as "a disciplined effort to produce fundamental decisions and actions that shape and guide what an organization (or other entity) is, what it does, and why it does it" (P. 6). That disciplined effort could be considered to be a strategic planning *project* undertaken by the organization.
2. Project Management Institute. 2004. *A Guide to the Project Management Body of Knowledge*, 3rd edition. Newtown Square, PA: Project Management Institute. P. 5. This book's definition of a public project includes both "service" and "result" under the category of "product."
3. Lewis, James P. 2007. *Fundamentals of Project Management*, 3rd edition. New York: American Management Association.
4. Bryson, John. 2004.
5. Werkman, Janet, and David L. Westerling. 2000. Privatizing Municipal Water and Wastewater Systems: Promises and Pitfalls. *Public Works Management & Policy* 5:1:52–68.
6. Lewis, James P. 2007.
7. Bryson, John. 2004. Pp. 224–227.
8. The "cornerstone" of budgetary control by Congress over executive agency contracting is the Anti-Deficiency Act (31 U.S.C. section 1341), which prohibits government employees from obligating spending that exceeds appropriated amounts. The act specifically prohibits agencies from entering into contracts before money has been appropriated. (Cibinic, John,

Jr., Ralph C. Nash, Jr., and James F. Nagle. 2006. *Administration of Government Contracts,* 4th edition. CCH, Inc.) At the state and local levels, similar requirements exist.

9. Transit Cooperative Research Program. 2003. *Financing Capital Investment: A Primer for the Transit Practitioner.* Washington, DC: Transportation Research Board. http://onlinepubs.trb.org/onlinepubs/tcrp/tcrp_rpt_89a.pdf

10. Werkman, Janet, and David L. Westerling. 2000.

11. Altshuler, Alan, and David Luberoff. 2003. *Mega-Projects.* Washington, DC: Brookings Institution Press. P. 41.

12. Westerling, David, and Steve Poftak. 2007. *Our Legacy of Neglect: The Longfellow Bridge and the Cost of Deferred Maintenance.* Pioneer Institute White Paper, No. 40.

13. Transit Cooperative Research Program. 2003.

14. Young, Trevor L. 2007. *The Handbook of Project Management,* revised 2nd edition. London: Kogan Page Publishers. P. 13.

15. In many cases, quasi-public agencies are exempt from state and federal procurement, civil service, and other laws that govern public agencies (State of Minnesota, Office of the Legislative Auditor, 1991).

16. *CommonWealth* magazine. 2006. *Learning from the Big Dig: What Lessons Can Be Drawn from an Engineering Triumph Now Marked by Tragedy? We Asked Eight Expert Observers for Answers.* Fall 2006. P. 61.

17. Chandrasekaran, Rajiv. 2006. *Imperial Life in the Emerald City: Inside Iraq's Green Zone.* New York: Vintage Books. P. 74.

18. Washington State, Joint Legislative Audit and Review Committee. 2005. *An Assessment of General Contractor/Construction Management Contracting Procedures.* http://www.leg. wa.gov/reports/05-9.pdf P. 25.

19. United States House of Representatives, Committee on Oversight and Government Reform. February 15, 2007. *Hearing on Iraq Reconstruction: An Overview. Preliminary Transcript.* http://oversight.house.gov/documents/20071114145606.pdf

20. Terry, Larry D. 2005. The Thinning of Administrative Institutions in the Hollow State. *Administration & Society* 37:4: 426–444. P. 430.

21. Terry maintained the NPM introduced two major new managerial approaches in the United States and many other governments around the world. The first, "liberation management," is based on the idea that managers must be liberated from burdensome bureaucratic rules and red tape. The second, "market-driven management," calls for increased privatization of governmental services and the use of private sector practices and technologies within government.

22. See, for instance, Fox, Charles J. 1996. Reinventing Government as Postmodern Symbolic Politics. *Public Administration Review* 56:3:256–262. Fox argues that much of the NPM or "reinventing government movement" of the early 1990s could be understood not as substantive reform of government, but as "symbolic politics," which papers over a number of contradictions between the schools of thought that make up the movement.

23. Terry, Larry D. 2005. P. 436.

24. Kelman, Steven. 1990. *Procurement and Public Management: The Fear of Discretion and the Quality of Government Performance.* Washington, DC: AEI Press.

25. Goldstein, Mark L. 1992. *America's Hollow Government: How Washington Has Failed the People.* Homewood, IL: Business One Irwin.

26. Terry, Larry D. 2005. Terry, drawing on the work of Milward, Provan, and Else, describes the "hollow state" as a transfer of power and decentralization of services from central governments to "sub-national governments" and to "third parties," such as nonprofit agencies and private firms.

27. Terry, Larry D. 2005. P. 439.

28. United States General Accounting Office. 2003. *Federal Procurement: Spending and Workforce Trends.* GAO-03-443.
29. *CommonWealth* magazine. 2006. *Second-Guesswork: Fred Salvucci Insists That the Big Dig Was the Right Project, Just Not Done Right.* Fall 2006. P. 72.
30. *CommonWealth* magazine. 2006. P. 73.
31. Goodsell, Charles T. 2004. *The Case for Bureaucracy: A Public Administration Polemic.* Washington, DC: CQ Press.
32. Piotrowski, S., and Rosenbloom, D. Nonmission-Based Values in Results-Oriented Public Management: The Case of Freedom of Information. *Public Administration Review* 62:6: 643–657
33. Curry, William. 2008. *Contracting for Services in State and Local Government Agencies.* Boca Raton, FL: Taylor & Francis.
34. Commonwealth of Massachusetts, Office of the Inspector General, 2001. *A Report on the Design and Construction of the University of Massachusetts Computer Science Center.*
35. Commonwealth of Massachusetts, Office of the Inspector General, 2001. P. ix.
36. Jackson, Barbara J. 2004. *Construction Management Jump Start.* San Francisco: Sybex, Inc.
37. Project Management Institute. 2004.
38. Baniszewski, John. *Government Contracting: A Project Manager's Perspective.* PowerPoint presentation. U.S. Department of Energy. Available online at *http://*management.energy. gov/documents/ProjectManagementContractingOfficers.pdf.

Chapter 2

A Strategic Framework for Public Sector Project Management

What are the most important ways to keep public sector projects on schedule and avoid cost overruns and other performance problems?

Responding to that written interview question, Paul Mlakar, a senior research scientist with the U.S. Army Corps of Engineers, wrote the following:

> Begin with a good plan for the work. Check the work continuously against this plan. Anticipate problems before they surprise you. Adjust the plan if conditions require it.

Mlakar has gotten to the heart here of both public and private sector project management. This advice lines up well with a number of strategic approaches to both project and organizational management, including the framework for public sector project management that forms the basis of this book. Now that we've introduced the concept of public sector project management itself, the objective of this chapter is to introduce the framework and discuss how it relates both to the major processes of project management and to strategic planning frameworks for both public and private sector organizations. The five elements of this framework address key aspects in our definition of public sector project management, including the application and integration of project planning, selecting agents, enacting agreements, and monitoring and controlling work to achieve a unique public sector project vision.

The framework elements are intended to apply to the major activities of a public sector project's life cycle and are a key part of our effort to reduce at least some of the confusion attendant on project management, which we first discussed in Chapter 1. Our expectation is that public sector managers, who approach projects with this framework in mind, will find the management process both more coherent and successful. The framework elements are portrayed in Figure 2.1.

Succeeding chapters of this book will give this framework more meaning by explaining how managers can apply the elements effectively to achieve their project visions successfully. It should be noted that a single project manager may not be concerned with all of the elements of the framework. Some organizations employ separate project managers for the project planning and execution phases, for instance.

1. A planning process is undertaken for the project that accurately identifies both the problem to be solved by the project and the project's scope of work.

2. The project manager selects the best agent(s) to undertake the project work based on the advance planning that has been done.

3. The manager and agent(s) enact and carry out mutually advantageous, clear, and lawful agreements regarding the project's scope of work.

4. The manager monitors the project work by ensuring an adequate and accurate flow of information from the agent(s); and the manager adjusts the work, resources, and project plans accordingly.

5. The manager maintains active involvement, if applicable, in the operation and maintenance of the asset or assets created by the project.

Figure 2.1   Five elements of successful public sector project management.

The Framework and the Principal–Agent Challenge

The key purpose of the framework is to help managers cope effectively with a salient challenge to public sector project management. If one views the project manager as the "principal" and those carrying out the project work under his or her direction as the "agents" in a principal-agent relationship, the principal's problem lies in ensuring that the agents faithfully carry out the agreed-upon work. The challenge in these relationships exists largely due to the fact that agents usually have more knowledge, information, and expertise about the specific work they do than does the principal. They also often do that work in locations that are remote from the principal, who is therefore not in a position to observe them at that work. In addition, some agents have different interests and incentives than does the principal. For instance, the principal goal of contractors and consultants is to make a profit, not to serve the public interest. So, how can a public sector manager be sure the people he or she hires do the work they were asked to do? As John Pratt and Richard Zeckhauser note:

> The challenge in the agency relationship arises whenever—which is almost always—the principal cannot perfectly and costlessly monitor the agent's action and information. The problems of inducement and enforcement then come to the fore.[1]

While a contractor is building a nuclear-powered submarine, how can the project manager in the public agency that is paying for the work be sure that the vessel is being built to the promised standards, that corners are not being cut? How can he or she be sure the pipes throughout the interior of the ship are welded correctly? As we will discuss in the case of the nuclear submarine Thresher in Chapter 10, that uncertainty can have fatal consequences.

Each element of the framework, therefore, is intended to address this principal-agent challenge, starting with the need for a planning process that accurately identifies the project problem and scope. Let's consider each of these elements in turn and how they address the challenge.

Framework Element 1—Starting with the Right Plan

As Paul Mlakar advises above, projects should begin with a good plan. Each of the four succeeding framework elements flows from this one. As many of the cases we will discuss in this book show, effective project planning is necessary in selecting the best agents, enacting mutual agreements, monitoring their work, and controlling the project execution. For instance, without a planning process that has resulted in a clear conception of what is to be done under the project, proposals submitted by contractors to undertake the work will be hard to compare because they are likely to refer to different scopes of work. Moreover, under those circumstances, a project manager will have no standard to use to determine whether contractors or other agents have done the work well, making monitoring the project a meaningless exercise.

It may seem obvious that adequate planning is necessary in project management, but it is surprising how often it is neglected. James Lewis maintains that in the private sector, 30 percent of the cost of product development and construction involves rework due to inadequate project planning. He adds:

> People adopt a ready-fire-aim approach in an effort to get a job done really fast and end up spending far more time than necessary by reworking errors (and) recovering from diversions down blind "alleys"…[2]

There is no reason to assume a similar problem does not exist in the public sector. As we will discuss in coming chapters, project planning has many aspects or steps to it. Those aspects are listed in Figure 2.2.

It should be noted that the steps listed in Figure 2.2 constitute a broad view of public sector project planning. Some analysts draw a distinction between project initiation, which might include as many as the first five steps, and project planning, which includes the last four. Yet other analysts separate the development of plans and specifications from the planning stage and place them in a separate design stage. For the purposes of this book, the broader view of project planning is taken, in part, to emphasize the importance of all of these steps in defining the project as clearly as possible.

Moreover, certain steps in the planning process can lead the manager back to earlier steps, making project planning an iterative process. For instance, Step 2, which involves questioning presumptions held about the project, should be

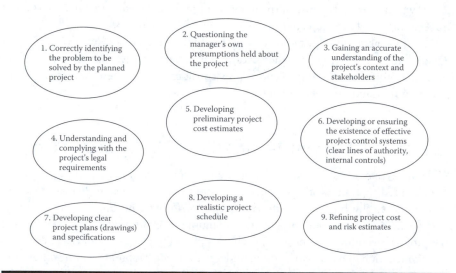

Figure 2.2   Key aspects or steps of public sector project planning.

continually applied during the planning process, and can therefore lead the manager back to Step 1, meaning he or she may then rethink the problem the planned project is expected to solve. Similarly, the results of Step 9 (refining cost and risk estimates) can lead the manager back to rethinking Steps 7 and 8 (developing the project schedule and developing project plans and specifications). These planning steps will be discussed in more depth in Chapters 3 through 5.

This iterative process, by the way, does not stop when the planning stage is formally complete and the project execution or construction phase begins. As we will discuss in later chapters, problems and issues that crop up during the project execution phase may cause the project manager to return to and rethink major aspects of the planning phase.

Framework Element 2—Selecting the Right Agents

As noted above, agents are those people who are hired or recruited by the principal to undertake the project work, which includes the project planning. We'll separate the discussion of agents into two parts. In Chapter 6, we'll discuss key aspects in selecting and building a competent and cohesive project management team. In Chapter 7, we'll discuss steps involved in selecting the best contractors and consultants when projects or key aspects of them are outsourced.

We don't mean to imply that there is a clear demarcation between this second element of the overall strategic management framework—selecting the best agents—and the first—undertaking adequate planning. Most members of the project management team are selected during the project's planning phase, and at least some outside agents, such as architects and planning consultants, are selected during the planning process as well. Other agents, such as general contractors and subcontractors, are selected once the planning process is complete.[3] But even this demarcation has become fuzzy with the advent of design-build construction in which a public agency hires a joint design and construction entity.

Just as it is hard to draw clear distinctions between the successive stages of the project management process, it is difficult to clearly categorize all the roles played by the actors in this process. But public sector project managers do have to be clear on which agents are hired to represent their interests and which aren't. For instance, while an architect and general contractor are hired to design and construct or execute a public construction project, respectively, they do not represent the owner's interests. As a result, many public agencies employ a separate architect or engineer to serve as an "owner's project manager" who provides advice and consultation to the public sector project owner on such things as the scope of work, cost estimating, the qualifications and selection of the general contractor and subcontractors, and monitoring project performance.[4]

Figure 2.3 depicts typical principal-agent relationships involving a public sector project owner agency, an owner's project manager, an architect, and a general contractor.

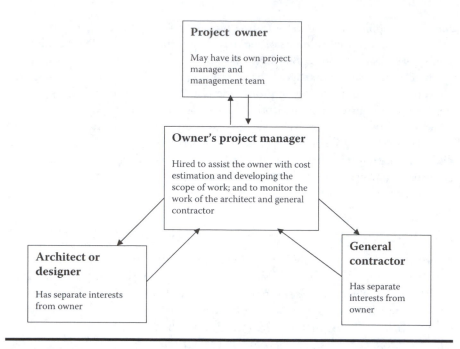

Figure 2.3 Principal-agent relationships in a public construction project. *Note:* **Arrows depict typical paths of information flow about project-related work. There is nothing, of course, to prevent direct communication between the owner and the general contractor or between the owner and the architect.**

In some cases, the roles and interests of various agents can become blurred. For instance, as we discuss in Chapter 4, the Port of Seattle often used contractors and consultants to work on project management teams in roles that made them "indistinguishable" from Port of Seattle engineers, contract managers, and other personnel, according to the Washington State Auditor.[5] The auditor noted that the Federal Acquisition Regulation (FAR 37.104) prohibits federal agencies from hiring contract personnel to perform "personal services" normally done by employees under direct management.[6] There are many cases, however, in which contract personnel, such as clerks of the works and owners' project or construction managers, are hired to assist project management teams without duplicating the services of agency employees. These external agents can be very valuable to have as part of the public sector management team.

Selecting the Most Experienced and Motivated Agents

Both Chapters 6 and 7 describe how public sector managers go about choosing the best agents to undertake their projects. Whether they are members of the project management team or external to it, the best agents are those who have the experience and motivation to carry out the planned project work efficiently and effectively. Thus, this second element of the public sector project management framework addresses the agency challenge in a direct way. If the agents are experienced and are motivated to carry out the work efficiently and effectively, the principal will probably need to use less inducement and enforcement to make sure the work gets done well, as Pratt and Zeckhauser would put it.

There are a number of ways to acquire experienced and motivated agents, and they can differ depending on whether those agents are internal or external to the agency. Project managers normally engage in a fairly straightforward process to determine the knowledge and experience their potential management team members have. In many cases, a manager will have worked with potential team members and will know their capabilities well. Managers can obviously interview and check references of team members who are recruited from other agencies or hired from outside. Motivation of these internal agents is something that can be imparted by a project manager. We will discuss these issues more fully in Chapter 6.

One of the best means of selecting the best external agents is through competition. As William Sims Curry points out, competitive contracting provides a significant incentive for contractors to deliver their services at competitive prices and to produce high quality services and adhere to schedule commitments.[7] John Donahue maintains that subjecting contracts to competition keeps contractors in a "state of healthy insecurity."[8]

The federal government and the states all have legal requirements for competitive selection in the public procurement of services and supplies, for those very reasons.[9] Sole-source contracting by public agencies is usually allowed only under very limited circumstances, such as a public emergency, which will not permit a delay resulting from a competitive solicitation, or the fact that an item or service is only available from a single source. Requirements for competition, however, run contrary to the instincts of some public sector managers. And competitive procurement rules have, in fact, been a major target for criticism from some who argue those rules cause delays and other performance problems in public construction and the delivery of public services (see our discussion of the New Public Management movement in Chapter 1). As a result, contract and other project managers may face internal opposition, particularly when trying to introduce competition in a previously noncompetitive environment.

Framework Element 3—Entering into the Right Agreements

This third framework element primarily applies to agreements between principals and *external* agents, which most often take the form of contracts between public agencies and contractors or consultants. Clear agreements, though, are also needed between principals and internal agents, i.e., the project management team; but it is usually not necessary that those internal agreements be as explicitly spelled out as are contracts with external agents.

In the private sector, *internal* project team agreements may be contained in what some analysts refer to as the project brief or charter, which is a series of preliminary project statements about project objectives and specifications. In addition to specifying preliminary objectives for project team members in the project charter or brief, Trevor Young recommends, in a private sector context, that project managers establish responsibility charts for their projects, which list the key project stages and the names of the team members responsible for work in each stage.[10] We discuss responsibility charts further in Chapter 6.

In a public sector context, responsibility charts combined with a project feasibility study (which we will discuss further in Chapter 3) may serve as sufficiently clear agreements in enumerating the team members' duties. The clarity of those duties and requirements is likely to be enhanced in the frequent meetings and discussions that normally occur among the team members and the project manager. If one or more of these things are not in place—no project feasibility study with clear objectives, no chart of clear responsibilities for team members, no regular professional contact among the team and the project manager, no clear lines of authority between the team and the manager—the project will be in serious trouble before it even begins.

Internal project management team agreements are usually made well before contracts with external contractors and consultants are signed, and are very much a part of the project planning process, although contracts with some external agents, such as the designer or architect and general contractor in a public building project, are signed both during and after the planning process. As noted, external-agent agreements are also likely to be much more complex than are the internal-agent agreements. The reason for this difference lies in the challenge that Pratt and Zeckhauser point to in the agency relationship. It is usually more difficult for a public sector manager to observe, monitor, and control a contractor or consultant's work—generally performed at a site outside the public-agency office—than it is to monitor and control the work done by his or her team members. This is why contracts, which clearly spell out the external agents' requirements, are usually necessary in the former case.

Allocating Contract Risk

As part of the contracting process, the allocation of risk between the public agency and its external agents takes on special importance. Curry maintains that "contracts should be drafted to identify potential risks and describe how these risks are to be mitigated."[11]

This brings up an important aspect of this third element of the public sector project management framework, which is that agreements between the principal and the external agents, in particular, should be clear and mutually advantageous. Regarding the clarity requirement: just as is the case in project planning, the project contracts must clearly specify the work that the agents are hired to do. In fact, contracts in public sector projects often incorporate the same specifications that were developed during the planning phase.

Contracts must also be drafted with pricing mechanisms that are appropriate to the type of project involved and the manner in which it is designed and constructed or produced. For instance, as we discuss in Chapter 8, fixed-price contracts are more often recommended when reasonably definite or detailed specifications are available for the contract work. In other cases, cost-reimbursement contracts may be recommended.

In addition to having clearly stated terms and requirements and appropriate pricing mechanisms, contracts between public agencies and external agents must distribute the project risks equitably—in other words, they should be as mutually advantageous as possible. Risks are uncertainties that have the potential to affect the project's cost, schedule, or scope of work. They can arise from many sources, such as unforeseen underground conditions at the site of a project, unanticipated changes in environmental or other laws or other circumstances that occur during the project's construction or execution, unanticipated increases in prices for supplies, and unanticipated public opposition to the project that might suddenly arise.

As will be discussed in subsequent chapters, potential risks must be assessed during the project planning stage and controlled or mitigated once the construction or project execution stage begins. Interestingly, one piece of advice often given about risk in private sector project management textbooks is that certain risks can be "transferred" to third parties. In contractual relationships involving public agencies and contractors, the project risks are frequently transferred to the public agency. While this is often appropriate to prevent contractors from having to include large contingency amounts in their bids to account for the risks they would incur, it is unwise for public agencies to take on responsibilities for risks that they cannot adequately assess.

Public agencies frequently take on risky contractual responsibilities under some long-term "design-build-operate" (DBO) contracts, according to Janet Werkman and David Westerling. Under these contracts, which often have terms of 20 or more years, private firms design, build, and operate assets ranging from tolled highways to water or wastewater treatment systems to prisons, and other facilities. Because major project risk factors are impossible to quantify accurately over such long periods of time, the financial risks of the projects are often contractually transferred to the public parties.[12] The contracts are sometimes referred to as "public-private partnerships," as discussed in Chapter 1; but, particularly at the local level, most of these arrangements should be viewed strictly as business transactions, Pamela Bloomfield contends.[13] In Chapter 8, we discuss two examples of these arrangements—the North East Solid Waste Committee public-private partnership and the Lynn, Massachusetts, wastewater and sewer privatization project.

As previously noted, many so-called public-private partnerships also involve nontraditional, contractual financing arrangements, such as concession arrangements under which the private contractors make up-front cash payments or loans to the public agencies at the start of the agreements. These loans must then be paid back by the public agencies in the form of service fees that can escalate substantially over the terms of the contracts. As Werkman and Westerling explain, some of these agreements allow the public agencies to incur expenses without legally incurring public debt. As a result, the agreements are often accompanied by public statements that the projects entail little or no risk or cost to the public. In fact, they many entail substantial costs over decades.

Example 2.1: Nontraditional financing risks in the Cranston, Rhode Island, wastewater treatment system

In 1997, the city of Cranston, Rhode Island's aging wastewater system was failing to meet federal and state environmental regulations. According to Werkman and Westerling, the city was facing serious financial problems as well, and did not have the funds to make the needed repairs to the wastewater treatment system.[14]

The city thought it had found the solution to its problems by entering into a 25-year DBO contract with a contractor who had agreed as part of its treatment plant upgrade to provide the city with an upfront cash advance of $48 million. Under the terms of the contract, Cranston would repay the cash advance through a stream of payments over the 25-year term.

The city signed an initial DBO lease contract with Triton Ocean State LLC. In 2001 Triton delegated its rights and obligations under the contract to U.S. Filter Operating Services, Inc., and the contract was extended for five years.[15]

An analysis that the city presented to the U.S. Environmental Protection Agency in 1997 projected that the city would save as much as the entire $48 million cash advance over the initial 25-year contract period. The analysis was based on a projected improvement in the city's credit rating due to the contract, and a projected lowering of wastewater service fees during the early years of the contract. The city planned to use the up-front financing to reduce a cumulative municipal deficit and pay off existing general obligation bonds.

However, the city's bond rating failed to improve after the DBO contract was signed. In fact, Cranston's general obligation bonds were downgraded from Baa-1 to Baa-2 in June 1997 due to a slight deterioration in the city's financial condition, and remained unchanged for the next two years. Werkman and Westerling concluded that

> focusing narrowly on perceived benefits without critically analyzing long-term cost projections and risks presented by a DBO contract can be misleading.[16]

Werkman and Westerling maintained that the city's prediction that the DBO contract combined with the up-front financing would improve its credit rating ran contrary to common sense and to criteria published by municipal bond rating agencies. While the city had avoided the need to issue general obligation bonds to finance the treatment system repairs, its long-term contractual obligations were the equivalent of debt in the eyes of the rating agencies. Moreover, the rating agencies tend to view "one-shot" budget fixes to meet recurring municipal expenses as unwise, Werkman and Westerling noted.

The city's bond rating did not recover to its pre-privatization level until 2008. In the meantime, the sewage treatment plant encountered several expensive problems, including spillages of 1.8 million gallons of untreated sewage into nearby waters, the spillage of thousands of gallons of sludge onto a city street in 2003, and numerous odor and arsenic and cadmium emissions problems in violation of environmental regulations. In the 10 years following the privatization contract, sewer rates jumped 55 percent. As Food and Water Watch, a nonprofit consumer organization, summed it up, "Cranston is paying too much for a bad deal."[17]

In addition to nontraditional financing arrangements, contract terms that can have significant impacts on project risk allocations are those that concern potential future changes in law, changes in circumstances, and differing site conditions. It may seem an obvious point to make that public sector project managers should ensure that contractual terms allocate project risks equitably between the public principal and external agents; but as a number cases we will discuss show, this is easier said than done. As in the Cranston case above, public agencies often find—or think—they have little choice but to enter into contracts with private contractors that saddle them with most of the project risks. As noted, some local governments, in particular, find they are not in a position to finance required wastewater treatment facilities due to taxpayer-imposed debt limits. Thus, public entities may also face strong political pressure to enter into expensive and risky contractual arrangements.

Contracts and Asymmetry of Information

We noted earlier that one of the characteristics of the principal-agent challenge is that private agents frequently have more knowledge, information, and expertise about the work involved in the project than does the public sector principal. That, of course, is why the private agent is hired in the first place; but this asymmetry of information also puts the principal at a disadvantage in the drafting of contracts for the work. Long-term DBO contracts, in particular, tend to be highly complex, and many public sector managers do not have the legal and engineering training to fully understand their key provisions. Ironically, this imbalance of expertise may have worsened in recent years as a result of government downsizing trends that we discussed in Chapter 1, and of the resulting loss in expertise and institutional memory in government in many areas. As long as this brain-drain from the public to the private sector persists, it will be an uphill battle for public sector project managers to fully protect the public interest in project contracting and consequently to maintain public trust and confidence in government.

Framework Element 4—Monitoring and Controlling the Project Execution

The fourth aspect of the project-management framework applies primarily to the production or execution phase of the project, after the planning is complete. While adequate planning and the enactment of mutually advantageous contract terms are necessary for effective public sector project management, they are, by themselves, not enough to ensure that the work gets done satisfactorily. Once the planning is done and the contracts are signed, public sector project managers must see to it that the actual project work is carefully monitored, that effective work-related adjustments are made to emerging risks and problems, and that project agreements are enforced. As Paul Mlakar notes at the opening of this chapter, the manager must check the work continuously against the plan, anticipate problems before they surprise him or her, and adjust the plan if conditions require it. Trevor Young notes three tasks of project control: measuring, evaluating, and correcting.[18] We will discuss these tasks in Chapter 9.

Ensuring Adequate Information about the Project Work

As part of the "measuring" task of project control, adequate and accurate information about the project work must flow from the agent(s) to the project manager and his or her team. The manager and the team must constantly assess that information and compare it to the project's specifications, schedule, projected cost, and other aspects established during the project's planning phase.

Again, the statements above may seem obvious, but project and contract monitoring is often an area of critical neglect in public sector management. Each of five states surveyed by the Government Accountability Office about privatized functions reported that monitoring contractors' performance was the "weakest link in their privatization process."[19] Once again, governmental downsizing and the resulting lack of personnel available in many public agencies with expertise in contract monitoring may be responsible for this. In many cases, public sector agencies, lacking in-house expertise, hire consultants and contractors to monitor the project-related work of other consultants and contractors. The danger in this practice is that the spreading pattern of privatization of public sector functions continually raises the principal-agent problem discussed earlier—how does the public sector manager ensure that the external agents he or she has hired to monitor other external agents are doing *their own* monitoring jobs satisfactorily?

Moreover, as public sector managers hire more and more contractors and consultants to do the work that used to be done in house, they lose their own capacity to manage projects, from planning through execution and monitoring. The result is the emergence of the "hollow state" that we discussed in Chapter 1.

As many of the cases we will discuss in this book show, while contractors and consultants perform important work on public projects, public sector managerial involvement continues to be vitally important, particularly when it comes to maintaining control during the project execution and operations phases. Among the issues that public sector managers must continue to track are:

- Compliance with the project's legal requirements
- Whether the project's many stakeholders understand and are satisfied with the progress being made on the project
- Whether the project objectives are being met and whether those objectives remain appropriate

- Whether project risks are under control
- Whether the project's cost estimates are being met or exceeded
- Whether the project schedule is being met
- Whether the project specifications are being met

The public sector manager may seek advice from private consultants on all of those issues, but he or she has to make his or her own judgments about them in the end. Federal regulations, in fact, forbid contractors and consultants from engaging in governmental policy making.[20] Thus, only public sector personnel can and should make final decisions about the types of projects to undertake and whether final plans and project-related work, once underway, are appropriate to the circumstances. If public sector managers and policy makers retreat from the scene once they hire external agents to undertake public projects, a critical aspect of their duty to serve the public interest is lost.

Enforcing Appropriate Agreements

A key part of project control involves making effective use of both leverage in terms of contract protections and of the information gained through contract monitoring. As Pratt and Zeckhauser note: "The parties whose interests are affected by others' actions [the principals] must be willing and able to oversee and influence the behavior of their agents."[21]

If the contract requires the contractor to complete the project by a certain date or specifies that the contractor must use materials of a specific quality in the construction of a building or a submarine, the public sector manager must be willing and able to enforce those requirements and specifications. Those enforcement actions usually take the form of penalizing or terminating agents who fail to abide by the terms and provisions of the contracts. Of course, those penalty and termination provisions must be in the contract as well.

If the public sector manager does not exercise those enforcement provisions when it is warranted, he or she sends a strong signal to the contractor (and to other contractors who do business with the manager's agency) that the agency's contract provisions can be disregarded with impunity. A contractor obviously has a strong incentive to reduce its costs and increase its profit. If a contractor knows that it can substitute lower-cost materials that are inferior to those specified by the contract and not be penalized, the contractor will have a strong incentive to do so. Certainly, not all contractors will succumb to that temptation. But why give them that temptation to begin with? Not only does nonenforcement of contract provisions enable contractors to either undercut the bids of other contractors who intend to fully comply with the provisions or cut costs during the project execution, but the use of those inferior materials could cause serious performance and even safety problems in the resulting product.

Despite those potential consequences, nonenforcement of contract provisions is yet another frequent weakness of public sector contract management. In Chapter

9, we discuss the failure of public agency project managers to enforce contract provisions in the construction of the University of Massachusetts Computer Science Center. There are many reasons that public sector agencies forego the benefits of enforcing contract provisions. In some cases, it is the result of an inappropriately close relationship between the contractor and the public agency. In other cases, it is simply a matter of cost. Local governments in particular may find themselves unable to afford the cost of monitoring and enforcement. It should be pointed out, however, that prior to signing a contract, a public manager and his or her team should carefully assess those potential costs, such as legal fees that might be incurred. A public agency should not enter into contracts whose provisions are deemed to be too expensive to enforce.

It is also important to note that a public sector manager's willingness to enforce contract provisions does not mean that the public sector manager cannot have a cooperative and mutually beneficial relationship with his or her contracting agents. "Partnering," in fact, is a growing practice in public and private construction in which key stakeholders—the project management team, contractors, designers, subcontractors, suppliers, and others—establish a "mutually acceptable protocol for communication and conflict resolution" early in the project.[22]

A partnering provision may, in fact, be included in the contract. But partnering does not mean that the public sector project manager waives or changes other contract requirements.[23] The ideal situation is one in which a spirit of trust and cooperation exists among all the players. But the contract provisions and their enforcement must remain as an option for the public jurisdiction if things do go wrong. As Peter Jackson, a citizen-manager of the construction of the new library in Harvard, Massachusetts, put it:

> We treated this (project) as a partnership between the architect, the (owner's) project manager, the contractor, and us. By having…meetings every week with everybody there, it really developed into a partnership, so no one grabbed the contract and said "no, it says it right here." We knew it (the contract) was there.

Framework Element 5—Maintaining Active Involvement in the Operation and Maintenance of the Asset or Assets Created by the Project

As a public project nears substantial completion, the project manager's attention will generally be fully absorbed in the closeout of the execution stage, which can include such things as completion of final "punch-list" items, testing of equipment and systems, and training of owner's personnel in the operation and maintenance of those systems. But once the closeout is complete, the manager's involvement with the project often does not come to an end. The focus now shifts to the long-term operation and maintenance of the asset or assets, if any, that have been created by the project.

In some cases, the same public sector manager or team that oversaw the design and construction or execution of the project will remain in place during the operations and maintenance stages. In other instances, the management team will change entirely, as will the public agency or agencies involved with the project. But in most cases, at least some public sector managers will need to maintain an active measuring, evaluating, and correcting process for months or years after the project execution stage has been completed. In Chapter 10, we will discuss operational issues as well as the all-too-common neglect by public agencies in this country of the long-term maintenance of public assets, and the dire consequences of that neglect. A public agency's managerial responsibilities clearly do not end once a bridge is constructed or a satellite is launched or a new computer system is installed in a government office.

Placing the Strategic Management Framework in Context

The strategic framework for public sector project management that we have just introduced is intended, as noted, to apply to the major activities of a public project's life cycle. Those activities can be grouped into phases that are common to both public and private sector projects. In the private sector, the Project Management Institute identifies five major project processes: initiating, planning, executing, monitoring and controlling, and closing. Those processes, in turn, are based on the "Plan-Do-Study-Act Cycle," which was developed under the influential business management model known as Total Quality Management.[24]

The private sector project management approach begins with attention to planning or initiating processes, which involve establishing a definition of the project and its objectives as well as the development of a detailed scope of work. This book's *public sector* management framework groups those activities under the first framework element involving a planning process that accurately identifies the project problem and scope of work.

The subsequent executing and monitoring and controlling processes in the private sector model concern the work done under the project and the measures taken to monitor the work and take corrective actions when the work deviates from the plan. The corresponding element in the framework in this book to those processes is element 4, which concerns the flow of adequate and accurate information about the project work to the principal and the enforcement of contractual agreements. Prior to those elements, however, this book's framework inserts two additional elements that are critical to public sector project management and which must be in place before major project work can begin: the selection of the best agents for the work (element 2) and the enactment of clear and mutually advantageous project agreements (element 3).

The elements of this public sector project management framework are also intended to correspond to strategic management approaches used in public sector organizations as a whole. John Bryson states that

> strategic **planning** (in public and nonprofit organizations) is first and foremost about clarifying (an agency's) mission, mandates, vision, goals, and the nature of the common good and public value to be created—doing the right things—whereas (strategic) **management** is about making sure those things are done well through strategies and operations at reasonable cost.[25]

Similarly, the framework in this book is intended to help public sector managers both do the right things with their projects through proper planning, and make sure they are done well and at a reasonable cost through proper project execution.

Endnotes

1. Pratt, John W., and Richard J. Zeckhauser. 1991. *Principals and Agents: The Structure of Business.* Boston: Harvard Business School Press. P. 3.
2. Lewis, James P. 2007. *Fundamentals of Project Management,* 3rd edition. New York: American Management Association. P. 3.
3. The terms *principals* and *agents* are not used in this book in a legal sense in which agents have a fiduciary duty to act on behalf of the principal. A principal and an agent are considered, as Pratt and Zeckhauser (1991) express it, to be "parties bound together by an agreement that attempts to align *divergent motivations*" (emphasis added) P. ix.
4. Commonwealth of Massachusetts, Office of the Inspector General. 2005. *Designing and Constructing Public Facilities: Legal Requirements, Recommended Practices, Sources of Assistance.* http://www.mass.gov/ig/publ/dcmanual.pdf.
5. Washington State Auditor. 2007. *Performance Audit Report: Port of Seattle Construction Management.*
6. The Washington State Auditor further criticized the Port of Seattle's consultant personnel practice as unduly expensive because certain Port of Seattle contracts stipulated that the consultants' salaries were to be increased by a fixed multiplier (Washington State Auditor, 2007, P. 78).
7. Curry, William. 2008. *Contracting for Services in State and Local Government Agencies.* Taylor & Francis.
8. Donahue, John D. 1989. *The Privatization Decision: Public Ends, Private Means.* New York: Basic Books. P. 218.
9. See for example Heisse, John R. (ed.) 1997. *The Design/Build Process: A Guide to Licensing and Procurement Requirements in the Fifty States and Canada.* American Bar Association.
10. Young, Trevor L. 2007. *The Handbook of Project Management,* revised 2nd edition. London: Kogan Page Publishers.
11. Curry, William. 2008.
12. Werkman, Janet, and David L. Westerling. 2000. Privatizing Municipal Water and Wastewater Systems: Promises and Pitfalls. *Public Works Management & Policy* 5:1:52–68.

13. Bloomfield, Pamela. 2006. The Challenging Business of Long-Term Public-Private Partnerships: Reflections on Local Experience. *Public Administration Review* 66:3: 400–411. Bloomfield explains that public-private partnerships encompass a "broad spectrum of creative, intersectoral initiatives," from the use of private philanthropy to achieve a public objective to business transactions that take the form of "novel contracting arrangements."
14. Werkman, Janet, and David L. Westerling. 2000.
15. City of Cranston, Rhode Island. Online information document. Available at http://www.cranstonri.com/pdf/fins_with_seal.pdf). Also, see Food and Water Watch. 2009. *Money Down the Drain: How Private Control of Water Wastes Public Resources.* http://www.scribd.com/doc/12765412/Money-Down-the-Drain.
16. Werkman, Janet, and David L. Westerling. 2000. P. 62.
17. Food and Water Watch. 2009.
18. Young, Trevor L. 2007. *The Handbook of Project Management,* revised 2nd edition. London: Kogan Page Publishers.
19. United States General Accounting Office. 1997. *Privatization: Lessons Learned by State and Local Governments.* GAO-97-48.
20. The Federal Acquisition Regulation (FAR 7.503) states that functions considered to be "inherently governmental" include, among others, determining federal program priorities for budget requests, determining what supplies or services are to be acquired by government, approving contractual documents defining requirements, and ordering changes in contract performance or quantities.
21. Pratt. John W., and Richard J. Zeckhauser. 1991. P. x.
22. Jackson, Barbara J. 2004. *Construction Management Jump Start.* San Francisco: Sybex, Inc. P. 167.
23. Washington State Auditor. 2007. The auditor cited the partnering policies of transportation departments in California, Arizona, and Washington State, all of which stated that partnering is not meant to negate contractual agreements.
24. Project Management Institute. 2004. *A Guide to the Project Management Body of Knowledge,* 3rd edition. Newtown Square, PA: Project Management Institute.
25. Bryson, John M. 2004. *Strategic Planning for Public and Nonprofit Organizations,* 3rd edition. San Francisco: Jossey-Bass. Pp. 15, 16.

Chapter 3

Project Planning, Part 1:
Getting the Concept Right

If you've ever played chess against a better player than yourself, you'll know the feeling that often begins fairly early in the game as you find yourself starting to run out of possible moves that don't result in the losses of your own pieces. As the game progresses, you make a series of increasingly desperate gambits only to watch each one go down in flames, and you finally watch as your forces collapse under your opponent's onslaught.

You may wonder later on where you first went wrong in the game—what your first careless move was that left you weak and exposed to your opponent's attacks. It may be that you went wrong at the very beginning. In chess, you must play the opening moves correctly or you will leave yourself immobile, vulnerable, and unable to make good choices throughout the game. And like the well-established opening combinations of moves in chess, there are certain guidelines in project management that will strengthen your position as your project progresses and help you succeed rather than act in continual desperation and finally futility as your project collapses around you.

That is the purpose of the strategic framework for public sector project management that we introduced in Chapter 2. The first element of the framework states that the public sector manager undertakes a planning process for the project that accurately identifies both the problem to be solved by the project and the project's scope of work. Much as if one were to employ a time-tested opening move in chess, engaging in careful and deliberate planning will give one a fighting chance for success in managing a public or private sector project.

Yet, as noted in the previous chapter, adequate planning is often neglected in the project management process. This neglect may occur even in some of the largest-scale public undertakings in which multiple projects are involved, as Example 3.1 illustrates.

Example 3.1: The lack of timely U.S. postwar planning in Iraq

The U.S. government's failure to undertake adequate postwar project planning in Iraq is evident in the run-up to the invasion of the country in March 2003. It was not until January 2003, just two month before the start of the invasion, that the Department of Defense created the Office of Reconstruction and Humanitarian Assistance (ORHA), a temporary organization established to coordinate existing reconstruction and humanitarian assistance plans.[1]

Rajiv Chandrasekaran points out that when Jay Garner, a retired lieutenant general, assumed command of ORHA in January 2003, "he had no staff and no blueprint for the job ahead."[2] Moreover, Garner claimed he never received postwar reconstruction plans or analyses that had been developed in secrecy at the Pentagon, the State Department, or the CIA. He said he was told by Douglas J. Feith, undersecretary of defense for policy at the Pentagon, that he should develop his own plans.[3]

As late as five years into the war, needed strategic planning for reconstruction of such things as Iraq's energy sector and development of its ministries had yet to be done, according to the Government Accountability Office. The GAO noted that the lack of a strategic plan for those undertakings resulted in a situation in which "multiple U.S. agencies (have been) pursuing individual efforts without overarching direction."[4]

As noted in Chapter 2, there are a number of aspects or steps of planning that we will consider in undertaking public projects:

1. Correctly identifying the problem to be solved by the planned project
2. Questioning the manager's own presumptions held about the project
3. Gaining an accurate understanding of the project's context and stakeholders
4. Understanding and complying with the project's legal requirements
5. Developing preliminary project cost estimates
6. Developing effective project control systems (clear lines of authority, internal financial controls)
7. Developing clear project plans (drawings) and specifications
8. Developing a realistic project schedule
9. Refining project cost and risk estimates

While these steps, as we previously stated, may not always proceed in the order listed and while some steps may lead managers back to earlier ones, we will discuss them in order. We have divided the overall discussion into three parts. This first chapter on planning will consider the first five steps, which together comprise the preliminary, conceptual stage of project planning. The chapter will close with a discussion of project feasibility studies, which are often a result or product of this initial phase of project planning. Chapter 4 will discuss steps 6 and 7, which are intermediate planning aspects concerning effective project internal control systems and accurate specifications; and Chapter 5 will conclude the planning discussion by examining the development of realistic schedules and refined cost and risk estimates.

As noted in Chapter 1, we will gear our discussion of these planning issues to "public sector project managers," keeping in mind that preliminary planning decisions, in particular, are often made by top administrators and others who would not be considered to be project managers or part of a project-management team.

Getting It Right: The Preliminary Steps of Public Sector Project Planning

As James Lewis points out, project planning is an attempt to answer the journalist's questions—who, what, when, where, why, and how—about a particular project prior to its execution.[5] (In this book, as noted, we are referring as well to program involving multiple projects or programs.) In Chapter 1, we used at least some of the journalist's questions to help define the concepts of public projects and public sector project management. The definition we came up with for a public project was that it is a temporary endeavor, undertaken, managed, or overseen by one or more publicly funded organizations to create a unique product of public value.

In *planning* a public project, a project manager must consider: who is going to create or produce the *particular* product or series of products; what is going to be created and where; in what period of time it will be created; what the nature is of the public value that will be created; and how it will be created.

To do this, the public sector project manager must engage in the nine planning steps listed above. For instance, in answering the questions what is to be created and why, the manager must engage in virtually all of the planning steps. He or she must first correctly identify the problem to be solved by the project. As part of that process, he or she must gain an understanding of the context of the project and stakeholders relevant to the project, all the while continually questioning his or her own presumptions about those issues. (These steps will be explained in more detail later in this chapter.) The manager must also brainstorm with the project management team and other stakeholders over the project's costs and risks and must either develop an effective project internal control system or ensure that an existing internal control system in the public agency applies to the project. Subsequently, the manager and his or her team must develop clear plans and specifications and a realistic project schedule and refine cost and risk estimates. In engaging in these planning aspects, the other journalists' questions will be answered as well.

This, in essence, is the purpose of public sector project planning: planning is meant to ensure, before the actual project execution phase begins, that the finished project will achieve the project manager's vision and thereby create public value.

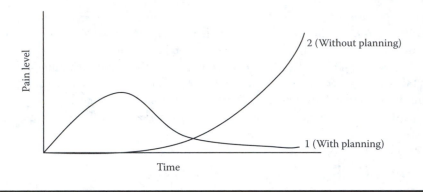

Figure 3.1 Two pain curves in a project over time. (From Lewis, James P. *Fundamentals of Project Management,* **2007.)**

Engaging in the nine aspects we've listed of public sector project planning may sound like a complex and painful process, and, in many ways, it is. But it is far less painful than the consequences of skipping this process. Lewis plots two "pain curves" that can occur in undertaking a project (Figure 3.1)—the first curve showing the amount of pain experienced over time if project planning is undertaken and the second showing the amount of pain without project planning.

The first curve shows a spike in the level of pain early in the project—the pain involved in the planning—which diminishes to zero as the project progresses. The second curve shows zero pain at the beginning—due to the fact that there is no planning—but the pain level rises quickly as the project progresses—due to inevitable project-related mistakes—until it approaches infinity. Clearly, it is better for the manager to be on the first curve.

It should be noted that while a full and accurate planning process will enable a project manager to achieve his or her project vision, it may also demonstrate that the vision is not feasible or achievable. In that case, the manager may have no choice but to cancel the project or—depending on what stage of the planning process he or she has reached—go back as far as the start and reconsider the problem and the concept of the project itself. Trevor Young points out that a decision to cancel a project before the project execution stage is a difficult one to make, but it should not be considered a failure. In fact, a decision to cancel an unviable project rather than go on with it and incur unnecessary costs is an indication that the planning process was successful.[6] As Richard Neustadt and Ernest May point out:

> Busy people in authority, when faced with complicated governmental problems and compelled to act under uncertainty, will not—cannot— escape an almost irresistible temptation to think first of what to do and only second, if at all, of whether to do anything.[7]

In the remainder of this chapter, we will take a closer look at how public sector project managers engage in the first five steps we've listed of project planning and the consequences of failing to engage in them.

Identifying the Correct Problem

This is the first key planning step. A manager's project at this point may be just a vague concept in his or her mind, but the reason it exists as a concept at all is that the manager recognizes the existence of a problem that the potential project might solve.

> **TIP FOR SUCCESS:**
>
> In planning a public project, a manager must frame the problem or problems correctly that the project is meant to solve. This involves correctly identifying the goals the project is meant to achieve and the obstacles in the way of achieving them.

In Chapter 1, we noted that all projects are undertaken to solve problems of some kind. Those problems can be considered to be obstacles in the way of reaching goals. The first planning issue that a public sector project manager (or other decision makers) must consider is identifying the problem correctly. This means not only framing the goals correctly, but correctly identifying the obstacles as well.

One way to ensure that the decision makers have identified the correct problem is to consider it in terms of the agency's overall strategic planning. As the federal Office of Management and Budget notes, a strategic plan includes long-term goals for the agency and should identify assets that are needed to meet the goals. If the decision makers determine that the agency's current assets are not sufficient to meet the goals, that gap becomes the problem that may be solved by implementing a new project or program.[8]

Example 3.2: Correctly identifying the problem: the Town of Harvard library project

The three citizen managers of the project begun in 2003 to build a new public library in Harvard, Massachusetts, viewed the problem they had to solve as one in which the existing town library was too small to accommodate its growing number of public uses and books. This simple explication of the problem allowed the managers to consider possible solutions to it in a rational and systematic way.

The managers brainstormed with a volunteer building committee, which two of them co-chaired, over possible solutions. They asked themselves first of all whether a new building was really needed, or whether the existing library building could be expanded. In other words, was the problem they were facing one which might be solved in a way that might be less expensive than undertaking a new construction project?

These questions were answered only after extensive consideration by the managers and the building committee of all the seemingly possible alternatives. The existing library could not be expanded, for instance, because it was landlocked. It was located close to several residences in the center of town. There was, moreover, no room at the existing library for the expanded parking that would be needed. Other locations around town were considered. In the end, the agreed-upon solution was to construct a new, larger building at the site of the Old Bromfield school, a historic but abandoned school building less than a quarter mile down the road that needed to be refurbished.

Ultimately, the managers achieved their vision of a new library building attached to the refurbished Bromfield School.

Identifying the problem correctly sets the stage for the right solution. That is what happened in the Harvard library case, but it did not happen in the U.S. reconstruction effort in Iraq, beginning in 2003. Clearly, the management of the reconstruction of Iraq's infrastructure is several orders of magnitude more complex than the management of the Harvard Library project. Yet, in both cases, a number of similar management dynamics applied, including the need to identify a problem or problems correctly during the initial planning stage, as Example 3.3 shows.

Example 3.3: Incorrectly identifying postwar problems in Iraq

In the aftermath of the U.S.-led invasion of Iraq in 2003, Iraq's governing structures had virtually collapsed and the country's infrastructure was severely dilapidated.

These were problems for which, as noted in Example 3.1, U.S. planners were largely unprepared. In part, this was because those planners had made a number of faulty assumptions prior to the invasion about the problems they were likely to encounter. The planners had presumed that the actual reconstruction of infrastructure that would be needed in Iraq after the invasion ended would be minimal because the infrastructure would largely remain intact and Iraqi oil revenue would be a primary source for reconstruction funds. They also presumed that the security environment in Iraq would stabilize once Saddam Hussein was removed from power; that U.S. and coalition forces would be greeted as liberators; and that government ministries would continue to function. All of those presumptions turned out to be wrong.[9] Some of the faulty presumptions may, in fact, have been responsible for the overall lack of planning for reconstruction in Iraq that we discussed in Example 3.1.

In an interesting bit of irony, one agency, which had done extensive postwar planning—the United States Agency for International Development—had done so in anticipation of a humanitarian crisis, and yet that crisis never materialized.[10] There were not large numbers of refugees in postwar Iraq and a general breakdown in the food distribution system did not occur. What actually turned out to be the case in the immediate postwar period was that the country's infrastructure was severely dilapidated and the country's oil production and export capabilities had disappeared, meaning that oil revenue would not be sufficient to fund the reconstruction program. Moreover, an insurgency started to develop almost immediately, which made reconstruction extremely dangerous. And widespread looting occurred, which further damaged infrastructure throughout the country. Little or no planning had been done to anticipate those contingencies because they hadn't figured in the planners' presumptions.

The U.S. planners in the example above failed to frame the problems they would face correctly. This led to major delays in needed reconstruction efforts—delays that inevitably pushed up project costs. As a RAND Corporation study pointed out, these faulty presumptions, while not unreasonable in themselves, persisted because they were never seriously challenged. The RAND study stated that

> those charged with planning for Iraq assumed that one particular scenario would play out and did not plan for other possible contingencies that had been identified both inside and outside the U.S. government.[11]

One thing that should be noted here is that although we have placed questioning presumptions second on our list of the aspects of public sector project planning (and will discuss it further in the next section), it is a practice that should begin immediately in the planning process and should accompany all of the other planning aspects. In fact, questioning presumptions should continue throughout the project execution phase as well.

Questioning Presumptions

Neustadt and May contend that decision makers' presumptions "shape objectives and influence options."[12] Presumptions often operate subconsciously and they involve cause and effect—if X then Y. They are often shot through with "muddled, often mistaken" perceptions of the past. And they are often associated with faulty historical analogies.[13]

We pointed out in Example 3.3 how U.S. planners in Iraq held a number of faulty and unquestioned presumptions about the likely postwar situation there. Those presumptions caused them to frame political and economic problems incorrectly and to propose the wrong public projects to address them. They also caused the planners to fail to anticipate real problems, such as looting and the insurgency, which resulted in additional unforeseen costs and schedule delays in planned reconstruction projects. Consider, for instance, the planners' presumption that the U.S. invasion would bring about a stable and secure political environment in Iraq. It would seem that even a cursory review by agency planners and staff of any number of other comparable situations in recent U.S. history would have alerted them to the possibility of looting and other breakdowns in security in Iraq.

James Dobbins, director of the RAND Corporation's International Security and Defense Policy Center, maintains that had the American planners for postwar

Iraq looked at previous U.S. and United Nations occupations in places such as
Haiti, Somalia, Bosnia, and Kosovo, in which rapid disintegrations of security
occurred, they would have realized a similar potential existed for a security breakdown in Iraq.[14] Dobbins argues that such an analysis would have prompted the
U.S. planners to pre-position large numbers of military police in Iraq and to prepare American military commanders to deal with the same situation there. Those
deployments were never taken, he notes.

Such deployments of military police in Iraq may well not only have prevented
the widespread loss of life that the insurgency caused, but would have probably
greatly reduced the devastation to the Iraqi infrastructure that the looting caused.
The massive scale of the destruction of the infrastructure coupled with the high
level of danger faced by U.S. contractors in attempting to repair it were major factors in the skyrocketing costs of those rehabilitation projects.

It appears that the U.S. planners in Iraq did use historical analogies in forming
their presumptions that the security situation would be stable there and that the
country's infrastructure would largely remain intact. The problem was they did not
properly analyze those analogies, did not ask needed questions about them, and did
not determine the similarities and differences between them and the situation in
Iraq, as Neustadt and May argue must be done.

Dobbins maintains that many high-level U.S. planners had looked to the
American occupations of Japan and Germany after World War II in developing
their presumptions about Iraq. Because little or no breakdowns in security had
occurred in those countries in the post–World War II period, the American planners in 2002 may well have expected a similar outcome in Iraq. But Dobbins points
out that Japan and Germany turned out to be faulty analogies. The U.S. planners
in Iraq should have considered their chosen analogies more carefully. Looting was
certainly unlikely to have occurred in Japan and Germany, Dobbins notes, because
both of those countries had been defeated in war with the U.S. and its allies and
both had formally surrendered. This was a major difference from the situation 60
years later in Iraq. In addition, the populations in Germany and Japan in 1945 had
been defeated by years of devastating warfare and were unlikely to resist the occupations. And those populations were largely homogeneous—they were not divided
by ethnic, cultural, religious, or linguistic conflicts as was the case in Iraq. Iraq, in
fact, resembled Yugoslavia in 1995 much more closely than it resembled Japan or
Germany in 1945, Dobbins maintains.[15]

As we noted, questioning presumptions is a practice that should occur
throughout the project's planning phase and even beyond it. Neustadt and May
explain that questioning presumptions can be a relatively simple process and can
be a part of a brainstorming process as well. Whenever options for action are
being considered during any stage of the project, posing some basic questions
about those options as a basis for group discussion can force many hidden presumptions out into the open. Two simple questions that Neustadt and May suggest that decision makers pose are, (1) What are the presumptions behind the

TIP FOR SUCCESS:

Managers should ask Neustadt and May's two questions regarding the options they are considering for public projects:

1. What are the presumptions behind the pros and cons for the options we're considering?
2. What experience, if any, validates those presumptions?

pros and cons for the options we're considering? and (2) What experience, if any, validates those presumptions?[16]

Two major options for the postwar period in Iraq involved either planning for a massive humanitarian assistance crisis or planning for a major infrastructure repair problem. Planners focused on the former option and largely ignored the latter. Those planners might have gathered people knowledgeable about the situation in Iraq together for a series of brainstorming sessions and posed Neustadt and May's questions: What are the presumptions behind the pros and cons of a massive humanitarian effort? What experience suggests that there will be one type of crisis and not another? RAND's study on the planning for the postwar situation in Iraq found that the American planners failed to convene those brainstorming sessions. Numerous people could have been found, the study suggested, who would have challenged the planners' presumptions, including individuals who had recently visited Iraq and scholars of Iraq and the Middle East, all residents in the United States. Interviewees in the study claimed that "knowledgeable individuals had been excluded from the planning process and that many of the Iraqi expatriates who provided much of the information about the condition of the Iraqi infrastructure had not been in Iraq for a considerable period of time."[17]

Had Neustadt and May's questions been asked in the Iraq planning case and had a wider range of experts been consulted, it seems likely that a different approach to the postwar situation would have been taken. The Defense Department planners would have seen their presumptions crumble quickly—particularly their view that the political environment in postwar Iraq would remain stable.

Example 3.4 presents another instance of unquestioned and faulty presumptions underpinning a public project. It shows how those presumptions can cause planners to pursue inappropriate solutions to problems for years, thereby compounding those problems and raising the costs of solving them exponentially.

Example 3.4: Faulty presumptions and the NESWC project

During the 1980s and 1990s, the Northeast Solid Waste Committee (NESWC) project became an expensive gamble for 23 Massachusetts towns that signed long-term agreements with a contractor to build a resource recovery plant that would incinerate their municipal waste. The contracts provided for the municipalities' waste disposal fees to be reduced by projected revenues from the sale of electricity produced by the incineration plant to a local utility. The contracts provided that these revenues would be based on the price of oil.

In the late 1970s, the state of Massachusetts prodded the communities to sign the agreements based in part on a presumption held by state planners that resource recovery projects were the answer to the problems of both rapidly declining landfill space and rising oil prices. That presumption is reflected in a January 1979 letter sent by the then Commissioner of Environmental Management to the manager of a town that was wavering on whether to join the NESWC coalition. The letter noted, in part:

> Stricter requirements will eliminate many landfills and increase the costs of those that remain. If municipalities do not make timely decisions now to assure the availability of the NESWC (resource recovery) facility, many municipalities...can be expected to enter a period of crisis management...[18]

State planners and their consultants also held a presumption that oil prices would continue to rise throughout the 1990s, causing them to make highly optimistic projections about the revenues that would be generated in the sale of electricity from the NESWC plant. These presumptions caused the state to endorse a provision in the NESWC contracts requiring each community to pay for a minimum number of tons of waste delivered to the resource recovery facility, regardless of whether each community actually produced that amount of waste.[19]

Yet, the state's presumptions began to change in the 1990s. Because oil prices did not rise as fast in the 1990s as had been projected, the revenues from electricity produced by resource recovery facilities did not meet expectations. Perhaps more importantly, states were beginning to become increasingly concerned about air pollutants emitted by resource recovery facilities. And by that time, recycling and composting had supplanted incineration as a preferred solution to refuse disposal. In 1994, the state of Massachusetts went so far as to criticize communities that had signed long-term contracts to dispose of set quantities of waste at incineration facilities—the very same contractual arrangements that the state had endorsed and prodded the NESWC communities to accept in the 1980s.[20]

It is easy to look back more than two decades and criticize the state of Massachusetts for its seemingly single-minded focus on refuse incineration in the 1980s. Yet, it seems that had state managers and their consultants been a little more reflective about their presumptions during that period of time, they might have counseled the NESWC communities to sign contracts that at least protected them from the potential financial risks of flat oil prices and "put-or-pay" refuse disposal fees at the resource recovery facility.

The unexamined presumptions that drove the state's resource recovery policy in the late 1970s and 1980s prevented state planners and policy makers from brainstorming over all possible solutions to the state's declining landfill problem. Those policy makers and managers appear to have viewed the problem solely in terms of one solution—resource recovery. They latched onto that solution to the virtual exclusion of all others. And it was only after the passage of several years, when events had clearly shown the weakness of that solution, that the state dropped its initial presumption and began criticizing those it had pushed into adopting that original solution.

Understanding the Project Context and Stakeholders

In discussing this third aspect of project planning, let's define the terms *context* and *stakeholders*. By *project context*, we mean factors involving history and politics that relate in some way to the project. In the case of the Harvard library project, recent town history and politics were important. The citizen managers and other proponents of the project were aware of this context. For instance, they understood, in approaching the town for funding, that a number of other recent public building projects had exceeded their budgets and had stretched the town's finances. Those problems had caused concern and skepticism among many elected officials in town about new project proposals, according to Peter Jackson, one of the library project's citizen managers. As a result, the library project proponents reached an agreement with the town to limit its financial exposure in the project. This agreement was to have a number of beneficial effects, including prompting the proponents to seek supplemental private financing for the project.

> **TIP FOR SUCCESS:**
>
> A key part of the planning process is understanding who the project stakeholders are and how to structure a positive relationship with them.

John Bryson defines a *stakeholder* as any person, group, or organization that can place a claim on an organization's (or other entity's) attention, resources, or output or that is affected by that output.[21] In the case of the library project, stakeholders included not only the citizen project managers themselves and the building committee, but also the members of the Harvard town Board of Selectmen (the Massachusetts towns' equivalent of a town council), its Finance Committee, and other town departments and officials that had some claim on the project, such as the town building inspector and legal counsel. The stakeholders also included the agents ultimately hired to design and execute the project, including the architect, general contractor, and subcontractors. In addition, all town residents could be said to have been stakeholders in the library project to the extent that their taxes helped fund the project and they continued to make use of the library. Other funding sources, such as the state Board of Library Commissioners, were stakeholders as well.

In the library case, the project's proponents and managers understood the project context and were sensitive to the concerns of the stakeholders. Public sector project managers cannot realistically consult with all potential stakeholders in planning their projects, nor do they have the time to research all possible history that might be relevant. Nevertheless, it is important to keep those contextual factors in mind throughout the planning and execution phases of the project. We will discuss different aspects of the project manager-stakeholder relationship in later chapters.

Understanding and Complying with Legal Requirements

In addition to the cost, time, and scope requirements that managers face in undertaking projects, all projects are constrained by legal requirements. Public sector managers must ensure that their project teams include legal experts, who are familiar with the many legal requirements that are likely to affect their particular projects. These requirements govern the procurement and contracting processes, and can include laws and regulations requiring bidding, specifications in bid documents, the avoidance of conflicts of interest, the payment of prevailing wages to workers, procedures for project changes, financial reporting by contractors, certifications by public agencies that appropriated funds are available for the contract, and much more. At the federal level, much of the body of requirements for programs and projects is codified in the Federal Acquisition Regulation (the FAR), a group of regulations that govern the purchase by the federal government of goods and services.[22] States enact their own laws and regulations governing programs and projects at the state and municipal levels.

Figure 3.2 is an only slightly exaggerated assessment of the differences between public and private sector legal requirements in the procurement of supplies and services for projects and programs.

In Chapter 1, we noted the political and academic controversy that has swirled around the issue of procurement and other legal requirements or rules that affect public projects. Critics have contended that these bureaucratic rules have become so onerous and complex in the public sector that they have hampered the performance of government and have contributed to a steadily declining level of public trust in government. Robert Behn, for instance, has argued that the reliance of public managers on rules evolved as a response to the corruption in government that was pervasive during the 19th century. He maintains that at the start of the 21st century, corruption has receded as a major problem in government in the

TIP FOR SUCCESS:

Complying with laws and regulations governing public projects is time-consuming, but evading the rules will ultimately prove to be even more time-consuming.

	Private	*Government*
What you can buy	Whatever is not illegal	Only what is authorized by law
Selection of sources	Whomever you want	Competition required by law
Contract terms & conditions	Whatever you write	Mandatory, pre-written clauses
Authority to enter into contracts	All that is implied by your position	Only what is explicitly stated in writing
Public information	It is generally totally private	It is generally publicly available
Socio-economic factors	None	Many

Figure 3.2   Private versus Government: Different Worlds. (From Baniszewski, John. Government Contracting: A Project Manager's Perspective. PowerPoint presentation. U.S. Department of Energy.)

United States and has been superseded by the problem of performance.[23] Thus, he argues, to the extent that rules hamper government performance, they should be loosened or eliminated and public sector managers should be given more discretion to achieve intended results.

It is undoubtedly true that the complexity of rules governing public sector management has continued to grow and that complying with these rules has become burdensome to managers in many cases. Behn and many others have cited numerous case studies in which rules have been associated with problems in performance.[24] However, rules are complex and have many characteristics. Many examples can be found, including Example 3.5, which show that *evading* rules can lead to performance problems in projects. These cases have led this author to suggest that the evasion of—or exemptions from—procurement and other rules in public projects can cause performance and accountability problems and, conversely, that compliance with such rules can ensure project success.[25] Procurement and contracting rules, in particular, are often intended to encourage public managers to undertake adequate project planning, select the best agents for the task, adopt mutually advantageous agreements, and monitor projects adequately—all elements of this book's framework for successful public sector project management.

Example 3.5: Noncompliance with rules in the Mount Hood public works project

In May 2000, trucks began transporting fill from underneath Boston Harbor to the Mount Hood Memorial Park and Golf Course in the city of Melrose, Massachusetts, about seven miles north of Boston. The fill had been excavated as part of Boston's

Big Dig project. Under an initially informal agreement, the fill-delivery contractor paid the city of Melrose 70 cents per ton of fill accepted by the city. Melrose city officials estimated they would garner more than $200,000 in revenues from the fill. The city's parks superintendent drew up a scope of work that called for the fill to be used to reconstruct the 12th fairway of the Mount Hood golf course.

City officials, however, failed to first do an adequate project plan or cost estimate for the acceptance and placement of the fill and the fairway reconstruction.[26] As the truckloads of fill continued to be delivered, wetlands in the park became flooded and sediment from the fill got into resource areas. Trees and other vegetation in several areas died or were stressed. Rather than completing the golf course reconstruction project with $200,000 in revenues from the fill, as had been projected, the project, which now included remediation of the unintended environmental impacts, was expected to cost $1.8 million.

The Massachusetts Inspector General's Office found that in 16 instances involving the procurement of construction and other services for the project, the city failed to comply with a law requiring written contracts. In six of those cases, the city also failed to comply with either of two applicable state public works bid laws. One of those instances involved the city's selection of a contractor to install a drainpipe in the 12th fairway of the golf course. The contractor, which was selected without the required bidding process, performed the work without a contract. The drainpipe installation subsequently failed and the city was forced to abandon the partially installed pipe, cover it with fill, and install a new drainpipe in the fairway, this time under a proper, competitive bidding process.

Figure 3.3 displays examples of alleged procurement violations in the Mount Hood project.

The Mount Hood case demonstrates the danger of undertaking public projects without adequate planning and without complying with key procurement and contracting laws. The drainpipe installation, in particular, shows how compliance with those legal requirements would likely have led to a different, more positive outcome for the city of Melrose.

The Massachusetts Inspector General's Office found that the drainpipe had been installed by the contractor in an area of the fairway where peat was present. Portions of the pipe became dislodged when the peat moved, or "heaved," underneath the pipe. An excavating machine belonging to the contractor became buried in the fairway. Silt deposits in nearby wetlands were found to have been caused by the drainpipe failure.

It is likely that had the city of Melrose complied with the public works bid laws, it would have hired an engineering firm to prepare plans and specifications for the drainpipe.[27] Those plans would have been likely to have been based on existing conditions of the fairway and the presence of peat there, and those conditions would presumably have been disclosed to all bidders on the project. The environmental problems and the expensive effort to correct them and reinstall the drainpipe could have been avoided.

Furthermore, had the city followed the requirements of the state's municipal finance law, it would have signed a contract with the drainpipe installation

Invoice	Date	Vendor	Supplies/Services	Payment	M.G.L. c. 43, §29 (Written contract)*	M.G.L. c. 30, §39M or M.G.L. c. 30B, §5 (Bidding)**	M.G.L. c. 149, §§26-27 (Prevailing wage)
						VIOLATION OF:	
	6/30/00	J.M. Cook Co., Inc.	Land clearing	$12,000	X	X	X
	7/19/00	S.R. Dodge, Inc.	Installation of volt service	7,750		X	X
	8/1/00	Camp Dresser & McKee, Inc.	Engineering services	20,100			X
	8/1/00	Greenwood and Sons	Machine rentals	5,375			X
	8/1/00	Nitro Dynamics, Inc.	Drilling, blasting ledge	7,100		X	X
	8/11/00	Environmental Landscape Management, Inc.	Clerk of the works and other services	20,008			X
	8/11/00	Environmental Landscape Management, Inc.	Hole #13 construction	24,835	X	X	X
	8/14/00	Greenwood and Sons	Machine rentals	7,270			X
	10/2/00	MDR Construction Co., Inc.	Water truck rental	9,900			X
	10/31/00	Environmental Landscape Management, Inc.	Clerk of the works and other services	17,804			X
	11/1/00	Millennium Maintenance and Power Sweeping	Construction Sweeping	10,455	X	X	X
	11/16/00	Nitro Dynamics, Inc.	Drilling, blasting ledge	22,900	X	X	X
	12/7/00	Greenwood and Sons	Hauling, dozer rental	5,340		X	X
	1/12/01	Greenwood and Sons	Construction services	5,698		X	X
	3/2/01- 3/15/01	Dami and Sons	Construction services	23,188	X	X	X
	3/28/01	Environmental Landscape Management, Inc.	Ball field irrigation installation	13,112	X	X	X
			Totals	$221,692	$221,692	$106,490	$141,235

Figure 3.3 Partial summary of apparent procurement violations by the Park Department in the Mount Hood public works project. *Required for contracts valued at over $5,000. **Required for public works contracts valued at over $10,000. (From Commonwealth of Massachusetts, Office of the Inspector General, 2002. *Review of the Mount Hood Public Works Project in Melrose.*)

contractor. Signing mutually advantageous contracts is the third of the five elements of our overall strategic framework for public sector project management. Without a contract with the original drainpipe installer, the city had no legal basis to seek any monetary or other redress from the original contractor for its failed work.

All of this is not to say that public sector project managers should follow rules blindly or that all rules are well thought-out and helpful to public managers. Yet, while it is no doubt burdensome at times to comply with rules governing public sector projects, the Mount Hood example suggests that a pain curve exists with regard to complying with rules that is similar to the pain curve for planning shown in Figure 3.1. The pain involved in following at least some rules governing public projects appears to be greatest at the start of a project and to gradually diminish with time. And while there may be no pain at the start if rules are evaded, that pain may well appear once the project is under way and is likely to get worse as the project progresses.

Developing Realistic Preliminary Project Cost Estimates

One of the critical points at which public projects go wrong occurs when project managers issue their first projections of the costs of their planned projects. Getting this final aspect of the initial planning stage right is vitally important.

The problems caused by unrealistic cost projections—in particular, projections that are overly optimistic—have been unrelenting and have done much damage to the credibility of government. In the 1990s, news stories about major cost overruns in major weapons systems, such as the B-1 and B-2 bombers, the Trident submarine, and the Navy's A-12 attack plane, outraged both the public and Congress, which then periodically sought to cut funding for those programs.[28]

Unrealistic and overly optimistic cost projections are not limited to projects undertaken by the Defense Department. Bent Flyvbjerg maintains that cost underestimation problems apply to a wide range of other public and private project types, from power plants to dams to water projects, concert halls, museums, sports arenas, convention centers, IT systems, oil and gas extraction projects, aerospace projects, and others.[29] Out of a sample of 258 public transportation infrastructure projects around the world worth $90 billion, Flyvbjerg, Holm, and Buhl reported that costs had been underestimated in 90 percent of them. They found that actual costs were 28 percent higher on average than estimated costs.[30]

What are the reasons for this continual underestimation of project costs? Flyvbjerg says that both psychological and political reasons have been advanced to explain the phenomenon. The psychological explanation is sometimes referred to as "optimism bias," a form of self-deception. The political explanation is that project planners purposefully underestimate project costs to get approval for their projects—in other words they lie about the potential costs.

Flyvbjerg discounts the psychological explanation, contending that the explanation that planners purposefully lie is the better one. The reason for lying is simple. Legislative and other decision-making bodies are more likely to approve projects if the projected costs are low. The result, however, is a "survival of the unfittest" projects. Flyvbjerg points out that "[i]t is not the best projects that get implemented, but the projects that look best on paper. And the projects that look best on paper are the projects with the largest cost underestimates and benefit overestimates, other things being equal."[31]

Example 3.6: Optimistic cost projections in the Future Imagery Architecture project

The Future Imagery Architecture project is one of several U.S. satellite programs that have failed in recent years, leaving the United States with outdated imaging technology, according to an investigation by the *New York Times*.[32] The nation's spy satellite system is considered to be integral to intelligence and military operations, including monitoring nuclear and missile installations in countries such as Iran and North Korea.

Boeing, which was selected in 1999 in a bidding contest with Lockheed Martin to undertake the electro-optical and radar-imaging spy satellite program, had never built that type of system before. Yet, Boeing claimed not only that it could undertake the project, it could do so within the tight $5 billion budget cap that Congress had set for it.

Boeing's design for the project was a major departure in technology from the traditional large, heavy satellites of the past. The company sought to replace the tripod system used by the heavy optical satellites to limit movement and vibration with an automatic system. The Boeing design also proposed a revolutionary zoom lens. In addition, Boeing planned to produce a radar-imaging satellite with a much stronger radar signal than any previous satellites had used.

Prior to the submission of the Boeing bid, Robert Kohler, a member of the Boeing project team, compared the Boeing design to a comparably complex system done before, and calculated that the $5 billion cost estimate for the Future Imagery project was $4 billion too low. His warning went unheeded.[33]

A few months after Boeing was selected for the project, two independent federal cost-estimating groups determined that the Boeing plan would "bust the budget caps," according to the *Times*. But by then it was determined to be too late to reopen the bidding. By the time the project was killed in September 2005—a year after the first satellite was originally to have been delivered—cost estimates had run as high as $18 billion.

Analogy-Based and Parametric Cost Estimating

The type of calculation done by Kohler on the Boeing project team in the example above involved taking data from a comparable project and using it to derive a preliminary cost estimate for a planned project. Known as analogy-based cost estimating, this is a relatively simple, yet effective way to produce an unbiased estimate.

> **TIP FOR SUCCESS:**
>
> Using analogy-based or parametric cost-estimating techniques are relatively simple ways at the outset of projects to derive unbiased estimates of their likely costs.

Peter Jackson, a former project manager with the U.S. Army Corps of Engineers, noted in an interview that his cost-estimating team members would examine bid prices for the most recent projects they could find in the same geographical area as their planned project, which happened to be New England. Similar physical and performance characteristics would be compared. The cost estimators would also examine the availability of contractor resources as part of their preliminary cost estimation process. For example, if several similar projects were underway at the time, Jackson said, the estimators would know that their planned project was likely to be more costly to undertake than would otherwise be the case.

A typical approach to preliminary cost estimation, particularly in building projects, is simply to multiply the planned square footage of the structure by a cost per square foot derived from historical data. Jackson maintains that this rough estimation process may not project the ultimate cost of the project with complete accuracy; yet, it still can be very valuable in comparing different options, and is thus very helpful in undertaking feasibility studies.

A number of experts suggest that using a statistically valid sample of comparable past projects and preparing a probability distribution for them can help produce a more accurate preliminary cost estimate than can the simple analogy method.[34] The GAO describes this "parametric" cost-estimating technique as involving the development of a statistical relationship between historical costs and the planned program or project's "physical and performance characteristics." Had parametric cost estimating been done prior to development of the Future Imagery project, it would have involved gathering data about specific characteristics of past projects, such as advanced optical or radar equipment that were used in them and that might have had similar characteristics to the planned Future Imagery project. Statistical methods would then have been used in determining the relative impact those characteristics had on the ultimate costs of those past projects. Those findings could then have been applied to the planned project to determine its probable cost.

More refined methods of estimating a project's cost than these statistical methods can be done only after a detailed schedule and specifications are developed for a planned project. We will discuss some of those methods in Chapter 5.

Life-Cycle and Independent Cost Estimates

In an effort to reduce over-optimism and bring clarity and accountability to cost estimating, the Office of Management and Budget requires federal agencies to fully estimate "life-cycle costs" for all major planned programs and projects. Life-cycle costs include all direct and indirect costs that are incurred over the life of those programs or projects. Those costs include the costs of planning, procurement, operations and maintenance, and disposal of those assets.[35]

David Westerling and Steve Poftak recommend the inclusion of life-cycle costs and a plan for extended maintenance at the outset of a project to ensure that an adequate maintenance plan is in place and can be funded.[36] The issue of long-term operations and maintenance issues is discussed more fully in Chapter 10.

For Defense Department programs and projects, federal law (Title 10 U.S. Code, sec. 2434) requires that "independent cost estimates" be done before the Secretary of Defense can approve the development or production of a major defense acquisition program.[37] The statute defines an independent cost estimate as one that is prepared by an office that is not under the supervision or control of the military department or agency directly responsible for the program's development or acquisition. One example of this is the Cost Analysis Improvement Group (CAIG), in the Office of the Secretary of Defense.

In addition, the Defense Contract Management Agency (DCMA) and the Defense Contract Audit Agency (DCAA) help agencies in the Defense Department undertake a wide range of program and project management activities, including undertaking valid cost analyses.[38] Unfortunately, civil agencies throughout the federal government have no comparable agencies to the DCMA and DCAA. At the state and municipal levels, there is nothing comparable either. Nevertheless, an owner's project manager or consultant experienced in cost-estimating techniques can help project managers develop accurate cost estimates.

Concluding the Preliminary Project Planning Phase with a Feasibility Study

As noted, the planning aspects we have discussed—defining the problem correctly, understanding the context and stakeholders, understanding and complying with legal requirements, and developing cost and risk estimates—are part of the preliminary, conceptual stage in planning public sector projects. During this time, managers and their teams have considered various project options and alternatives and may have selected a preferred alternative. In many cases, the management team must present a feasibility study at this point concerning the proposed project to a decision-making body. In the public sector, that decision-making body may consist of top agency administrators; or the decision maker may be a separate public agency that coordinates or oversees public construction or other projects at the state level; or it may be a local school board or a legislative body, ranging all the way from a town or city council at the local level to Congress at the federal level. The presentation of the feasibility study for a public project is comparable to the presentation in the private sector of a project business case or project charter to a corporate decision-making body, sometimes referred to as a program or project steering team. In the public sector, the feasibility study may well be produced by an architectural or engineering firm hired by the public agency.

In Massachusetts, state agencies undertaking construction projects must produce feasibility studies that contain elements such as the following:[39]

1. Existing conditions at the site of the proposed project. Are there environmental or soil conditions at the site that could affect the construction of the project?
2. A list and evaluation of alternatives and the preferred option for the project.
3. Comparative cost analyses of the various alternatives.
4. A recommendation of the preferred project solution.
5. A detailed statement of design and operational criteria for the preferred solution.
6. All codes and public regulations required for design and construction of the preferred solution.
7. A schematic design of the planned project, which outlines major site and architectural features, construction systems and materials. This level of design is not as detailed as the final design level that must be achieved before construction can begin in most public projects.
8. A cost estimate for the project based on the schematic design. The cost estimate must include labor and equipment costs and a projected cost for the contractor's and subcontractors' overhead and profit, and a 5 to 15 percent contingency for possible changes in the project's final design. An acceptable overhead rate is 10 percent for contractors and 15 percent for subcontractors. The cost estimate must also include a projection of annual maintenance, utilities, and staffing costs for the asset created by the project. This cost estimate would be further refined during the project's final design stage.
9. The project schedule or duration, from approval to occupancy.

The Massachusetts guide on feasibility studies notes that the purpose of the feasibility study is "to investigate, justify and define projects before design begins."[40] Thus, a study may well recommend the cancellation of a proposed project. As we noted previously, such a recommendation should not be considered a verdict on the success or failure of the project manager or his or her team. A key purpose of feasibility studies is to prevent the undertaking of wasteful or unnecessary public projects. The studies also serve as a guide to legislative bodies in making decisions on appropriating funds for design and execution of the projects.

In the case of the Future Imagery spy satellite project, discussed in Example 3.6, the *New York Times* reported that the National Reconnaissance Office (NRO), the nation's satellite development agency, had put the Future Imagery contract out for bid in 1998 despite an internal feasibility assessment that questioned "whether its lofty technological goals were attainable given the tight budget and schedule."[41] In early 1997, as the project began to move from the conceptual stage to concrete planning, the NRO's acquisition board, which reviews programs at an early stage, had questioned the feasibility of the project, particularly given an expected $5 billion budget cap for its first five years. Yet, the NRO ultimately gave the project the green light to proceed to the bidding stage.

The Future Imagery project demonstrates a breakdown in the federal government's approval process for major technological programs and projects. Billions of dollars were wasted because a public agency was allowed to proceed with a project that its own internal experts had concluded was not feasible. Clearly, changes are warranted to a system under which a major public project is allowed to proceed under those circumstances.

If a feasibility study does recommend, however, that a proposed project be undertaken and that recommendation is adopted by the appropriate decision-making body, the project management team can then move on to the final design and subsequently the construction or execution of the project. That process begins with the intermediate planning aspects that we discuss in Chapter 4.

Endnotes

1. Office of the Special Inspector General for Iraq Reconstruction. 2007. *Iraq Reconstruction: Lessons in Program and Project Management.*
2. Chandrasekaran, Rajiv. 2006. *Imperial Life in the Emerald City: Inside Iraq's Green Zone.* New York: Vintage Books. P. 33.
3. Chandrasekaran, Rajiv. 2006.
4. United States Government Accountability Office. March 2008. *Stabilizing and Rebuilding Iraq, Actions Needed to Address Inadequate Accountability over U.S. Efforts and Investments.* Statement of David M. Walker. GAO-08-568T. P. 3.
5. Lewis, James P. 2007. *Fundamentals of Project Management*, 3rd edition. New York: American Management Association.
6. Young, Trevor L. 2007. *The Handbook of Project Management*, revised 2nd edition. London: Kogan Page Publishers.
7. Neustadt, Richard, E., and Ernest R. May. 1986. *Thinking in Time: The Uses of History for Decision Makers.* New York: The Free Press. P. xvii.
8. Office of Management and Budget. 2006. *Capital Programming Guide.* Supplement to Circular A-11, Part 7.
9. See for example, Office of the Special Inspector General for Iraq Reconstruction. 2007; also, RAND Corporation. 2008. *After Saddam: Prewar Planning and the Occupation of Iraq.*
10. Office of the Special Inspector General for Iraq Reconstruction. 2007. RAND Corporation. 2008.
11. RAND Corporation. 2008. P. 237.
12. Neustadt, Richard E., and Ernest R. May. 1986. P. 136.
13. Neustadt, Richard E., and Ernest R. May. 1986. P. 136.
14. FRONTLINE. 2006. *The Lost Year in Iraq: Key Controversies and Missteps of the Postwar Period.* http://www.pbs.org/wgbh/pages/frontline/yeariniraq/analysis/fuel.html.
15. FRONTLINE. 2006.
16. Neustadt, Richard E., and Ernest R. May. 1986. P. 137.
17. RAND Corporation. 2008. P. 215.

18. Commonwealth of Massachusetts, Office of the Inspector General. 1997. *The North East Solid Waste Committee Project: Planning and Development of a Public-Private Partnership.* P. 18.
19. Commonwealth of Massachusetts, Office of the Inspector General. 1997.
20. Commonwealth of Massachusetts, Office of the Inspector General. 1997.
21. Bryson, John M. 2004. *Strategic Planning for Public and Nonprofit Organizations,* 3rd edition. San Francisco: Jossey-Bass.
22. The FAR appears in the United States Code of Federal Regulations (CFR) at 48 CFR Chapter 1. The chapter is grouped into eight subchapters: (A) General; (B) Competition and Acquisition Planning; (C) Contracting Methods and Contract Types; (D) Socioeconomic Programs; (E) General Contracting Requirements; (F) Special Categories of Contracting; (G) Contract Management; and (H) Clauses and Forms. The regulations can be found online at http://www.arnet.gov/far/.
23. Behn, Robert D. 2001. *Rethinking Democratic Accountability.* Washington, DC: Brookings Institution Press.
24. See for example, Osborne, David, and Ted Gaebler. 1992. *Reinventing Government: How the Entrepreneurial is Transforming the Public Sector.* Reading, MA: Addison-Wesley; also, Kelman, Steven. 1990. *Procurement and Public Management: The Fear of Discretion and the Quality of Government Performance.* Washington, DC: AEI Press; and, Anechiarico, Frank, and James B. Jacobs. 1996. *The Pursuit of Absolute Integrity: How Corruption Control Makes Government Ineffective.* Chicago: University of Chicago Press.
25. Kassel, David S. 2008. Performance, Accountability, and the Debate over Rules. *Public Administration Review* 68:2: 241–252
26. Commonwealth of Massachusetts, Office of the Inspector General, 2002. *Review of the Mount Hood Public Works Project in Melrose.*
27. In the drainpipe installation, the city had a choice of following Massachusetts General Laws chapter 30, section 39M, which requires public agencies to award public works contracts over $10,000 in value to the lowest "responsible and eligible" bidder; or Massachusetts General Laws chapter 30B, section 5, which applies to public works contracts between $10,000 and $25,000. The legal necessity of including adequate specifications in bid solicitations is set out in a Massachusetts Supreme Judicial Court Case—*Sweezey v. Mayor of Malden,* 273 Mass. 536, (1931). In that case, the court invalidated an award for a street paving contract after finding that the City of Malden's specifications for the contract failed to include the required grade, quality, and type of material to be used or the manner in which the paving surface was to be applied. (For a fuller explanation of Massachusetts court cases involving specifications, see Werkman, Janet, and Lisa Price. *Bid Protests under M.G.L. c. 30B: The Uniform Procurement Act.* Massachusetts Office of the Inspector General. http://www.mass.gov/ig/publ/c30bprot. htm.)
28. Goldstein, Mark L. 1992. *America's Hollow Government: How Washington Has Failed the People.* Homewood, IL: Business One Irwin.
29. Flyvbjerg, Bent. 2005. Policy and Planning for Large Infrastructure Projects: Problems, Causes, Cures. World Bank Policy Research Working Paper No. 3781.
30. Flyvbjerg, Bent, Mette Holm, and Soren Buhl. Summer 2002. Underestimating Costs in Public Works Projects: Error or Lie? *Journal of the American Planning Association.* http://pqasb.pqarchiver.com/planning/access/128776261.html?dids=128776261:128776261:128776261:128776261&FMT=ABS&FMTS=ABS:FT:TG:PAGE&type=current&date=Summer+2002&author=Bent+Flyvbjerg&pub=American+Planning+Association.+Journal+of+the+American+Planning+Association&edition=&startpage=279&desc=Underestimating+costs+in+public+works+projects%3A++Error+or+lie%3F.

31. Flyvbjerg, Bent. 2005. P. 15.
32. Taubman, Philip. 2007. In Death of Spy Satellite Program: Lofty Plans and Unrealistic Bids. *New York Times.* November 11, 2007. http://www.nytimes.com/2007/11/11/washington/11satellite.html?hp#step1
33. Taubman, Philip. 2007.
34. See for example Flyvbjerg, Bent. 2005; also, United States Government Accountability Office. 2009.
35. See Office of Management and Budget. 2006; also, United States Government Accountability Office. 2009. *GAO Cost Estimating and Assessment Guide: Best Practices for Developing and Managing Capital Program Costs.* GAO-09-3SP.
36. Westerling, David, and Steve Poftak. 2007. *Our Legacy of Neglect: The Longfellow Bridge and the Cost of Deferred Maintenance.* Pioneer Institute White Paper, No. 40.
37. United States Government Accountability Office. 2009.
38. United States Government Accountability Office. 2009.
39. Commonwealth of Massachusetts, Division of Capital Asset Management. Guidelines for the Preparation of Studies for Building Projects for Commonwealth of Massachusetts State Agencies, Building Authorities, Counties. Revision October 2000. http://www.mass.gov/cam/dlforms/STUguide.pdf.
40. Commonwealth of Massachusetts, Division of Capital Asset Management. 2000.
41. Taubman, Philip. 2007.

Chapter 4

Project Planning, Part 2:
Developing and Refining the Process

At the intermediate stage of the project planning process, the preliminary planning discussed in Chapter 3 has largely been done. The project manager and his or her team have, we hope, clearly identified the problem their planned project is meant to solve. They have agreed on the basic outlines of a solution after having examined all the project alternatives they could think of and thoroughly examined their presumptions in doing so. They have obtained an understanding of the key stakeholders in the process as well as an understanding of the applicable legal requirements. They have undertaken a preliminary cost and risk analysis of the project and have obtained approval to proceed to the project procurement and execution stage by the legislative or other approval body that authorizes funding for the undertaking.

Now, the project manager and his or her team must begin to refine the project concept. If they haven't already done so, they must also develop a clear structure of accountability with regard to the project team itself and the external agents, e.g.,

TIP FOR SUCCESS:

Key practices in intermediate project planning:

Establish a clear and effective project accountability structure and project plans and specifications.

consultants and contractors, who will be involved. And they must refine the up-to-now conceptual design for the project.

The Project Accountability Structure

Development of a clear and workable accountability structure helps answer the key questions: How does the project manager ensure that project-related information will flow smoothly from the external agents to the management team and back again? How can a manager control project funding to prevent waste and fraud and deliver the most cost-effective product to taxpayers? How does the manager structure the principal-agent relationships involved to ensure that his or her project vision is successfully achieved?

The answers to these questions are not only complex, but they vary based on the types of projects being undertaken. Even for similar project types, there is often disagreement over what constitutes the best accountability structures. Gareth Morgan argues, for instance, in a business context, that the traditional hierarchical or bureaucratic accountability structure that most organizations use in planning and executing projects and other business initiatives is not conducive to innovation or successful project execution, particularly in turbulent and unpredictable environments.[1] In a version of the argument made by the New Public Management movement, which we discussed in Chapters 1 and 2, Morgan suggests that it is advantageous to have project management teams that are small and autonomous and that require a high level of discretion and expertise in different areas among individual team members. Morgan even goes as far as to argue that successful project teams should be given less rather than more direction to innovate.[2]

We've argued previously that managers do need to maintain a level of control and authority over public projects that is sufficient to prevent those projects from spinning out of control. Yet a balance clearly has to be established. In this chapter, we will discuss the balance that is needed both in the development of a project accountability structure and in the development of project specifications. We'll consider each of these project planning aspects in turn and discuss some of the key relationships that exist between them. Our discussion will specifically involve steps 6 and 7 of the project planning process: establishing an effective internal control structure regarding the project and establishing clear project specifications.

Establishing the Right Project Internal Control Structure

As noted above, a balance has to be struck in the management or accountability structure of a public sector organization to ensure that project team members are given sufficient discretion and autonomy to be innovative, without allowing the

TIP FOR SUCCESS:

GAO's key aspects of internal control are:

- Create a working environment that stresses ethics and competence
- Identify all project risks
- Establish controls over management procedures
- Establish controls over information systems
- Ensure a management system that allows for a free flow of information
- Monitor the internal control system periodically

process to descend into chaos or corruption. This is where an agency's internal control procedures come into play.

The United States Government Accountability Office defines internal control as a "component" of an agency's management that provides reasonable assurance that three objectives will be met: (1) operations will be efficient and effective; (2) financial reporting will be reliable; and (3) laws and regulations will be complied with.[3] Internal controls involve the "plan, policies, methods, and procedures" to achieve those objectives. From that perspective, one might argue that the overall purpose of this book is to provide guidance to public sector managers on establishing effective internal control over their projects.

To ensure proper internal control, GAO identifies five internal control standards. The following are a few words about each of them and how they relate to the discussion in this book of public sector project management.

The GAO's Five Standards for Internal Controls

Control Environment

Public managers must strive to create a working environment for both internal and external agents that promotes ethical behavior and competence. This involves both ensuring that project staff have the proper training and experience for their roles and that key areas of authority and responsibility and appropriate lines of communication are established. (We discussed some of the unique ethical issues that apply to public sector project managers in Chapter 1. We will discuss project team training and experience issues more fully in Chapter 6.)

Risk Assessment

Managers must "comprehensively identify risks" facing their projects, and should "consider all significant interactions" they might have internally and externally.

(We will discuss risk assessment as a key step in public sector project planning in the next chapter.)

Control Activities

Managers must establish a system of effective and efficient controls over management procedures. These include such things as approvals and authorizations (sign-offs), verifications, periodic evaluations of project performance, and the creation and maintenance of project-related records. (We will say more about project-related authorizations and record keeping below. Evaluations of project performance will be discussed in Chapter 9.)

One example of a critical control activity is the safeguarding of public-agency assets, such as cash, securities, inventories, and equipment, which might be vulnerable to the risk of loss or unauthorized use. Managers must make sure these assets are periodically counted and compared to control records. Managers must also be careful to divide or segregate key duties and responsibilities among staff, particularly with respect to authorizing, processing, recording, and reviewing financial transactions. For instance, an individual who has custody of assets such as cash or checks should not also have access to the accounting records for those assets. In Chapter 1, we noted a clear example of an internal control failure to protect assets. It involved the failure of the U.S. government–led reconstruction authority in Iraq to keep accounts of the hundreds of millions of dollars of cash in its vault intended for reconstruction and other rebuilding projects.

Control Activities Specific for Information Systems

Managers must also ensure control over computer information systems and software. This includes control over everything from data center operations to system software acquisition and maintenance. For instance, managers must make sure that adequate "firewalls" exist in their computer systems to prevent unauthorized entry from hackers. Control is also needed to ensure that internally developed or commercially purchased software meets the users' needs and is properly installed and used.

Information and Communications

Managers must ensure that the management structure they put together to undertake their projects allows for a free flow of information, not only from external agents undertaking project-related work, but from stakeholders in the project and within the project management team itself. This internal control standard will be discussed in more detail in Chapters 6, 7, and 9.

Monitoring

The internal control structure itself should be periodically monitored. Monitoring can range from self-assessments to internal and external audits. Serious problems uncovered during this process should be reported to top management.

TIP FOR SUCCESS:

Two important project control activities:
   Public sector project managers should

- Maintain adequate and proper project documentation
- Keep contract administration duties separate from day-to-day project management duties

---

Project Documentation

Proper documentation is such a critical aspect of effective management of public projects that we will take a little time to discuss it separately here. In its discussion of internal control, the GAO groups project documentation under its third internal control standard (listed above) and specifically notes that all transactions and other significant events need to be clearly documented and that documentation should be readily available for examination. Moreover, project-related transactions should be recorded promptly "to maintain their relevance and value to management in controlling operations and making decisions."[4]

Analysts recommend that project managers set up a file for all documentation related to a project. The file should contain at a minimum the following records:

1. The project feasibility study and any changes made to it.
2. A project organization chart that lists the names and key responsibilities of all members of the project management team. (An example of a project responsibility chart is provided in Chapter 6.)
3. Project plans and specifications.
4. Project schedules and updates to the schedules as the project progresses.
5. Contracts and amendments.
6. Shop drawings and as-built drawings, if a construction project is involved. (Shop drawings are detailed drawings done by the general contractor or subcontractors of components or systems within the project. As-built drawings identify changes or adjustments to the original plans and specifications that are made during the actual construction or project execution work.)

7. Project logs and daily reports. These reports record such things as phone calls, material and equipment deliveries, and daily activities.
8. Change orders. (Change orders are changes approved by the project owner to the contract that affect the project's price, scope, or schedule.)
9. Work authorizations.
10. Invoices and payment requisitions.
11. Project-related correspondence, including faxes, letters, memoranda, and e-mails, sent and received.
12. Contractor warranties.

Project managers may find it helpful and convenient to maintain both hard copy and computerized versions of these records. It is important that the hard copy and computerized record-keeping systems correspond. Example 4.1 lists several instances of poor internal control practices alleged to have occurred within a quasi-public organization, including instances of missing and noncorresponding project records.

Example 4.1: Failings in internal control procedures in Port of Seattle construction contracts

A 2007 state audit of the Port of Seattle (POS), a quasi-public municipal corporation, which operates both seaport facilities and the Seattle-Tacoma International Airport, alleged numerous internal control deficiencies involving a wide range of agency projects and contracts.[5] The audit was done by consultants to the Washington State Auditor's Office.

The following are some examples of the audit findings:

- Incomplete management records: The Washington State Auditor reviewed POS software management information systems for 35 separate POS projects as to whether they provided key project and contract information, schedule information, change order information and logs, actual costs and invoices, and work authorizations. Various divisions within the POS used as many as four separate management information systems, according to the auditor. Yet, in virtually all of the categories reviewed, information was either missing, incomplete, or conflicted with information provided in hard-copy project records. For instance, in several of the projects sampled, invoices were either missing from project files or did not reconcile to amounts entered in the computerized information systems. The auditor reported that no controls appeared to exist to ensure that the information systems were correct and updated on a regular basis.
- In one case involving the POS Seaport information management system, the auditor's report stated that the auditor was unable to find change-order amount information for several projects. The system reportedly tracked critical issues, but no costs were shown for those issues, and thus there was "no ability to forecast the POS's exposure to potential cost overruns."[6]
- Segregation of duties: The auditor found that the POS did not employ independent and professional contracting officers whose responsibilities would

include negotiating and awarding contracts, approving contract changes, and settling disputes. Instead, those duties fell by default to various engineering, construction management, and project management personnel who worked directly with contractors and consultants on a day-to-day basis.
• Failure to notify the Commission: The auditor stated that POS internal control policies require management to notify the Port Commission whenever a low bid on a construction project was greater than 10 percent above an engineer's estimate so that the Commission could intervene in the procurement decision if deemed necessary. The Commission is an elected, five-member board that governs the POS (see our discussion in Chapter 1 of quasi-public agency projects).

According to the auditor, the Commission-notification policy was ignored by POS management, which had improperly negotiated with the sole bidder on a Third Runway construction project at the Seattle-Tacoma International airport. The auditor found that top POS managers had improperly met with a principal of a construction company bidding on the work after the bids were opened, to persuade the principal to lower his bid. The bid had come in more than 10 percent higher than a cost estimate by a POS engineer.

A follow-up review of the state audit by a "Special Investigative Committee," which was led by a former United States Attorney, concluded in December 2008 that several aspects of the Third Runway procurement and other activities by the Port of Seattle constituted fraud.[7] As of early 2009, a federal grand jury was continuing to consider possible criminal charges relating to Port procurement activities.

Example 4.1 demonstrates both the importance of, and limitations of, internal control measures. Even if those measures are in place, project managers must also comply with them. A project manager may go to the trouble of purchasing an information management system software package (or more than one in the Port of Seattle case); but if he or she then does not see to it that the software is used for its intended purpose, it will prove to have been a useless expense. Similarly, while internal control policies may be in place in an agency, the policies might as well not exist if they are routinely evaded by project management staff.

The failure to establish and comply with workable internal control policies in project planning can leave public sector managers vulnerable to major problems, from an inability to track or control project cost increases to losses due to fraud. The Washington State Auditor noted, for instance, that if senior project management is unaware of budget discrepancies or schedule delays because it does not have a policy in place or adhere to a policy to track them, "it can no longer effectively manage projects and staff or initiate timely corrective actions."[8] In addition, inappropriate budget transfers cannot be monitored or controlled if the systems are not regularly updated, the auditor stated.

The Washington State Auditor also maintained that the failure by the POS to employ independent contract officers with the sole authority to award contracts and approve contract changes left the agency open to a wide range of potential fraud. In response to a query from this author, the authors of the state auditor's report maintained that agencies should ideally keep the duties of their contract procurement and administration staffs separate from the duties of their day-to-day project management staff. At the federal level, a contracting officer (CO) has the authority to award contracts and approve change orders, for example. The project management staff, including engineers and other project management specialists, are able to review proposed contracts and make recommendations to the CO. But only the CO has the authority to approve actual expenditures (FAR 1.602, 2.101, and 42.302).

Outside the federal government, rules and policies governing contract administration and project management duties, and whether they must be kept separate, vary widely. Example 4.2 provides an illustration of two such contrasting arrangements.

Example 4.2: Contract administration and project management on the Boston Harbor cleanup and Big Dig projects

The Boston Harbor cleanup project in the 1990s, which was managed by the quasi-public Massachusetts Water Resources Authority (MWRA), employed a very different contract administration and project management process than did the Big Dig project in the same city. The Boston Harbor cleanup project was a $6 billion undertaking in the 1980s and 1990s to upgrade sewage treatment facilities serving Boston and surrounding communities. The project is credited with cleaning up Boston Harbor, once described as "the dirtiest harbor in America."[9] Background on the Big Dig project is provided in endnote 6 in the introduction to this book.

Steven F. Wojtasinski, an attorney with a Boston-based law firm, was previously involved in both the Boston Harbor and Big Dig projects. He was administrative manager in the Contracts and Claims Department on the Big Dig for the last 6 years of the project, and was a construction changes and claims manager on the Boston Harbor cleanup project during most of that 11-year undertaking. On the Big Dig project, he worked as an employee of Bechtel/Parsons Brinckerhoff, the design and construction management consortium; and on the Boston Harbor project, he was an employee of Kaiser Engineers, which was employed by the MWRA as its construction manager.

In an interview, Wojtasinski noted that the MWRA employed a traditional separation on the Boston Harbor project between contract and change order administration, on the one hand, and project and construction management on the other. Project managers had no authority to directly approve project change orders. Wojtasinski maintained that because of the "inflexibility of the existing administrative and bureaucratic institutions," it took on average nearly four months at the MRWA to get a change order documented, approved, and processed, "whether it was for $1,000 or $100,000." There were dozens of steps and signoffs involved, and ultimately, the MRWA Board of Directors approved any significant change orders.

In contrast, resident engineers, who worked for Bechtel/Parsons Brinckerhoff and other joint venture subconsultants, had limited authority to approve moderately priced change orders in the field (up to $50,000) on the Big Dig project. Wojtasinski added that under a "creative and flexible Integrated Project Team" arrangement, employees of Bechtel/Parsons were delegated the authority to work alongside construction management staff of the Massachusetts Turnpike Authority[10] in the Contracts and Claims Department, as well as in other project control and design oversight units. Both executive level consultants and MTA officials signed off on those higher dollar change orders. There was little or no differentiation among consultant staffs and MTA employees in preparing the change order and claim validations or for approval steps in the change-order authorization process.

Wojtasinski contended that there was a "strict written set of protocols for documenting, evaluating and approving change orders" on the Big Dig project and that the combined consultant-MTA teams "successfully managed nearly 20,000 construction changes during the life of the project." Toward the end, he acknowledged, the blended public-private management process became controversial, particularly after allegations surfaced that a major projected cost increase in the project had been concealed from the public and from bondholders.[11] "At this stage of the project, all unorthodox administrative systems were suspect," Wojtasinski said.

Many observers such as the Massachusetts inspector general and Fred Salvucci, former Massachusetts transportation secretary, have been sharply critical of the Big Dig accountability structure. Salvucci maintained that the MWRA, with its internal conflict and cumbersome series of contract administration approvals reaching as high as the Board of Directors, was nevertheless a more successful approach, even from a cost and performance standpoint. "The apparent peace at the Big Dig was because no one was asking basic questions," Salvucci said. "They were just throwing good money after bad..."[12] Salvucci maintained that while both projects were estimated in 1990 to cost $6 billion apiece and to be completed by the year 2000, the Boston Harbor project was completed on time and "slightly below budget." The Central Artery/Tunnel project was still not completed as of 2006 and was estimated at that time to cost $15 billion.

Wojtasinski counters that the Big Dig Integrated Project team system actually worked well and has been unfairly blamed for cost increases that were due to many factors outside the project's control, including the need to satisfy numerous constituents. Had the Big Dig project used the traditional change-order approval process, the project would never have been completed due to the long delays that would have occurred, he maintained. On the Boston Harbor cleanup project, had the contractors not as a group "unilaterally assumed the risk of nonpayment for changes, and, in contradiction to the contract, moved forward to execute pending changes, the change-order system would have crashed and the delays and resulting job impacts and costs would have been disastrous," Wojtasinski maintained.

Wojtasinski's assessment of the difficulties inherent in following a traditional change-order accountability process on complex projects, such as the Big Dig and Boston Harbor cleanup projects, is compelling. Nevertheless, it should be noted that when "flexible" or "integrated" approaches are used that depart from those traditional approaches, new risks can develop, including the risk that project managers will be blamed for departing from traditional approaches.

In smaller public construction projects at the state and municipal levels it is sometimes difficult to achieve segregation of duties with respect to contract administration and day-to-day project management for another reason. There may simply not be enough people involved to easily segregate those duties. The public official who oversees the project on a daily basis may also be the person who signs off on contracts and change orders. Contractors and consultants, however, are generally prohibited from having such sign-off authority. In Massachusetts, the state's public construction agency specifies that owners' project managers must only provide advice and counsel regarding contract awards, change orders, and progress payments.[13]

In the case of the Port of Seattle, the Washington State Auditor maintained that engineering, construction management, and project management personnel who worked directly with contractors and consultants on a daily basis had improperly been delegated authority to negotiate and award contracts, approve contract changes, waive contractual requirements, and settle disputes. This lack of proper segregation of duties resulted in "vulnerability to a wide array of potential fraud to occur and not be detected."[14] There were no controls in place, according to the state auditor, to deter, prevent, or detect bribery, kickback, illegal gratuity, or bid-rigging schemes. Among the auditor's specific findings were that on some contracts, change order amounts were consistently the same as the contractors' proposed amounts. In some cases, change orders were approved without evidence of evaluation or negotiation.

Preventing Fraud in Public Projects

As illustrated in the examples above, fraud is, or should be, an ever-present concern to public managers in undertaking their projects; and effective internal control procedures can provide a reasonable assurance to them that fraud will not occur. The Auditing Standards Board notes in its Statement on Auditing Standards (SAS) Number 99 that

> it is only those organizations that seriously consider fraud risks and take proactive steps to create the right kind of climate to reduce its occurrence that have success in preventing fraud.[15]

Yet, despite clear statements of guidance from authoritative sources such as the Auditing Standards Board, concern over the potential for fraud is often lacking in public agencies. The federal Office of Management and Budget, for instance, provides federal managers with a series of best practices in planning for and acquiring capital assets, which are defined as land, structures, equipment, and intellectual property with a useful life of at least two years.[16] Yet, the OMB's Capital Programming Guide says little or nothing about deterring fraud or implementing internal control procedures. In a written response to a query from this author, an OMB deputy administrator maintained that the OMB Guide "must be read in conjunction with other policy documents, including the FAR (Federal Acquisition Regulation)." Recent and pending OMB rules, the deputy administrator added, "reflect unprecedented steps to strengthen contractor ethics and combat fraud in government contracting."[17] Nevertheless, the Guide does not appear to mention the word *fraud* and does not instruct readers that it should be read in conjunction with other policy documents such as the FAR. While the Guide notes on page 1 that it provides "updated best practices and lessons learned regarding more efficient project and acquisition management of capital assets," it does not discuss methods of tracking and safeguarding assets.

Mark Zepezauer and Arthur Naimen have estimated that $172 billion of a total $327 billion in military spending per year by the United States could be attributed to waste and fraud.[18] The Project on Government Oversight (POGO) maintains a database (at http://www.contractormisconduct.org/), which lists total numbers of dispositions and amounts of military contractor misconduct involving fraud, environmental, ethics, and labor violations. As of October 2008, the top 100 contractors listed in the POGO database had engaged in 638 instances of misconduct totaling $23.6 billion since 1995. That was out of $226.5 billion in contracts since that time. We noted in Chapter 1 that in Iraq alone, there was alleged to have been more than $10 billion in questioned and unsupported costs related to U.S. reconstruction and troop support contracts.

Among the more common types of fraud in public contracting are the following categories of false claims:

■ Submitting below-cost bids and seeking to make up the difference through change-order requests
■ Bid-rigging, collusive bidding, and kickback schemes
■ Billing for work not performed or defective work
■ Submitting false schedule updates, such as showing progress ahead or behind its actual position
■ False representations on payment applications, such as prevailing wage certifications or certifications about subcontractor payment
■ False representations about good-faith attempts to obtain minority, women, and small-business participation
■ Asserting a false subcontractor claim on a pass-through basis to the public agency[19]

To the extent that public sector project managers institute measures during the project planning process to promote an ethical environment, safeguard assets, segregate staff duties, and ensure adequate documentation of activities, they will go a long way toward lessening their agencies' vulnerability to fraud. In doing so, they will go an equally long way toward ensuring the success of their projects.

Developing Clear Project Specifications

Developing project specifications lies at the heart of project planning. The seventh step in our discussion of planning, it is the point at which project managers answer definitively the journalists' questions involved in the definition of public projects.

TIPS FOR SUCCESS:

■ Specifications define the project.
■ Specifications should be clear and precise.

The specifications describe in detail the design or other characteristics of the product of public value that is created by a public project.

Some analysts use the broader term *scope* or *scope of work* to encompass the depiction of all of the actual work required to complete the project successfully. Specifications describe the project work as well as all of the project's systems and components. In public construction projects, specifications are usually accompanied by plans, which are detailed architectural drawings of the buildings or facilities and all of their components.

Plans and specifications are an integral part of the solicitations for bids, Requests for Proposals, and other competitive solicitation documents for public projects that are issued by public agencies; and they become an integral part of the contracts signed to undertake the project work. Public agencies generally hire architects or engineers to develop project plans and specifications.

As the examples we will discuss later in this chapter show, the development of clear project specifications gives public agencies a basis on which to select the best agents to undertake the project work. It also gives the agencies a basis on which to evaluate the work actually done. Without these standards for evaluating contract work, in particular, public agencies have little basis on which to monitor projects or enforce project agreements. Janet Werkman and David Westerling note, for instance, that research data indicate that a decision by a public agency to contract out for work is likely to produce lower costs than in-house operation only when (1) the "*scope of work is precisely specified in advance*," (2) the contractor's performance can be readily evaluated, and (3) the contractor can be replaced (or penalized) if it fails to perform[20] (emphasis added).

John Cibinic et al. point out that the federal government has traditionally included

> significant amounts of detail in its (contract) specifications for a number of reasons, including obtaining standardization, avoiding duplication of costs of design, ensuring fair competition, creating a firm baseline for measuring contractor performance, and ensuring contractor performance.[21]

If specifications remain vague by the time the contract with the general contractor is made final, significant problems and higher costs in public projects may well be the result, as Example 4.3 shows.

Example 4.3: Vague technical specifications lead to major contract cost increases at the Port of Seattle

In 1998, the Port of Seattle (POS) awarded a one-year contract to a firm for architectural and engineering services.[22] The contract contained a vague scope of services, with few specifications, according to the Washington State Auditor. Among the specifications were that the consultant would assist the POS in implementing a capital improvement program at the airport. The scope of services stated that the services would include "a broad range of planning, technical, project and construction management services as requested by the POS..."[23] It also stated that the consultant would prepare specific work authorizations, subject to the approval of the POS, which could add new tasks or services to the authorizations at any time.

According to the state auditor, an initial work authorization specified a budget for the consultant, mobilization (equipment and personnel setup) services to be provided, and direction to proceed. However, no additional work authorizations were ever issued or approved containing detailed scopes of services, schedules, or budgets. Instead, the POS authorized the contractor's personnel as well as subcontractors to "carry out day-to-day activities side-by-side with" POS employees. In addition, the POS later allowed the contract personnel to charge hourly rates for their services based on salaries multiplied by an agreed number. Over the next 10 years, the contract was routinely extended without competition or written work authorizations. The size of the contract grew during that time from $10 million to more than $120 million.

The auditor estimated that had the POS hired employees rather than the consultant to perform day-to-day work, the agency would have saved $14.5 million during the period from 2004 to 2006 alone.

In the case above, the Special Investigative Committee that followed up the Washington State audit report concluded that fraud was *not* established to have occurred in the award of the contract and in the amendments that increased its cost and scope. However, the Investigative Committee report stated that the contractor had failed to provide it with requested documentation, and that the Committee was therefore unable to conduct a complete evaluation of the matter.

Whether or not fraud occurred in the arrangement described in Example 4.3, the lack of specifications in the contract left the POS vulnerable to nearly unrestrained cost increases, according to the state auditor. Moreover, this example provides a lesson in how project specifications or the lack of them can affect a public agency's internal control procedures. The original POS contract did not specify the work that the consultant would do, but instead left it to the consultant to come up with those specifications, subject to the agency's approval. This lack of specifications eventually led to a situation in which the employees of the consultant and its subcontractors began working as expensive de facto employees of the POS.

> **TIP FOR SUCCESS:**
>
> Construction projects using delivery methods in which the design and specifications are not complete can pose an increased risk of cost increases.

Specifications and Alternative Project Delivery Methods

Public construction projects have traditionally involved sequential bidding phases: (1) a designer prepares 100 percent complete plans and specifications for a project, and (2) construction bids are solicited, based on those plans and specifications. A number of states and the federal government allow public agencies to use alternatives to this traditional "design-bid-build" approach to public construction. For instance, "design-build" delivery allows owners to "fast-track" the design and construction process by permitting some construction to proceed before the design is complete. In design-build, the owner signs a single contract for design and construction with a single entity, such as a design-contract joint venture. Design and construction are combined into a single stage, with no separate bid for construction based on complete plans and specifications.

Fast-tracking, however, can pose risks to public project owners. The Massachusetts inspector general and the *Boston Globe* both noted, for instance, that construction on many of the Big Dig project's major contracts began with incomplete and inaccurate designs, causing costly delays in the project.[24] Interestingly, the Big Dig was not contractually intended to be a fast-tracked project, yet the incomplete-design issue nevertheless proved to be a major problem, according to the inspector general.[25] Ironically, Bechtel/Parsons Brinckerhoff's purpose in proceeding with incomplete designs was for "catching up to the Big Dig construction schedule because of prior design related delays."[26] In Example 5.1 in the following chapter, we discuss a similar mistaken presumption by planners of the University of Massachusetts Computer Science building that sidestepping the traditional design-bid-build process by fast-tracking would shorten the project's design and construction schedule. In fact, the opposite occurred.

One alternative project delivery method that resolves some of the issues caused by proceeding with an incomplete design and specifications is the construction management at risk (CM at risk) method. In CM at risk, the contractor is hired early in the project's design stage and is separate from the designer. During the design stage, the contractor advises the owner on planning issues, including the budget and schedule and the development of the design. Also, the owner and contractor agree during this stage on a guaranteed maximum price for the construction work. Once construction begins, the contractor takes on the role of general contractor and assumes the risk of constructing the project in accordance with the design specifications.[27] In both design-bid and CM at risk, the public agency usually issues a Request for Qualifications (RFQ) and a subsequent Request for Proposals (RFP) that usually contain preliminary concept designs for the project. Both the owners' RFPs and the contractors' proposals often do not contain detailed specifications.[28]

One advantage of the CM at risk approach is that by keeping the contractor separate from the designer, yet giving the contractor input into the design, the owner can fast-track some project elements while ensuring that the design is constructible from the contractor's standpoint. However, even CM at risk can be problematic for a public owner if the owner tries to negotiate a guaranteed maximum price for the construction before the plans and specifications are reasonably complete. Claude Lancome, executive vice president of Coast & Harbor Associates, Inc., an owner's project management firm in Massachusetts, suggests that in CM at risk contracts, the public agency wait until the project design is complete or reasonably close to it, or else until subcontractor prices are approved, before negotiating a guaranteed maximum price with the CM at risk firm. That way the price is based on complete and fully understood specifications.

Lancome adds that the less the public owner develops its own specifications and the more it relies on the contractor to come up with its own plans and specifications, "the more risk the project won't come out as intended by the owner or meet the owner's needs." In design-build, in particular, there should be some definition of the project by the time the contractor is hired, he says. "If you let the contractor figure out the job, you can't say 'you didn't build what we intended or what we need,'" Lancome contends. In Example 4.4 below, we see the potential risks that can develop when a public agency essentially cedes the development of the project specifications to the contractor.

Example 4.4: Unclear specifications in the Lynn water and sewer privatization project

In 1999, the Lynn, Massachusetts, Water and Sewer Commission issued requests for proposals for long-term contracts both to undertake a major sewer separation project in the city and to design and build improvements to and operate the city's wastewater treatment plant.

The Commission's objective in the sewer separation project was to reduce or eliminate combined sewer overflows and to alleviate flooding in a number of city neighborhoods. According to a report by the Massachusetts inspector general, the development of an adequate plan to achieve those objectives would have required that the Commission obtain information on the sources and amounts of excess water entering the existing sewer system. Despite that, the Commission did not conduct field investigation work prior to issuing its RFP for the sewer separation project. Instead, the RFP called for the selected proposer to conduct the field investigations as part of the design-build contract.[29]

In addition, the Commission chose an open-ended design approach to the project. The RFP invited proposers to develop a design based on any technology that would accomplish the project objectives. As the inspector general's report noted, the intent was to promote competition among firms to develop the most cost-effective design. However, the Commission received only two proposals in response to the RFP, and those proposals were submitted by companies owned and controlled by the same corporate entity. Moreover, the proposals submitted by each company were so different from each other that they could not be reasonably compared.

The inspector general's report stated that one of the two proposers, Modern Continental Construction Co., proposed to construct a new storm-water system and rehabilitate the existing combined sewer to serve as a sanitary-only sewer. The other proposer, U.S. Filter, proposed essentially the opposite approach—it would construct a new sanitary-only sewer and rehabilitate the existing combined sewer to serve as the storm-water system. The two proposers proposed dramatically different lump-sum prices for their work. Modern Continental's lump-sum proposal was $82 million and U.S. Filter's proposal was $48 million.

As Example 4.4 shows, there was a lack of clear specifications in at least two major respects involving the Lynn sewer separation contract. One was that proposers were not provided with information about the existing conditions of the sewer system. As the Massachusetts inspector general noted, this lack of crucial specifications made the prospect of submitting a price for undertaking the work a risky proposition for the proposers. The proposers would either have to inflate their prices to allow for worst-case scenarios, or they would have to include contract terms that would allow price increases. Secondly, the open-ended RFP provision that the proposers submit their own designs resulted in proposals for two completely different scopes of work. Thus, the inspector general concluded that the two lump-sum prices themselves could not be meaningfully compared.

Indefinite Delivery/Indefinite Quantity Contracts

As is the case with certain alternative project delivery approaches, Indefinite Delivery/Indefinite Quantity Contracts (IDIQ), which are authorized at the federal level under the Federal Acquisition Regulation, are associated with an initial lack of detailed specifications.[30] These contracts involve the awards of unspecified amounts of future work to preapproved contractors. Specifications are developed after the contracts are signed and take the form of task orders for the delivery of services, and delivery orders for the delivery of supplies. Critics, such as the Project on Government Oversight, charge that some of these contracts, which have been used extensively in the U.S. reconstruction efforts in Iraq, have effectively guaranteed a small number of favored contractors billions of dollars in noncompetitive awards. The contractors acquire effective monopolies in providing services under the contracts, in many cases for years.[31]

Many project experts contend that IDIQ contracts offer an advantage to public agencies in that they allow the agencies to develop productive relationships with a small number of contractors that are experienced in the work involved. Thus, the arrangement can save time in bidding and can offer an assurance that the contractors know how to do the work. Moreover, selected contractors will have an incentive to perform well or risk losing the IDIQ contract. However, if task orders under these contracts themselves have vague specifications or are not issued in a timely manner, the potential risks of IDIQ contracting can be realized. In some respects, the Port of Seattle contract referred to in Example 4.3 operated much like an IDIQ contract. In that case, there were apparently not even any work authorizations (similar to task orders) issued during the 10-year period following an initial authorization.

The limited competitive nature of IDIQ contracts combined with their lack of initial specifications appear to have resulted in high costs of many reconstruction projects in Iraq. Example 4.5 illustrates a number of problems associated with three IDIQ contracts awarded to one of the major U.S. contractors in Iraq.

Example 4.5: KBR IDIQ contracts are subject to cost overruns in Iraq

Kellogg Brown and Root (KBR), a subsidiary of Halliburton, Inc., was first awarded an IDIQ contract with the U.S. Army Corps of Engineers in 2001.[32] As the Office of the Special Inspector General for Iraq Reconstruction reported, KBR initially received a one-year contract under the umbrella Logistics Civil Augmentation Program (LOGCAP), with nine one-year options to extend it. LOGCAP is intended to coordinate contractor-based logistical, engineering, and construction services in wartime situations. In 1992, LOGCAP was converted into "an umbrella support contract with a single worldwide provider."[33]

In November 2002, the Army awarded a task order under the LOGCAP contract to KBR to develop contingency plans for the repair and operation of Iraq's oil infrastructure, should it be destroyed or damaged. The original value of the task order was only $1.9 million. Then, four months later, prior to the U.S. invasion of Iraq, KBR was awarded a separate, sole-source IDIQ cost-plus contract with a ceiling of $7 billion, to carry out its plans and to restore the oil infrastructure. The GAO noted that task orders under this contract were not even negotiated until some six months after the actual construction work began. As a result, the DoD paid more than $220 million in "questioned costs" under this contract to KBR.[34]

Regarding the KBR LOGCAP contract, an Army Audit Agency report in November 2004 found that the company had "inflated" its estimates, charged "excessive costs," billed for equipment that "wasn't necessary," and submitted millions of dollars in "duplicate costs."[35] The Army audit faulted the Defense Department for disregarding its own independent cost estimates for task orders under the program and relying on KBR's cost estimates. In one task order, for operations and maintenance at Baghdad International Airport, the government had estimated the cost at $1.9 million and KBR had billed the government for $12.8 million.

KBR received yet another Iraq IDIQ reconstruction contract worth $1.2 billion in January 2004 to rebuild the oil infrastructure in southern Iraq. According to the Special Inspector General for Iraq Reconstruction, the company received only a mobilization task order under the contract in February 2004, and did not begin substantial work until November of that year. During that nine-month period of inactivity, KBR billed the government $52.7 million in administrative costs and $13.4 million in project costs.[36]

The rationale for entering into IDIQ contracts in Iraq was that it was difficult or impossible to specify in advance the precise details and quantities of services or supplies needed in that complex, wartime situation. IDIQ contracts were needed to give the government and experienced contractors the flexibility to act quickly in difficult and fluid circumstances. However, it does not appear that the use of IDIQ contracts in Iraq always helped the U.S. government save either time or money in its reconstruction efforts. The Special Inspector General for Iraq Reconstruction, for instance, detailed numerous delays in the issuance of task orders under the IDIQ contracts and blamed these delays on security and funding issues, "inappropriate" scopes of work, and indecision.[37] Compounding the problem was the fact that the task orders themselves often lacked specifications. As the special inspector general noted:

> The failure to definitize contracts—essentially to come to a final agreement on what will be done, how much it will cost, and when it will be completed—significantly inhibited the government's ability to control costs within the (reconstruction) program.[38]

Performance versus Design Specifications

Two major types of specifications in bid documents and contracts are design and performance specifications. The difference between these two types of specifications is well summarized in a U.S. Court of Federal Claims decision (*Travelers Casualty and Surety of America v. The United States*, No. 02-584C & 03-1548C). The court stated that design specifications dictate the "how" governing a contractor's tasks, in contrast to performance specifications, which concern the "what" that is to be done. According to the court, details concerning measurements, tolerances, and materials—in other words "elaborate instructions on how to perform the contract"—qualify as design specifications. In those instances in which the specifications are described in precise detail and permit the contractor no discretion, they are labeled "design." In contrast, where the specifications set forth simply an objective or standard and leave the means of attaining that end to the contractor, they are "performance."

The federal claims court also referred in that same decision to the landmark Supreme Court case, *Spearin v. United States* (248 U.S. 132, 1918), which found that contractors cannot be held responsible for defective plans and specifications that have been provided by the government. The case underscores the care public

TIP FOR SUCCESS:

A mix of performance and design specifications is often used in complex public projects. Disputes can arise if performance specifications, in particular, are unclear.

agencies must exercise in developing specifications. Defects will often come back to haunt them.[39]

There is considerable debate over design and performance specifications, and which type is better to use. The federal Office of Management and Budget's Capital Programming Guide, referred to earlier in this chapter, argues in favor of managerial discretion and specifically advises against the use of design specifications in competitive bidding solicitations. The Guide, for instance, describes a renovation program at the Pentagon, which was undertaken in several phases. In the first phase, the design plans included 2,600 pages of detailed design specifications. The second through fifth phases used a "performance-based contract," and needed just 16 pages to communicate performance-based requirements. The OMB Guide states that the use of performance-based specifications (PBSs) "is a mandatory requirement for all major (federal) acquisitions."[40] OMB, perhaps in reference to the Spearin Supreme Court decision, contends that "design and specification detail" actually increases the risk assumed by the public agency for the project's success.

Other analysts maintain, however, that the use of performance specifications can actually be more risky to both the public and private entities in complex projects—particularly in cases in which there might be differing interpretations of the specifications. Example 4.6 shows how differing interpretations of an apparently simple performance specification can lead to costly disputes in a public project.

Example 4.6: Risks imposed by a performance specification in the University of Massachusetts Computer Science Center project

Performance specifications are frequently used in the design-build approach in construction projects in which the design lacks specificity prior to the selection of a design-build contractor (see our discussion of design-build contracting earlier in this chapter). In the design-build construction of a computer science building, which was completed at the University of Massachusetts at Amherst in 1999, several disputes between the contractor and owner arose because of the lack of specificity of the requirements.[41] The state's public construction management agency—the Division of Capital Asset Management (DCAM)—planned, procured, and administered the contract for the project.

This example focuses on problems arising from just one performance specification involving the installation of a cable tray system in the building. The RFP issued by DCAM for the construction of the computer science building contained a performance specification that trays for computer and other electronic cables were to be "accessible" to allow the building's users to reconfigure the computer cabling easily. The cable trays, along with HVAC ductwork and other mechanical systems, were to be installed above a suspending ceiling with removable panels to permit access. There was no design specification, however, stating that the cable trays must be installed with a certain minimum clearance to ensure that accessibility.

After the contractor, Suffolk Building Corporation, began to install cable trays in the building that allowed only 2½ inches of clearance between the trays and the ductwork, the University of Massachusetts, the user agency, objected, stating that it required eight inches of clearance. According to the Massachusetts inspector general, DCAM also objected to the cable tray installation and ordered Suffolk to remove, refabricate, and reinstall it at no additional cost to the state. Suffolk, however, denied responsibility for correcting the problem and continued to install the cable trays for another month.

At that point, however, Suffolk proposed to lower the ceiling panels in the main corridors and drop the cable trays downwards to allow the eight inches of clearance between the trays and the ductwork. The state accepted the solution, but continued to hold to its position that Suffolk was responsible for correcting the cable tray access problem without additional compensation. Suffolk then discontinued the cable tray work for approximately six weeks—a hiatus that began to affect other subcontract work.

Nearly three months after Suffolk began installing the cable trays, the company submitted a proposed change order for more than $33,000 for all costs associated with improving access to the trays. DCAM rejected the change order and Suffolk later resubmitted it as part of an overall claim, seeking a $2.7 million increase in the total contract price for the building. (This claim is discussed in detail in Chapter 9, Example 9.3.)

In Example 4.6, the requirement that the cable tray be "accessible" showed *what* was wanted by the University of Massachusetts, not *how* it would be done. Thus, it was a clear example of a performance specification. Had the requirement been that there must be at least eight inches of clearance above the cable tray, that would have been a design specification. The problem in this case is that the objective of the specification that the cable tray be accessible was vague enough that it was open to interpretation and therefore to dispute. The contractor was able—or at least considered itself in a position—to argue that it was complying with the contract by providing 2½ inches of clearance.

For reasons such as those illustrated in Example 4.6, this author would suggest that a reliance on performance specifications is appropriate in cases in which the project design is relatively simple, straightforward, or standardized, such as in modular or simple buildings. When specifications are vague or open to interpretation, they invite disputes between owners and contractors. For that reason, a mix of design and performance specifications is often preferable, particularly in complex projects.

Concluding the Intermediate Planning Stage

Once the project manager has developed clear project specifications and effective internal control procedures, the project planning process is almost complete. The major planning tasks that remain include developing the project schedule and refining cost and risk estimates (both of which we will discuss in the next chapter). As noted above, clear specifications will not only help the project manager in subsequently selecting the best external agents, entering into advantageous agreements with them, and evaluating their work effectively, but they also contribute to an effective internal control structure for the project. The specifications help accomplish that by detailing the work to be done and, in many cases, who is to do it. As Example 4.3 involving the architectural-engineering contract with the Port of Seattle shows, a lack of specifications regarding the work to be done by the contractor resulted in the inappropriate assignment of contractor staff to day-to-day Port agency duties. Not only was this arrangement unduly expensive, but it very likely resulted in confused lines of authority within the project management staff. The arrangement would therefore be unlikely to have met the first of the GAO's five internal control standards, discussed above.

With effective internal control standards and specifications established, the project management team should find itself in a strong position to meet the pressing demands of the project that lie ahead.

Endnotes

1. Morgan, Gareth. 2006. *Images of Organization.* Thousand Oaks, CA: Sage Publications, Inc.
2. Morgan (2006) maintains that organizations "must possess a certain degree of 'space' or autonomy that allows appropriate innovation to occur." Managers, he says, "should define no more than is absolutely necessary to launch a particular initiative or activity on its way." Pp. 110–111.
3. United States Government Accountability Office. 1999. *Standards for Internal Control in the Federal Government.* GAO/AIMD-00-21.3.1.
4. United States Government Accountability Office. 1999. P. 15.
5. Washington State Auditor. 2007. *Performance Audit Report: Port of Seattle Construction Management.*
6. Washington State Auditor. 2007. P. 140.
7. McKay, Mike, Krista Bush, John Keller et al. 2008. *Report of the Special Investigative Team* [Port of Seattle audit case]. December 3, 2008. McKay Chadwell, PLLC.
8. Washington State Auditor. 2007. P. 143.
9. Massachusetts Water Resources Authority. *The Boston Harbor Project: An Environmental Success Story.* Website information on the Boston Harbor cleanup project. http://www.mwra.com/01news/2008/bhpenvironentalsuccess/bhpenvsuccess.htm.
10. The Massachusetts Turnpike Authority, which built and operates the Massachusetts Turnpike, is a quasi-public agency, which was placed in charge of the Big Dig project in 1997. Prior to that year, the Massachusetts Highway Department was in charge of oversight of the project.
11. See Palmer, Thomas C. Cerasoli charges Big Dig Coverup. *Boston Globe.* March 21, 2001. http://boston.com/globe/metro/packages/bechtel/archives/032101.htm.
12. *CommonWealth* magazine. 2006. *Second-Guesswork: Fred Salvucci Insists That the Big Dig Was the Right Project, Just Not Done Right.* Fall 2006. P. 73.
13. Commonwealth of Massachusetts, Division of Capital Asset Management. *Owners' Project Manager Guidelines.* December 2004. http://www.mass.gov/cam/Creform/Own_PM_Guide.pdf.

14. Washington State Auditor. 2007. P. 185.
15. The Auditing Standards Board is the senior technical body of the American Institute of Certified Public Accounts (AICPA), a national professional organization for all CPAs. The Auditing Standards Board issues Statements on Auditing Standards, which provide guidance to accountants, auditors, and auditing organizations around the country.
16. Office of Management and Budget. 2006. *Capital Programming Guide.* Supplement to Circular A-11, Part 7.
17. The OMB deputy administrator wrote to this author in November 2008 that one OMB rule, finalized the previous year, requires federal contractors to have a written code of business ethics. A second rule, which was being finalized, was intended to address requirements to disclose violations of criminal law and the False Claims Act in connection with the award and performance of government contracts. OMB, the deputy administrator added, was also looking at how controls on supply chain management might be strengthened to reduce some forms of information technology security risks.
18. Zepezauer, Mark, and Arthur Naimen. 1996. *Take the Rich off Welfare.* Odonian Press.
19. Gay, Sean. 2008. Commentary: Examining Fraud and Public Contracting. *Daily Journal of Commerce.* AllBusiness.com, Inc. June 20, 2008. Available online at http://www.allbusiness.com/company-activities-management/contracts-bids/11464093-1.html
20. Werkman, Janet, and David L. Westerling. 2000. Privatizing Municipal Water and Wastewater Systems: Promises and Pitfalls. *Public Works Management & Policy* 5:1:52–68.
21. Cibinic, John, Jr., Ralph C. Nash, Jr., and James F. Nagle. 2006. *Administration of Government Contracts,* 4th edition. CCH, Inc. P. 272.
22. Washington State Auditor. 2007.
23. Washington State Auditor. 2007. P. 76.
24. Lewis, Raphael, and Sean P. Murphy. Easy Pass: Why Bechtel Never Paid for its Big Dig Mistakes. *Boston Globe.* February 9, 10, 11, 2003. http://www.boston.com/globe/metro/packages/bechtel/.
25. Bechtel/Parsons Brinckerhoff contended that the Big Dig project was intended as a fast-tracked project and that as the construction manager, it had the authority to approve some construction work prior to the final design. The Massachusetts inspector general countered that after a 12-year review of hundreds of thousands of project documents, the Office was "not aware of any verification of B/PB's claim that a 'fast track' system was implemented to supersede B/PB's contractual obligations to promulgate preliminary designs and to accept or reject final designs to facilitate construction" (Commonwealth of Massachusetts, Office of the Inspector General, 2003. P. 13).
26. Commonwealth of Massachusetts, Office of the Inspector General, 2003. P. 7.
27. Commonwealth of Massachusetts, Office of the Inspector General. 2005. *Designing and Constructing Public Facilities: Legal Requirements, Recommended Practices, Sources of Assistance.* http://www.mass.gov/ig/publ/dcmanual.pdf.
28. In Construction Management at Risk, Massachusetts law requires that the design for individual work packages be 100 percent complete before construction can start on them; however, some preliminary construction work is allowed to begin before the design of the rest of the project is complete (Massachusetts General Laws, chapter 149A).
29. Commonwealth of Massachusetts, Office of the Inspector General. 2001. *Privatization of Wastewater Facilities in Lynn, Massachusetts.*
30. Project on Government Oversight. *Federal Contracting and Iraq Reconstruction.* http://www.pogo.org/p/contracts/co-031001-iraq.html.
31. Project on Government Oversight. 2003. *Iraq Reconstruction Contracting Abuses.* October 27, 2003 Press Release. http://www.commondreams.org/news2003/1027-07.htm.

32. Office of the Special Inspector General for Iraq Reconstruction. 2006. *Iraq Reconstruction: Lessons in Contracting and Procurement.*
33. Office of the Special Inspector General for Iraq Reconstruction. 2006. P. 15.
34. United States Government Accountability Office. March 2008. *Stabilizing and Rebuilding Iraq, Actions Needed to Address Inadequate Accountability over U.S. Efforts and Investments.* Statement of David M. Walker. GAO-08-568T.
35. United States House of Representatives, Committee on Oversight and Government Reform. February 15, 2007. *Hearing on Iraq Reconstruction: An Overview. Preliminary Transcript.* http://oversight.house.gov/documents/20071114145606.pdf
36. Office of the Special Inspector General for Iraq Reconstruction. 2007. *Iraq Reconstruction: Lessons in Program and Project Management.*
37. Office of the Special Inspector General for Iraq Reconstruction. 2007. P. 79.
38. Office of the Special Inspector General for Iraq Reconstruction. 2007. P. 72.
39. In the Spearin case, the federal government had provided plans and specifications to a contractor to build a dry dock at the Brooklyn Navy Yard and to divert a section of a sewer that ran through the construction area. About a year after the sewer relocation, a sudden downpour of rain caused flooding, which backed up inside the sewer pipe and broke it, flooding the dry dock. It was later found that the flooding had been caused by a dam inside a portion of the sewer. The government's plans provided to the contractor had not shown the dam. The contractor refused to continue with the dry dock construction until the government assumed responsibility for the damages or changed the sewer system. The Supreme Court ruled in the contractor's favor, concluding that contractors cannot be held responsible for defects in public agencies' plans and specifications. In Massachusetts, a comparable Supreme Judicial Court case concerning the need for adequate specifications is *Sweezey v. Mayor of Malden,* 273 Mass. 536, (1931) (see discussion of *Sweezey* in endnote 27 in Chapter 3).
40. Office of Management and Budget. 2006. P. 37. The statement in the OMB Capital Programming Guide that performance specifications are required in all major federal acquisitions does not appear to be completely borne out by the Federal Acquisition Regulation. (See FAR 11.101, 37.6 and 37.102.) FAR 37.102, for instance, states only that performance specifications are the "preferred method for acquiring services" (Public Law 106-398, section 821); that federal agencies must use performance specifications "to the maximum extent practicable," and that exceptions include architect-engineering services and construction.
41. Commonwealth of Massachusetts, Office of the Inspector General, 2001. *A Report on the Design and Construction of the University of Massachusetts Computer Science Center.*

Chapter 5

Project Planning, Part 3:
Finalizing the Process

As we've previously discussed, the success or failure of public projects ultimately comes down to the project manager's success or failure in balancing three major factors—scope, schedule, and cost. We examined project scope, in the form of plans and specifications, in the last chapter, and will focus in this chapter on two final planning steps that must be taken in the planning phase—development of the project schedule and refinement of cost and risk estimates.

Developing the Project Schedule

The project schedule is the projected amount of time it will take to complete the project's scope of work, which is the total amount of work involved in completing the project successfully. The schedule is expressed in terms of objectives or goals, which are often referred to as "milestones." Milestones are significant events, such as the starting point or completion of a phase of the project or the delivery of a product created by the project.

Like the final estimated cost of the project, the final schedule can be fully developed only when the scope of work is fully known and specified. And as is the case with the projected cost, it is crucial that the estimate of the project schedule be realistic, i.e., based on realistic estimates of the amount of time it will take to complete the project scope.

Early in the conceptual stage of planning, the schedule may be very preliminary. The project management team, often with the assistance of an owner's project manager, will continually refine the schedule estimate, particularly as the project

TIPS FOR SUCCESS:

■ The project schedule becomes more fully developed as the project design is refined.

■ The public sector project manager should develop a "macro-schedule" that stresses strategic goals and objectives.

■ The contractor's schedule covers all construction or project work activities.

design nears completion and more data become available on which to base it. As with a realistic cost estimate, a realistic schedule estimate will help the project manager in evaluating competing proposals from contractors should major aspects of the project work be outsourced. Once construction or project execution begins, the schedule will then serve as one of the principal bases on which to measure the contractor's performance.

It is important to note that project schedules can come in a number of different forms, and not everyone involved in a particular project develops or makes use of the same form of schedule. George Ritz notes in a private sector context that in outsourced projects, the owner and contractor have differing scheduling goals and priorities. The public sector project manager's or owner's schedule tends to be a "macro schedule" that stresses strategic planning goals. The contractor's schedule is "a fully detailed operational schedule covering all the construction or project work activities and finishing within the owner's strategic end date."[1]

The Defense Department refers to an owner's schedule in military-based procurements as an "Integrated Master Schedule" (IMS).[2] We will mainly discuss the owner's scheduling issues in this chapter, but will touch on some contractor scheduling issues. Ultimately, the milestones in the owner's schedule need to match up with the contractor's own schedule. Karen Richey, a GAO senior cost analyst, pointed out in an interview that the owner's schedule often includes a number of activities that are outside the public agency's contract with a general contractor, such as furnishing equipment, program management activities, and testing.

In general, the project owner and the public sector project manager and his or her team will develop a preliminary owner's schedule before detailed plans and specifications are developed for the project. However, the very development of those plans and specifications will necessitate updates to the schedule. For that reason, we've listed scheduling as a planning activity that follows our discussion in the previous chapter of the development of plans and specifications.

It's important to note that in construction projects in particular, the order of the owner's schedule-based milestones varies depending on the project delivery approach. In previous chapters, we've discussed three major delivery approaches: traditional design-bid build, design-build, and construction management at risk. Let's first consider the owner's schedule in a traditional design-bid-build public construction project. In all of these cases, we'll consider the project schedule to begin at the point at which the project's preliminary or conceptual planning stage is complete.

Owner's Schedule in a Design–Bid–Build Public Construction Project

In a traditional design-bid-build delivery approach, the major milestones that make up the owner's schedule would be as follows:

1. Select an architect or designer and develop detailed plans and specifications on which the prospective general contractor will bid. (In an in-house project, of course, there would be no such selection step in the owner's schedule.) Architects or designers for public building projects are generally selected under a qualifications-based selection process.[3] In addition to developing detailed plans and specifications, the architect or designer may also conduct field surveys and tests to provide detailed information about conditions at the site and may consult with the project's users, abutters, and other stakeholders. The likely duration of all of these activities should be considered when calculating the total duration of this phase of the owner's schedule.

2. Select a general contractor to undertake the project work. General contractors bidding on traditional design-bid-build projects are generally selected on the basis of the lowest bid. Prospective contractors submit their bids based on complete plans and specifications for the project.[4]

3. Institute redesign by the architect if necessary to meet budgeted costs, and/or rebid the new design. Once the bids from the general contractor and, in some cases, subcontractors are opened, they must be compared to the cost estimate provided by the architect or designer. (We will discuss the development of the cost estimate later in this chapter). It is possible that the general contractor's low bid will be significantly higher than the estimated construction cost. In that case, the project manager may decide to rebid the project or return to the design stage and possibly reduce the project scope. An owner's schedule should include a contingency for those potential occurrences.

4. Award the contract. A number of steps are involved in this stage of the procurement process, and the owner's schedule should reflect the time needed for those activities. For instance, once the general contractor and subcontractors are selected, the contract award may be subject to approval by a board or even a separate public agency. The owner's schedule should also take into account the possibility that things can still go wrong at this point. In Massachusetts,

for instance, the lowest bidder must provide the owner with performance and payment bonds to ensure against failure to perform the contracted work and failure to pay suppliers or subcontractors, respectively. If, for some reason, the low bidder fails after a prescribed time period to submit those bonds or to sign the contract, the owner must select the next lowest bidder and start the contract execution and bond submission process over again.

5. Give contractor(s) notice to proceed. From this point on, the contractor is responsible for completing the project work within the period of time specified in the contract. As noted above, the contractor must develop a detailed operational schedule of its own that covers all the project work activities to meet the contractual finish date.

6. Monitor schedule performance and changes. The duration of this phase of the project is, of course, among the most difficult to estimate. Completing the project scope of work on time is subject to a wide variety of risks—as we will discuss later in this chapter—and schedule slippage is a constant concern of the project management team. The schedule should therefore contain a contingency for those risks.

7. Final inspection and facility or project acceptance.

A significant amount of time must be allocated by the project management team to the design phase of a traditional design-bid-build construction project. That is one reason alternative delivery approaches have become popular in recent years—their purpose being to allow the first two schedule milestones above, relating to the design and selection of the contractor, to overlap. Thus, the owner's schedule would differ from the design-bid-build schedule above if the project used a design-build or CM at risk approach.

Key milestones in an owner's schedule for a CM at risk project are the following:

1. Select an architect or designer to develop detailed plans and specifications for the project.[5]

2. Select a construction management at risk firm on the basis of a qualifications-based process and a request for proposals. (The CM at risk firm is selected before the plans and specifications are completely developed by the architect.)

3. Negotiate a Guaranteed Maximum Price for the project. As noted in Chapter 4, at least one expert advises owners to negotiate a Guaranteed Maximum Price only after the project design is close to being complete or the trade or subcontractor prices are approved by the owner.

4. Start preliminary construction activities on which design has been completed.

5. Complete design of the rest of the project with the input of the CM at risk firm and possibly an owner's project manager.

6. Monitor the CM at risk firm's schedule performance on the project.

7. Final inspection and facility or project acceptance.

Although there are the same number of steps in the above owner's schedule of a CM at risk project as in the schedule above of a traditional design-bid-build project, the CM at risk schedule duration may be shorter primarily because Milestone #2, the selection of the CM at risk contractor, is reached before the project design is complete. Also, Milestone #3 in the traditional design-bid-build schedule—involving the need for redesign if the contractors' bids come in too high—will not be a risk to the schedule in a CM at risk project. Nevertheless, it is important in a CM at risk project for the owner to be closely involved in coordinating the efforts of the designer and CM at risk firm in finalizing the project design. The State of Washington Joint Legislative Audit and Review Committee states that project management on the part of the owner must be "as great or more intensive" with the CM at risk method as it is with the design-bid-build method.[6]

It is also important to keep in mind that project scheduling is not an exact science and that fast-tracking plans do not always work as intended. Example 5.1 discusses two preliminary projected owner's project schedules that were part of a feasibility study done for the University of Massachusetts Computer Science Center project. (This project was previously discussed in Chapters 1 and 4.) As the example below shows, project managers should not automatically assume, in developing their project schedule, that the design-build approach to project delivery will be faster than the traditional design-bid-build approach.

Example 5.1: Underestimating the design-build schedule for the UMass Computer Science Center

In developing the feasibility study for the University of Massachusetts Computer Science Center project, the study designer determined that the university had placed a high priority on completing the project quickly.[7] The study predicted that a design-build approach would shorten the project schedule by allowing construction work to begin before the design was complete. As a result, the study designer recommended that the state Division of Capital Asset Management (DCAM), the state's public construction management agency, use design-build procedures authorized by the state's modular building procurement law.[8]

Figure 5.1 shows the feasibility study's comparison of a projected modular (design-build) construction schedule with a projected design-bid-build schedule for the Computer Science Center.

As Figure 5.1 shows, the feasibility study designer for the Computer Science Center projected that it would take nine months—or 50 percent longer—to complete the project using the traditional design-bid-build method than the modular design-build method. The designer assumed the modular schedule would be shorter primarily because of the lack of a need for a complete design in a modular project. However, the feasibility study's projected schedule was not realized. The project actually took a total of 37 months to complete—19 months longer than the projected modular construction schedule and 10 months longer than the projected design-bid-build schedule.

Projected Modular (Design-Build) Construction Schedule		Projected Design-Bid-Build Schedule	
Milestone	Duration in months	Milestone	Duration in months
1. Prepare and issue the RFP	2	1. Select the designer	3
2. Select the contractor and negotiate the contract	1	2. Complete the design for the project	9
3. Review and approve the design	3	3. Undertake bid process and select the contractor	3
4. Undertake and complete construction	12	4. Construction	12
Total	18		27

Figure 5.1 UMass Computer Science Center feasibility study owner's project schedule comparison. (From Commonwealth of Massachusetts, Office of the Inspector General, 2001. A Report on the Design and Construction of the University of Massachusetts Computer Science Center.)

One reason for the delay is that the lack of a complete design in this project resulted in numerous disputes between the owner and the design-build team, according to the Massachusetts inspector general (see the dispute over the cable tray installation in Example 4.6).

There are many reasons why an owner's project schedule can go wrong before it even takes effect, and Example 5.1 illustrates one of them. If the project management team is basing its projected schedule on a faulty presumption, then the projected schedule is unlikely to be a viable one. This is one reason that the project management team needs to examine its projected schedule closely and question all of the presumptions that may lie behind it. Questioning presumptions, as we discussed in Chapter 3, is one of the early steps in project planning to which the project management team should frequently return.

In the case of the Computer Science Center, there was a presumption by the project study designer that undertaking a complete design prior to construction would significantly delay the project. Had the designer carefully examined that presumption, he or she might have asked whether, in fact, proceeding without a complete design works in situations involving buildings such as a computer science building, which is expected to have relatively complex laboratory and other functions. It may be that the study designer presumed that such a building could indeed be completely constructed using a modular process. In that case, the university and the state agency managing the building construction might have more carefully questioned a subsequent decision by the contractor to build the first two floors by conventional methods. That, in turn, might have changed their presumption that a complete design was not needed before construction could begin.[9]

Scheduling the Project Work

Simply listing the owner's project milestones, as we've done above for public projects, is, of course, not sufficient in project scheduling. The owner and contractor must estimate the likely amounts of time it will take to reach each milestone. To accomplish that, both the owner's and the contractor's project scheduling generally proceeds in three phases: (1) development of a Work Breakdown Structure for the project, which breaks the scope of work into detailed work packages; (2) development of a logic diagram, which establishes a time sequence for the work packages; and (3) determination of the schedule's "critical path." Carrying out these three phases will enable the owner and contractor to develop realistic schedule projections.

TIP FOR SUCCESS:

Effective project scheduling involves:

1. Developing a project Work Breakdown Structure to determine all work activities.
2. Developing a logic diagram to determine activity durations.
3. Determining the schedule's "critical path."

The Work Breakdown Structure

In complex projects and programs, both scheduling and cost estimating often begin by organizing the project work according to levels of detail in what is referred to as a Work Breakdown Structure (WBS). Each descending level of the WBS depicts smaller pieces of the work in increasing detail. At the lowest level are separate "work packages," which are used to generate detailed cost and schedule information for the project.

The Government Accountability Office's Cost Estimating and Assessment Guide for federal programs describes the WBS as "the cornerstone for every program [and consequently every project], because it defines in detail the work necessary to accomplish a program's objectives." It does this by "reflecting the requirements, resources, and tasks that must be accomplished to develop a program."[10] The WBS is generally developed with input from the designer or architect or engineering team in a public project.

In many public projects, the WBS is organized according to 50 divisions established by the Construction Specifications Institute (CSI), a national organization that establishes construction-related standards.[11] Selected CSI project work divisions, all of which are often referred to as the MasterFormat, are listed below:

1. **General Requirements:** This includes overhead items directly associated with the project such as job trailers, supervision, field testing, security fencing, and project cleanup.
2. **Existing Conditions:** Includes such things as site demolition, grading, site utilities, landscaping.
3. **Concrete:** Includes cast-in-place concrete, reinforcing steel, concrete finishing.
4. **Masonry:** Includes brick, concrete block, stone, and mortar.
5. **Metals:** Includes steel beams, girders, columns, metal decking, and pipe railings.
6. **Wood and Plastics:** Includes rough carpentry, interior trim, cabinets, shelving, and stairs.
7. **Thermal and Moisture Protection:** Includes insulation, roofing, waterproofing, gutters, downspouts, flashing, and caulking.
8. **Doors and Windows:** Includes metal and wood doors, windows, skylights, and glass.
9. **Finishes:** Includes drywall, paint, carpet, wall coverings, and tile.
10. **Specialties:** Includes items such as flagpoles, toilet partitions, fire extinguishers, and bathroom mirrors.
11. **Equipment:** Includes items such as kitchen appliances, medical and recreational equipment.
12. **Furnishings:** Includes draperies, art, murals, bookcases, stadium seating, plants, and planters.
13. **Special Construction:** Includes such things as swimming pools, tennis courts, and security systems.
14. **Conveying Equipment:** Includes elevators and escalators.
22. **Plumbing:** Includes plumbing pipes and pumps, facility sanitary sewers, storm drains, vacuum piping for laboratory and healthcare facilities.
23. **Heating, Ventilating, and Air Conditioning:** Includes duct work, central heating equipment, boilers, furnaces, refrigerant compressors, central HVAC equipment.
26. **Electrical:** Includes electrical distribution systems, electrical generating equipment, wiring, transformers, light fixtures.
27. **Communications:** Includes structured cabling, data communications network equipment, data communications software, voice communications systems, audio-video and electronic digital systems.

Each of the major divisions in the MasterFormat comprise one level of the WBS in many public construction projects. Those divisions are broken down into

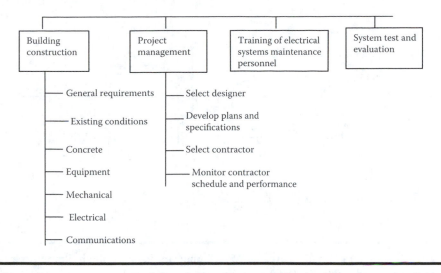

Figure 5.2   A Program Work Breakdown Structure for a public computer science building project.

increasingly detailed elements or items of work. In addition, an owner's level or program WBS consists of a number of common elements to all programs or projects, such as "program management," training, and system test and evaluation elements. The GAO defines the program management element as "planning, organizing... controlling and approval actions" that are needed for the project.[12] For our purposes, we will refer to this element as a project management element.

Figure 5.2 shows a simplified program WBS for a public building construction project, with some selected owner's level elements and construction-related MasterFormat elements included in it.

Development of a Logic Diagram

Once the WBS has been developed, the next step in the scheduling process is to take the elements of the WBS and determine their sequence in time and their durations. One way to do this is by means of a Program Review and Evaluation Technique (PERT) diagram. As Figure 5.3 shows, each work activity in a PERT diagram is represented by a "node box," which lists four "characteristic" times for each work activity. The PERT diagram in the figure represents a limited portion of the owner's schedule.

The top left square within the node box lists the earliest time at which the particular activity can start (EST). The bottom left square lists the latest time at which it can start (LST). The top right square lists the earliest time at which the activity is expected to be finished (EFT), and the bottom right square lists the latest estimated finish time (LFT).

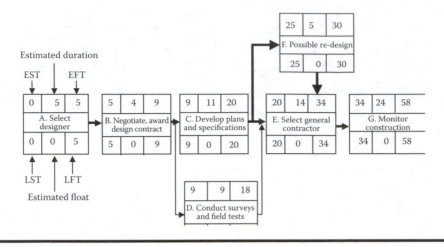

Figure 5.3 Selected node boxes in a PERT diagram for a public building project owner's schedule. (Numbers represent weeks.)

The estimated duration of the activities listed in the node boxes in Figure 5.3 are equal to the difference between the EST and the EFT and are listed in the middle square at the top of each box. If the EST and the LST are different for a particular work activity—in other words, if there is leeway for the activity to begin within a specified period of time after the EST—then that amount of spare time is called the "float" for that activity. The float is the difference between the EST and the LST and is listed in the middle square at the bottom of the box. In Figure 5.3, the activities in box D has a float associated with it. A number of software packages are available to help project owners and contractors to construct logic diagrams easily.

Determination of the Schedule's "Critical Path"

The final and key element in project scheduling is the determination of the schedule's "critical path." The fundamental purpose of critical path scheduling, which has been in use on projects for some 30 years, is to enable the scheduler to find the shortest possible time in which to complete the project.[13] George Lewis defines the critical path as "the longest series of activities (that can't be done in parallel) and which therefore governs how early the project can be completed."[14]

In Figure 5.3, the activities linked by the heavy-lined arrows (boxes A, B, C, E, possibly F, and G) are considered to be on the critical path because they have zero float, meaning that they must be completed as scheduled, or the entire project will fall behind schedule. The project manager must pay even closer attention to these activities than to those which have float. A schedule bar chart, often referred to as a Gantt chart, such as the one shown in Figure 5.4, is usually developed on the basis of a critical path scheduling process.

Figure 5.4 shows a bar chart owner's schedule of the milestones listed above for the same hypothetical public project using the traditional design-bid-build project delivery method.

Most of the activities in the *owner's* schedule (as depicted in Figure 5.4) occur in series with each activity serving as a predecessor to the following one. Thus, most of those activities are on the critical path. George Ritz suggests that the owner must

							Months								
	1	2	3	4	5	6	7	8	9	10	11	12	13	14	15
Design phase															
Select designer	▬														
Negotiate and award design contract		▬													
Develop plans and specifications			▬▬▬												
Conduct surveys and field tests			▬▬												
Contractor selection phase															
Select general contractor					▬▬▬										
Possible re-design					▬										
Award contract and notice to proceed								M							
Construction phase															
Monitor construction									▬▬▬▬▬▬						
Substantial completion														M	
Final inspection														▬	
Project acceptance															M

Legend: ═══ Float   **M** Milestone activity   ▬▬▬ Scheduled time

Figure 5.4   Owner's schedule chart for a design-bid-build public construction project.

insert a "nominal float" into these project activities if the schedule is to have any chance of being successfully met.[15] Monitoring the critical path is a key element in controlling projects once the work is underway.

Putting It All Together: The Importance of Realistic Scheduling

The critical path scheduling method allows public sector managers and contractors to compare the value of the work actually completed on a project at given milestones to the value of the work budgeted for that period. (We will discuss that progress-monitoring process in Chapter 9.) As many analysts point out, it is better for both the owner and contractor to project realistic schedules that have a good chance of being met than to project unrealistically tight schedules (with no contingency reserves) that are likely to be exceeded once the project is actually underway. The Catch-22 is that project planners have a strong incentive to project overly optimistic schedules just as is the case with project costs to make their projects more attractive to potential funding sources. Similarly, contractors submitting bids or proposals for projects have a strong incentive to claim to be able to meet an overly optimistic schedule to increase their chances of being selected for the contract.

The project planner who is honest about the likely duration of a project may face opposition from certain stakeholders who want the project done quickly and cheaply. Similarly, the contractor who honestly states that the owner's projected schedule may be impossible to meet may not get the contract. This sometimes results in situations in which project managers and contractors are forced either to lie about or "game the schedule" or else to allow the adherence to the schedule to drive the project. Projecting overly optimistic schedules can result in a cascade of problems once the projects are underway.

Refining Project Cost and Risk Estimates

In Chapter 3, we noted that preliminary cost estimates of projects are often highly optimistic and that this is one of the first ways in which projects go wrong. Yet, as that chapter discussed, there are ways of avoiding the optimism trap early on, particularly through the use of historical data and "parametric" cost estimating techniques that involve the development of a statistical relationship between historical costs and the planned program or project's specifications.

In this half of this chapter, we will discuss methods of refining those preliminary cost and risk estimates as the project's design progresses. As is the case with the project schedule, the degree of refinement in cost and risk projections depends on the level of completeness of project plans and specifications. The more complete the plans and specifications are, the greater the potential for accurately projecting the project cost and the greater the degree of confidence the management team can have in that projection. That higher confidence can, in turn, lead to a lowering of the risk of a cost overrun on the project, thus allowing the setting of a lower cost contingency as the design progresses.

Refining cost and risk estimates is the final step in the planning element of this book's strategic framework for public sector project management. Nevertheless, as we discussed earlier, these elements of project management do not always have clearly identifiable starting and ending points. For instance, the project management team may develop a complete project design and thus a refined project cost estimate prior to seeking bids from general project contractors. However, under alternative project delivery approaches, the project management team may hire the general contractor prior to the completion of a complete project design, and thus may not arrive at a final project cost and risk projection until after the general contractor or possibly contractor-designer is hired and that final price has been negotiated.

Refining the Cost Estimate

Ritz describes project cost estimating as proceeding in stages, which he identifies as feasibility estimating, appropriation estimating, capital cost or budget estimating, and definitive estimating. Those stages describe the purposes for the cost estimates. The most preliminary estimates are usually made for project feasibility purposes and for comparing options or alternatives, as we discussed in Chapter 3.

> **TIPS FOR SUCCESS:**
>
> - The degree of refinement of project cost projections depends on the level of completeness of the plans and specifications.
> - Just as each element of the Work Breakdown Schedule is used to develop the project schedule, each element of the WBS is used to compute a project cost estimate.

As the project design is developed, it becomes possible to derive more and more accurate cost estimates and to use them for the purposes Ritz describes, such as estimating appropriations for the project and projecting the project budget. Peter Jackson, a former project manager with the U.S. Army Corps of Engineers, points out that a more detailed design allows the cost estimators to itemize materials that will actually be used on the project, such as drywall or electronic components or topsoil. The cost estimators can then call suppliers, who can tell them exactly how much those components will cost.

The Government Accountability Office explains that a refined cost estimate depends on how well the project or program is defined, and that this definition process begins with the development of the project or program's specifications, performance characteristics, Work Breakdown Structure, and schedule. As we noted above, the WBS depicts the project work in increasing levels of detail and is an important first step in developing both the project schedule and cost. Just as a time frame for each element of the WBS is projected in determining the project schedule, a cost can be projected for each element as well. When the estimated costs of the elements are added together, a total project cost or "point estimate" is made for the project. Those individual work package costs are often listed in a "schedule of values," which can be used to determine payments to contractors, based on the percentage of completion of each work package.[16]

The GAO recommends that these work package costs include labor and materials costs that have a contractor's overhead and fee attached to them. As is the case with more preliminary types of cost estimating, historical costs are often used in basing a cost estimate on elements of the WBS. Peter Jackson points out that the resulting point estimate can be further refined by considering information about the market, particularly for materials such as steel, concrete, and glass and for electronics. The estimate can then be compared to bids that come in from contractors, providing the project manager with an apples-to-apples comparison.

Refining Risk Assessments

In addition to developing realistic cost estimates, the development and refinement of risk assessments can help managers avoid unexpected cost overruns on their projects. A risk assessment or analysis is based on an expectation that unforeseen problems will always occur in undertaking a project, and these problems are likely to affect the expected cost and/or the schedule. The problems can include unexpected changes in legal requirements for the project, unforeseen increases in the cost of supplies and materials needed, technology failures, and unanticipated work stoppages, and changes in site conditions, weather conditions, and much more.

TIPS FOR SUCCESS:

■ In assessing project risks, the project management team should brainstorm over everything that might possibly go wrong on the project.
■ Sensitivity and uncertainty analyses can help cost estimators establish a range of probabilities for the project's potential cost, based on known risks.

J. Davidson Frame identifies four "functional" categories of project risk in the private sector. These risks also manifest themselves in public sector projects. They include:

1. **Technical risks**: These are risks associated with the development or operation of the product or deliverable created by the project. Frame points out

that the technical risk level is highest when projects "tread new terrain or when they entail working with highly complex systems."[17] We discuss technical or technology risks more fully below.

2. **Market risks:** This is the risk that the product will fail in the marketplace. Market risk can be realized in the public sector if the long-term viability of public projects depends on revenues from users and those revenues fail to meet projections. For instance, the Boston Convention and Exhibition Center, which was opened in 2004, had generated only about half the projected revenue from associated hotel room stays as of 2007. That higher hotel room revenue projection had been a key factor in the decision to authorize construction of the convention center in 1997.[18]

3. **Financial risks:** These risks are centered on cash flow and profitability. While profitability is not an issue in the public sector, cash flow is. In Chapter 10, we will discuss the realization of cash-flow risks in the operation of the publicly financed Millennium Dome project in the United Kingdom.

4. **Human risks:** Frame notes that projects are "constantly plagued with problems of human resource reliability, competence, and availability," as well as by "the consequences of political struggles, the turnover of key players, and the fickleness of customers."[19] All of these factors create a long list of potential project risks.

Technology Risks

Technology risks are often underestimated in the development of both project schedules and cost estimates, particularly when major leaps in project technology are involved. The GAO has found that a major source of cost overruns and delays can be attributed to the development of aggressive project schedules in those instances. As a result, both the GAO and the Office of Management and Budget recommend an "incremental" or "evolutionary" development approach in projects as a best practice. Under the incremental approach, programs and projects features and capabilities are developed in stages on the basis of "mature technologies," rather than all at once. This is inherently less risky than development in a single step of a major technological capability, or what is sometimes referred to as the "big bang" approach.[20]

The GAO reported that the development by the U.S. Air Force of the F/A-22 tactical fighter was initially based on a big-bang strategy in which full capability was sought in one step rather than over a phased period. Cost, schedule, and performance problems resulted. The Future Imagery Architecture Project, discussed in Example 3.6 in Chapter 3, is another case of an inappropriately applied big-bang approach to project development. That project's problems were compounded by the fact that Boeing, the company selected to develop the satellite system, had never developed that type of system before.

Brainstorming and Sensitivity Analysis in Assessing Risks

Project managers have an obligation during the planning phase of a project to compile a list of possible risks and assess their likely impact on the project's cost and schedule. One effective way to accomplish this is by having the project management team members brainstorm over everything that might possibly go wrong on the project. It is helpful if the project manager can turn to one or more members of the team who are qualified to perform sensitivity and uncertainty analyses to determine which risk and other factors are likely to have the most impact on the project's cost.[21] One source of certifications for project cost estimators is the Society of Cost Estimating and Analysis, which has established training and certification programs for project and program cost estimators. Another is the American Association of Cost Engineers. In addition, the GAO notes that the Defense Acquisition University offers a variety of project and program cost-related certification programs. (Appendix 3 lists Website addresses for these and other organizations of interest to public sector project management.)

Sensitivity and uncertainty analyses can help cost estimators establish a range of probabilities for a project's potential cost. These analyses, which use statistical methods to predict the likelihood of possible project-related risks and costs, can help cost estimators add appropriate contingency reserve amounts to their cost estimates to cover expected risks. Public sector project managers must make sure that these contingency reserves are built into their project cost estimates.

One of the more powerful statistical techniques used to determine the uncertainty associated with a project cost estimate is to subject the individual cost estimates in the WBS to a Monte Carlo simulation. A Monte Carlo simulation involves calculating probabilities of different "what-if" scenarios that might pose a risk of increasing the project cost or schedule. Under the simulation, a statistical software program calculates a probability distribution of costs for each element of the WBS. It then draws values at random from each probability distribution and adds the results together. These random drawings among distributions are repeated thousands of times to create an overall probability distribution for the project's costs.[22] That normal distribution can be converted to an S curve such as the one shown in Figure 5.5.

The S curve projects probability levels for a range of possible costs of a particular project, determined through uncertainty analyses. According to the S curve in Figure 5.5, there is a 40 percent probability of meeting the primary project cost estimate of $825,000. The Government Accountability Office recommends that project cost estimates be budgeted to at least the 50 percent confidence level. Thus, in this case, the project manager should add a contingency reserve of at least $82,900, or about 10 percent, to the primary cost estimate, bringing the total projected budgeted cost for the project to $907,900. As the S-curve demonstrates, the contingency amount rises dramatically to achieve a confidence level of 80 percent or higher.

Peter Jackson said that his project management team at the U.S. Army Corps of Engineers frequently used the Monte Carlo method to estimate project risks. He

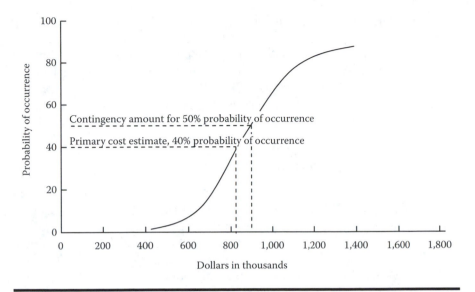

Figure 5.5 **A cumulative probability determination, or S curve, of a project's potential costs. (From** *Cost Estimating and Assessment Guide***, GAO, GAO-07-1134SP.)**

noted that cost projections based on those Monte Carlo risk analyses were generally
highest early in the project planning process. At that point, he said, it was common
to add a contingency reserve as high as 25 percent to the project's estimated cost.
As the design progressed and the WBS elements became better defined, the project
management team's could lower the contingency reserve and still achieve the same
level of confidence in the cost estimate, Jackson said. It might not be lowered, however, if certain risks, such as rising costs of materials, were realized.

TIPS FOR SUCCESS:

- The project management team should continually question presumptions that underlie risk and cost estimates.
- Realistic cost estimates, budgets, and affordability assessments are
  key to preventing a vicious cycle leading to schedule delays and cost
  overruns.
- Project stakeholders should be kept informed of project risks and
  changes in assumptions underlying project costs.

Putting It All Together: Developing Realistic
Presumptions behind Cost and Risk Estimates

As is the case in project scheduling, the project management team can refine its project
cost estimates based on detailed WBS data and subject those estimates to statistical

and uncertainty analysis and still come out with a cost projection that is significantly wrong. This can happen if cost estimators and project managers fail to account for certain risks or fail to question certain presumptions or assumptions underlying their cost estimates. Among those presumptions are that planned project technology, such as software, will be available and sufficiently developed when needed; that legal requirements that might affect the project will not change; that project stakeholders will accept major changes in the project design, and many others.

Questioning Presumptions

As we noted in our discussion of the preliminary steps in project planning in Chapter 3, it is often helpful or necessary for project managers to take a step back and question the presumptions that support their planning decisions. Cost and risk estimates are no exception. Neustadt and May's two questions about presumptions apply here as well: What *are* the presumptions that underlie a particular cost estimate, and what is the evidence for those presumptions?

As Example 5.2 shows, a faulty presumption that the technology needed for complex projects will be fully developed by the time the project is under development can have major ramifications on cost.

Example 5.2: Estimating software technology costs in satellite systems

The failure to produce accurate estimates of the cost of software and other information technology programs has helped fuel major cost increases and schedule delays in many space-based satellite and weapons systems. Costs for Defense Department space acquisitions over the past several decades have consistently been underestimated—sometimes by billions of dollars.[23]

Regarding satellites, the Defense Department has increasingly focused on developing fewer, but heavier, large and complex systems that perform a multitude of missions rather than larger groups of smaller, less complex systems that gradually increase in sophistication. According to the GAO, this has stretched technology challenges beyond existing capabilities in some cases and vastly increased complexities related to software.

For instance, the cost estimate for developing a Global Positioning System navigational satellite program was built on the presumption that the military code signal being developed would fit on a single microchip. However, the GAO noted that once development started, "interface issues" arose and the subcontractor had to move to a two-microchip design, which took eight months to resolve and increased the cost of the program.

In another instance, the GAO reported that cost estimators relied on data from the previous Milstar satellite system to estimate the cost of a new Advanced Extremely High Frequency communications satellite program (AEHF). The problem was that AEHF program officials presumed that certain satellite antennas would have the same performance capabilities as those on the predecessor Milstar satellite, requiring little if any development. In fact, because of parts obsolescence, personnel turnover, and other issues, the AEHF antennas had to be redesigned at nearly the same cost as the Milstar antennas. Moreover, there were presumptions that Milstar-based processing technology could be used in the AEHF system, which turned out not to be possible. According to the GAO, almost all of the AEHF payload software had to be rewritten to support the new hardware. As a result, there was much less technology transfer from Milstar II to AEHF than had been assumed, even though the contractor was the same.[24]

Moving from a Realistic Cost Estimate to an Affordable Project Budget

Accurate cost and risk estimates are critical to the process of developing budgets for projects. As we will discuss in Chapter 9, budgets and project schedules become the baseline against which the progress of the project is measured. If actual costs and work completed begin to diverge from the planned costs in the budget and the planned schedule, the project manager knows that corrective action must be taken.

A realistic budget also indicates whether a project is affordable. In determining affordability, the project manager must consider how the planned project fits in with other projects or programs that may be ongoing or planned by his or her agency, particularly if they compete for the same funding. This affordability assessment should take into account the project's entire life cycle costs.

In its report on space technology acquisitions referred to in Example 5.2, the GAO noted that for the fiscal years 2006 through 2011, budgets for the Defense Department's major space acquisition programs were unrealistic because they were based on cost estimates that were later increased by roughly $12.2 billion. In other words, these programs were not as affordable as they had been portrayed.

In discussing the interplay between cost estimates and budgets, the GAO report pointed out a vicious cycle that begins with over-optimistic cost estimates. Those estimates result in the approval of too many projects or programs for the amount of funding available. The result is extremely or unrealistically tight budgets for each program or project, resulting in decisions later on in many cases to stop planned activities, compress schedules, or reduce scopes. The ultimate result of those decisions, however, is usually more cost overruns and schedule delays.

As the GAO noted in the case of the Defense Department's space acquisition programs:

> DoD starts more weapon programs than it can afford, creating a competition for funding that encourages low cost estimating, optimistic scheduling, over-promising, suppressing of bad news, and, for space programs, forsaking the opportunity to identify and assess potentially better alternatives. Programs focus on advocacy at the expense of realism and sound management. Invariably, with too many programs in its portfolio, DoD is forced to continually shift funds to and from programs—particularly as programs experience problems that require more time and money to address. Such shifts, in turn, have had costly, reverberating effects.[25]

The GAO clearly considers the DoD's budgets for its space-based weapons programs and projects to be unstable. The Future Imagery Architecture satellite project, discussed in Chapter 3, provides a particularly clear case of this. In that case, Congress had set a budget cap of $5 billion for the first five years of the project, with spending limited to $1 billion a year. The contract with Boeing, the developer, imposed penalties for delays or cost overruns. In addition, the National Reconnaissance Office, the federal satellite agency, under pressure from Congress to control costs, did not establish a contingency reserve fund for the program.[26]

As development of the Future Imagery program progressed and costs rose, Boeing hesitated to report setbacks or ask for additional financing. An internal Reconnaissance Office postmortem concluded that because of the budget cap and the penalties for exceeding it, "the cost of an overrun was so ruinous that the strongest incentive it provided to the contractor was to prove they were on cost," according to the *New York Times*.

Presenting Cost Estimates and Budgets to Project Stakeholders

In addition to developing a realistic budget, it is important, as the project design and cost estimating process progresses, to present those numbers clearly to key stakeholders, such as the top management of the agency managing the project, potential users of the project, and the decision making body that may have approved the project or appropriates funding for it. Peter Jackson maintains that those clients should be made to feel they understand the risks and probability of success of the project. Those factors can often be hidden in the cost estimate. "You want to let them know how comfortable they can be with the estimate and what assumptions underlie it," he said. The project manager should also inform those stakeholders every time there is a refinement of the cost estimate and let them know if the underlying assumptions have changed. For instance, does the estimate reflect a plan to build Class A office space, or has the plan been changed to Class B space since the previous estimate was provided? Does the estimate reflect a different schedule, labor rates, or inflation indices? Does it reflect new legal requirements? Those are just some of the ground rules and assumptions that underlie cost estimates.

In Example 5.3, we can see some of the costly consequences of an apparent failure by public sector project managers to keep key stakeholders informed of planned changes in a project's scope. The example also illustrates the importance of realistically assessing project risks in developing the owner's cost and schedule.

Example 5.3: Failure to obtain budget authorization for a scope expansion of the L.A. District Courthouse construction project

In 2000, the General Services Administration, the federal government's primary asset acquisition and management agency, projected that it could build and take occupancy of a new federal courthouse in Los Angeles in six years. As of

September 2008, that schedule had slipped to 14 years, with occupancy projected by Fiscal Year 2014 at the earliest.[27]

According to the GAO, the schedule delays began after the GSA decided to design a courthouse much larger than what was authorized by Congress. In Fiscal Year 2001, Congress had appropriated $400 million for design and construction of a 41-courtroom structure. In November 2001, however, without informing Congress or the Office of Management and Budget, GSA increased the scope of the project to a 54-courtoom building. The GSA then took a year and a half to conduct environmental assessments and purchase the site.

When the OMB later balked at the larger scope and did not include the larger building plan in the president's Fiscal Year 2005 budget, the GSA was forced to redesign the project. GSA and Los Angeles court officials were slow to reduce the scope, however, which caused additional delays. Those delays caused the estimated costs for the new courthouse to nearly triple to over $1.1 billion, according to the GAO.

In July 2005, the GSA advised the Judiciary that the project could not be built for the originally appropriated amounts because of material shortages and other market factors, including an unforeseen, rapid increase in construction costs. The GSA calculated that each day of delay was costing the government $54,000. As of September 2008, the GSA was examining a number of options for further scaling back the scope of the project.

As Example 5.3 shows, by increasing the project scope without obtaining authorization from Congress or the OMB, the GSA was running a significant risk that Congress or the OMB would not approve the expanded scope and that significant delays and cost increases would result. In this case, that risk was fully realized.

Pulling Together the Planning Steps

Starting in Chapter 3, we began discussing nine key steps in successful public sector project planning. To reiterate, those steps are:

1. Correctly identifying the problem to be solved by the planned project
2. Gaining an accurate understanding of the project's context and stakeholders
3. Questioning the manager's own presumptions held about the project
4. Understanding and complying with the project's legal requirements
5. Developing preliminary project cost and risk estimates
6. Developing effective project control systems (clear lines of authority and other internal financial controls)
7. Developing clear project plans (drawings) and specifications
8. Developing a realistic project schedule
9. Refining project cost and risk estimates

As we've noted, it is important for project managers and their teams to engage in all of these steps—sometimes repeatedly—to ensure that their projects get done successfully. Example 5.4 discusses how managers in one municipal government agency used many of these planning steps effectively in completing a complex software technology project on time and on budget.

Example 5.4: Using key planning steps in successfully managing a public sector software technology project

In 1997, the City of Seattle was facing the need to upgrade its outmoded and inefficient computer mainframe system. It had become clear by that year that the system would no longer even function after the year 2000 due to Y2K issues, according to Claudia Gross Shader, who was the assistant director of the project to replace the old system. Shader helped manage 35 full-time city staff and 30 contractor and subcontractor staff in undertaking the computer replacement project. Shader said that the installation in 1991 of the earlier system had run 34 percent over budget. Many of the staff in 1997 "painfully recalled" the problematic 1991 computer project and wanted to do things better the second time around.

Shader said staff brainstormed about the problems the old system posed and the various options that might be available to solve it. The problems extended beyond the Y2K issues. The existing system had high operating costs and "poor interfaces" with other city agencies, and it couldn't even perform certain basic functions, such as keeping track of purchasing. Nevertheless, Shader and the other agency staff didn't automatically presume that an entirely new system was needed.

"We took about six months to evaluate the situation," Shader said. They considered the feasibility of fixing the existing system, but rejected that option as having too many obstacles. The project team hired an information technology consultant with experience on public sector projects, who prepared a project risk assessment model and a life-cycle cost model to help the project team sort through possible options for fixing or replacing the existing system.[28] The consultant also later helped the project team draft a request for proposals for a computer systems integrator. The integrator acts like a general contractor in managing the subcontractors on computer projects, managing the reporting on the project schedule and budget, leading the development of interfaces with other systems, and helping the city develop requirements for hardware procurement.

With the help of the consultant, the project team produced a benefit-cost analysis that projected $16.5 million in quantified benefits over a 10-year period in replacing the system. Among the projected benefits were a projected reduction in paper reports and external consultant fees and the elimination of the need for a mainframe central processor and its replacement with a lower-cost, server-based system.

Shader said the proposed computer replacement project obtained high-level sponsorship. It was supported by the mayor of Seattle and by a city councilmember who had previously been an executive at Microsoft. The City Council, in fact, passed an ordinance to provide bonuses for city staff for reaching key project milestones. In addition to getting the sponsorship of the mayor and the city councilmember, the project managers established a steering committee consisting of project stakeholders from several city departments.

As part of the process of selecting the software developer, the project team and steering committee held "mock strategy sessions" with the finalists in the process. They garnered information from those sessions about how to set up effective computer systems. In June 1997, the team recommended replacing the existing system with software from PeopleSoft, a Windows-based financial data software system. IBM was selected as the systems integrator. The project team contacted at least eight other public jurisdictions that had implemented the PeopleSoft system to determine their satisfaction with the system.

Figure 5.6 shows the projected budget, including contingency reserve, for the computer replacement project.

The budget was later reduced to $25.6 million. Shader noted that "spending up-front time on planning and on the RFP process were things that paid off down the line." In July 1999, the new system went live. It came in $1.5 million under its budget of $25.6 million and within the 22-month project schedule.

The Seattle computer example above demonstrates the effective use of several of the project planning elements we've discussed. For instance, the project team carefully defined the problems they were facing and conducted a benefit-cost analysis before selecting a preferred alternative as a solution. They were also careful to involve key project stakeholders on a project steering committee and enlisted the support of the mayor and an influential city councilmember in seeking funding for the project.

In addition, the project team hired a consultant with professional expertise to undertake a cost and risk analysis, help draft the RFP, and subsequently assist the Finance Department in contracting with the selected systems integrator. This step is analogous in many ways to the decision in public construction to hire an owner's project manager who assists the project management team in selecting the designer and general contractor. In complex, public sector IT projects, just as in complex public construction projects, the hiring of expert consultants can be an important step in protecting the public agency's interests during both the planning and execution stages of projects. The Seattle project team also employed due diligence in the

Consultant Labor	$13,350,000
City Labor	$4,800,000
Development Environment	$4,200,000
Project Facilities	$2,930,000
Production Environment Costs	$1,700,000
Time and Attendance	$750,000
Contingency	$2,785,867
Total	**$30,515,867**

Figure 5.6   Projected budget as of June 1997 for Seattle Finance Department computer replacement system.

selection of the software developer by contacting other jurisdictions that had used it. We will discuss due diligence in procurement in Chapter 7.

As we noted in Chapter 3, paying attention to project planning steps may entail some initial effort and pain, but it is nothing compared to the pain involved when the planning isn't done (just consider the federal courthouse project in Example 5.3 to remind yourself of the widespread pain resulting from the lack of attention to these critical phases in project planning).

In the following chapter, we will discuss the selection of the project management team. While it could be argued that this is a topic that precedes project planning, we are placing it after the planning discussion to keep it together with a discussion on the selection of project contractors and consultants (in Chapter 7).

Endnotes

1. Ritz, George J. 1994. *Total Construction Project Management.* McGraw-Hill. P. 110.
2. Department of Defense. *Integrated Master Plan and Integrated Master Schedule Preparation and Use Guide.* October 21, 2005.
3. In Massachusetts, public agencies must also use a qualifications-based process to select an owner's project manager for public building projects estimated to cost more than $1.5 million (Commonwealth of Massachusetts, Office of the Inspector General 2005. *Designing and Constructing Public Facilities*). A qualifications-based selection process involves the issuance of a Request for Qualifications, which allows the public agency to rank prospective designers and architects on the basis of their experience, the quality of their work and other criteria. The selection process is *not* based on the lowest bid, but rather on a set fee or a not-to-exceed fee limit. More will be said about this process of selecting designers and architects in Chapter 7.
4. For public building projects in Massachusetts estimated to cost more than $10 million, both general bidders and trade contractors must undergo a prequalification process, which involves the issuance of a Request for Qualifications that has some similarities to the RFQ issued for designers and architects. The prequalification process results in the selection of at least three qualified general contractors to submit bids on the construction contract (Office of the Inspector General, 2005).
5. In Massachusetts, the owner is also required to hire an owner's project manager to assist in procuring the design contract and to provide other management services for the project (Office of the Inspector General, 2005).
6. Washington State, Joint Legislative Audit and Review Committee. 2005. *An Assessment of General Contractor/Construction Management Contracting Procedures.* P. 25. http://www.leg.wa.gov/reports/05-9.pdf.
7. Commonwealth of Massachusetts, Office of the Inspector General, 2001. *A Report on the Design and Construction of the University of Massachusetts Computer Science Center.*
8. At the time the feasibility study for the Computer Science Center was done in 1995, design-build delivery could only be used in public building construction in Massachusetts if public contract awarding authorities obtained an exemption from the public building construction law requiring a traditional design-bid-build approach (Massachusetts General Laws chapter 149) or if a "modular" construction approach was used. The state's modular procurement law, M.G.L. c. 149, s. 44E, allows a one-step Request for Proposals process in modular, or

prefabricated, construction, which uses pre-engineered metal building systems. The modular procurement process is similar to the procurement process in design-build in that it allows construction to proceed without the need for a separate design process. The feasibility study recommended that the state procure the Computer Science Center project under the modular procurement law rather than seek an exemption from the Chapter 149 design-bid-build requirements. In 2004, the Massachusetts Legislature adopted procedures allowing design-build and construction management at risk delivery in certain types of projects with an estimated construction cost of $5 million or more.

9. One of the reasons for the disputes over the design in the Computer Science Center project was that the building was not actually constructed as a modular building. The Massachusetts inspector general determined that the first two floors of the Computer Science Center were conventionally constructed and that pre-engineered metal building systems were used only for the third floor and roof structure (Commonwealth of Massachusetts, Office of the Inspector General, 2001). As a result, the inspector general determined that the building had been improperly procured under the modular procurement law.

10. United States Government Accountability Office. 2009. *GAO Cost Estimating and Assessment Guide: Best Practices for Developing and Managing Capital Program Costs.* GAO-09-3SP. P. 61.

11. See Construction Specifications Institute. *MasterFormat: 2004 Edition Numbers and Titles.* http://www.csinet.org/s_csi/docs/9400/9361.pdf; Also, Jackson, Barbara J. 2004. *Construction Management Jump Start.* San Francisco: Sybex, Inc.

12. United States Government Accountability Office. 2009. P. 69.

13. Young, Trevor L. 2007. *The Handbook of Project Management*, revised 2nd edition. London: Kogan Page Publishers.

14. Lewis, James P. 2007. *Fundamentals of Project Management,* 3rd edition. New York: American Management Association. P. 73.

15. Ritz, George J. 1994.

16. Jackson, Barbara J. 2004. P. 177.

17. Frame, J. Davidson. 1994. *The New Project Management.* San Francisco: Jossey-Bass. P. 81.

18. Primack, Phil. Meeting market. *CommonWealth* magazine. Fall 2008.

19. Frame, J. Davidson. 1994. P. 81.

20. United States Government Accountability Office. 2009. P. 61; also, Office of Management and Budget. 2006. *Capital Programming Guide.* Supplement to Circular A-11, Part 7.

21. United States Government Accountability Office. 2009.

22. See United States Government Accountability Office. 2009; or Project Management Institute. 2004. *A Guide to the Project Management Body of Knowledge*, 3rd edition. Newtown Square, PA: Project Management Institute.

23. United States Government Accountability Office. 2006. *Space Acquisitions: DoD Needs to Take More Action to Address Unrealistic Initial Cost Estimates of Space Systems.* GAO-07-96.

24. United States Government Accountability Office. 2006.

25. United States Government Accountability Office. 2006. P. 6.

26. Taubman, Philip. 2007. In Death of Spy Satellite Program: Lofty Plans and Unrealistic Bids. *The New York Times.* November 11, 2007. http://www.nytimes.com/2007/11/11/washington/11satellite.html?hp#step1

27. United States Government Accountability Office. 2008. *Federal Courthouse Construction: Estimated Costs to House the L.A. District Court Have Tripled and There Is No Consensus on How to Proceed.* GAO-08-889.

28. Pacific Consulting Group. Report for the City of Seattle on SFMS Redevelopment Project. June 1997.

Chapter 6

Selecting the Best Agents, Part 1:
Building the Project Team

The managerial organization is the backbone of any project, public or private, in an almost literal sense. Like bundles of nerve fibers running through the spine of a living organism, management teams transmit information from the top of a project organization to the bottom and back again. If that information becomes blocked at any point—particularly at a point high up in the management structure—paralysis of the organization can easily develop.

As we will discuss in this chapter, public sector project teams can take many forms, and their roles and responsibilities are continuing to shift. As more and more of the work of public sector projects is outsourced to contractors and consultants, public sector project teams find that their major responsibilities comprise planning for, procuring, and managing those contracts. As we discussed in Chapter 1, this shift to contact management has been accompanied by the downsizing of public sector staff. Many types of in-house projects do remain in government, though, and in those cases, project teams are responsible for both managing and undertaking the project work.

As we noted in Chapter 2, there is no clear demarcation between the first two elements of this book's public sector project management framework—ensuring adequate planning and selecting the best agents to undertake the work. At least some members of the project team must be in place, for instance, to brainstorm with the project manager over the conceptual plans for the project. Nevertheless, the processes involving agent selection are different enough from the project planning processes that they merit a separate discussion in this and the next chapter.

Who Is on the Project Management Team?

In Chapter 1, we pointed out that there are many types of both private and public sector projects, and their management structures can vary considerably. Public sector projects, in particular, vary because of the wide variety of public agencies at all levels of government that undertake them. We previously noted at least three different types of public sector managers: public-agency managers, quasi-public agency and public authority managers, and private-citizen managers in conjunction with building committees. The project teams in these cases can look very different from each other. They can range from a handful of people to hundreds, depending on the complexity of the project involved, although, as we will discuss later in this chapter, the public sector team members on large projects can sometimes be greatly outnumbered by the private sector consultant and contract personnel assigned to those projects.

This leads to a second cautionary word here that it is often difficult on public projects to differentiate between public and private sector personnel on project teams. We discussed the Port of Seattle case in Chapter 4 in which consultant personnel had been hired to work in roles that were virtually indistinguishable from public sector staff. We also discussed a similar arrangement on the Big Dig project in Boston in which personnel employed by Bechtel/Parsons Brinckerhoff, the project's design and construction management consortium, worked alongside construction management staff of the public sector Massachusetts Turnpike Authority. In that case, both executive level consultants and MTA officials signed off on high-dollar change orders. Even on small public projects, an owner's project manager, who is often hired from the private sector, can be considered part of the public agency's management team.

What Are the Team Dynamics?

Despite all that variety among public sector project teams, there are a number of dynamics that teams of all sizes and varieties appear to have in common. A manager's success in assembling an effective team may well depend on how he or she deals with these dynamics:

1. Project managers must often "borrow" team members from other functional departments or divisions within their agencies. As a result, managers often find it a daunting task to build a team that is cohesive and committed to the project.

2. Like project managers themselves, members of their team must have a mix of expertise and skills in technical and other areas relating to the project, such as finance, accounting, law, organizational management, environmental regulation, and health and safety practices. The project manager's job is to assemble a team that has the requisite skills, experience, and expertise to manage the project successfully.

3. Clear and unimpeded communication among team members and with the project manager is essential for successful projects. Lines of authority must be clear, and the project mission or vision must be understood and shared by all. As we will discuss below, some project management arrangements, such as the Port of Seattle and Big Dig cases, in which the roles of public and private sector personnel are indistinguishable, can create blurred lines of communication and authority. In the Big Dig case, in particular, it has been argued that there was no public sector manager who was clearly in charge.

4. Project managers and their teams must operate under an appropriate managerial accountability system. In some cases, this accountability system is a hierarchical one in which the project manager makes key project-related decisions and transmits them down the line. In other instances, it may be more appropriate for team members to operate in a more flexible and autonomous manner.

5. An understanding among the team members of the project's legal requirements and of ethical business practices is necessary to ensure project success. As part of that, the team must be aware of project-related internal control policies and procedures that we discussed in Chapter 4.

6. The motivation of team members to get the job done and done well is essential to project success.

In the remainder of this chapter, we will examine these dynamics in more detail:

TIPS FOR SUCCESS:

Project managers can establish team cohesion and commitment by:

- Communicating clearly with the team members at the outset about the nature and importance of the project.
- Establishing open lines of communication throughout the project.
- Addressing the dual-loyalty problem in matrix organizations.
- Holding regular and productive meetings with the staff.

Establishing a Cohesive and Committed Team

Managers want their teams to be committed to their projects. This is often accomplished by recruiting teams whose members are able to form cohesive units that allow for close collaboration.[1] That is not always easy to ensure. One issue that appears to arise often in projects of all types is the potential threat to team cohesion when team members are brought together from other offices or divisions within an agency or from other agencies to work on a particular project. Because they are "borrowed" from those other "functional units," they must still report to their bosses in those units. This often leads to dual loyalties among team members.[2]

Team cohesion can be affected by a number of other factors as well, such as whether the personalities of the team members and the project manager fit well together. Cohesion can also be greatly influenced by the organizational "culture" that the manager helps establish; and it can be influenced by managerial leadership qualities, the clarity of members' roles and responsibilities, and the nature of the communication that takes place among the team members and with top management in the public agency.

Dual loyalty problems often arise in organizations that combine the structure of functional units found in bureaucracies with project-team structures. These increasingly common arrangements—often referred to as matrix organizations—can be effective in overcoming communication blockages that can occur when projects are undertaken exclusively by functional departments. However, James P. Lewis notes that it is often difficult for a project manager to ensure commitment among team members to project goals when a project manager does not have clear authority over all the team members, which is often the case in matrix organizations.

Figure 6.1 depicts the structure of a project team operating in a matrix organization. Solidly shaded boxes represent staff engaged in project activities. Boxes with a square pattern within them represent functional units within the agency.

Many experts suggest that in matrix organizations, in particular, the project manager must communicate clearly and effectively with the members of the team about the nature and importance of the project to overcome some of the initial resistance he or she may encounter. Also, unless roles and responsibilities on the project are clearly understood and agreed to by the team members and their functional unit bosses, conflicts can occur. The team members themselves may not take the project as seriously, at least initially, as they do their roles within their functional units because they may not know or have a history of interaction with the project manager and the other project team members. In that sense, the manager must exercise a key quality of leadership at the outset of the project planning stage. He or she must find a way to communicate the project vision, which we talked about in Chapter 1, to the team and make them feel as though they all have a stake in it.[3] The project manager must also communicate the project vision to stakeholders outside the project team.

J. Davidson Frame suggests that holding productive meetings is one important way to build team cohesion in these situations. He notes that of particular importance is the project kickoff meeting in which the project manager presents the team with the project charter, which defines project goals and authority; identifies team

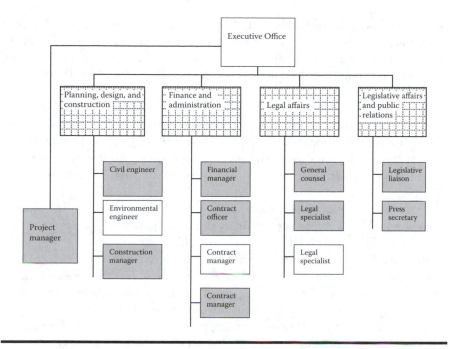

Figure 6.1   A project team-based matrix arrangement in a public agency.

players and provides a roster with their addresses and phone numbers; identifies key milestone dates; and establishes rapport among team players.[4] Frame also suggests holding regular status review meetings to measure project progress.

Lewis similarly lists four steps in building a new project team:

1. Introduce members to each other.
2. Together, develop a mission statement for the team.
3. Develop specific goals and objectives that the team must achieve.
4. Develop a plan to achieve those goals.[5]

Interestingly, Frame's suggestions for the project kickoff meeting appear to imply that the team has been selected only after the project charter has been developed. In Chapter 3, we noted that the project charter or business case appears to be the private sector equivalent of the project feasibility study in the public sector. By the time the project charter has been developed, at least some of the project team may already be in place. As Lewis points out, it is the process of involving team members in project planning itself that helps create team cohesion. The project manager should involve his or her team in the development of the business case or feasibility study.

Peter Jackson, a former project manager with the U.S. Army Corps of Engineers, discussed in an interview how he selected management teams for Army Corps projects, such as one to dredge Boston Harbor in the 1990s to make it suitable as a regional port for large vessels. He described a typical matrix organizational arrangement in those instances. The key to success in team building, according to Jackson, lay in finding the right people for the teams and integrating the teams well with personnel from functional departments and user agencies and with stakeholders in the projects.

Jackson said that on most of his projects, there would be a need for a construction manager as well as an expert in environmental engineering, a contract officer, and an expert from the legal office. Most of these people worked on several projects at once. "I would go to the engineering division, for instance, and say I needed a hydraulic engineer and ask the supervisor to assign someone with that expertise," he said.

Once the team was brought together for a particular project, the first order of business would be to prepare a preliminary project management plan, Jackson said. Planning would begin with a discussion about the likely scope of work and would then involve the initial development of the project's work breakdown structure, schedule, and budget. Each team member would have input into those planning elements.

Jackson said his core project teams would normally consist of about five people each. Joining each team, however, would be three to four people from outside user agencies. On the Boston Harbor dredging project, for instance, the user agency was the Massachusetts Port Authority (Massport), a public authority that manages Logan Airport in Boston and a number of harbor facilities. The entire team consisted of about 10 people; but each of those team members consulted with other people in their own functional departments or agencies in conducting fieldwork or writing reports. Jackson pointed out that the Boston Harbor project team was particularly fluid in that many of the members would join it or leave it at different times. As project manager, Jackson was officially the head of the management team and would have final say on major management decisions. But he said he referred to his counterparts at the user agencies as co-project managers.

In addition to establishing relationships with user agency members, Jackson had to be cognizant of other stakeholders in Army Corps of Engineers' projects. In the Boston Harbor project, he helped organize a citizens advisory committee, which included members of several organizations concerned about environmental conditions in the harbor. When the dredging project began in the 1990s, the advisory committee provided input to the Corps of Engineers in drafting an environmental impact statement. At the kickoff meeting of the advisory committee, Jackson recalls that "everyone agreed with the need for the project, but no one was in agreement on how it should be done."

Within the core project team, one other strategy for solving the dual loyalty problem is to arrange for the team members to work full time on the project. This strategy was used effectively in the Seattle computer software case that we discussed in Chapter 5. Claudia Gross Shader, the assistant director of that project, explained that the total project cost of $25.6 million included the cost of hiring temporary workers. However, these workers were not hired to work on the project itself but rather to "backfill" positions in functional departments from which expert staff needed for the project were recruited. This backfilling enabled the recruited staff to work on the project full time and to devote their undivided attention to it. It cost more up front to backfill the functional positions, Shader said, but it helped the project in the long run by eliminating the dual loyalty problem.

There is a potential downside to cohesiveness in groups, and that is the potential for such groups to develop *groupthink,* which Debra L. Nelson and James Campbell Quick describe as a dysfunctional process characterized by "a deterioration of mental efficiency, reality testing, and moral judgment."[6] Nelson and Quick contend that groups that lack of diversity among their members or that face time constraints in making high-impact decisions may succumb to groupthink. Symptoms can include a false sense that there is consensus or unanimity in the group's decisions as well as a failure to consider alternatives to those decisions and a failure to question presumptions behind decisions.

Thus, while a project manager must work to develop cohesiveness within his or her management team, it is important to watch out for the emergence of groupthink in decision making. Ways to avoid groupthink include establishing a mindset or culture within the team that encourages the questioning of presumptions and is open to differing points of view among the team members. We will discuss these qualities further later in this chapter.

TIPS FOR SUCCESS:

- Public sector project managers must recruit qualified personnel to their management teams and should *not* make hiring decisions based on political connections or friendships.
- Project management teams must have sufficient numbers of staff to manage projects effectively.

Ensuring That Team Personnel Are Qualified

As previously noted, the technical and other skills, experience, and expertise of the management team members are critical to the success of any project. This isn't to say that large staffs are necessary for all projects. One of the key decisions managers must make involves determining the appropriate size of the management team. In many cases, good decisions about team size and expertise can only come with experience. While too many managers can cause confusion and delay in a project, too few can result in insufficient project control and oversight.

In all cases, teams must include people with relevant technical, legal, and fiscal knowledge and experience. If team hiring or recruiting decisions are made on the basis of friendships or business or political connections rather than on the basis of appropriate qualifications, it stands to reason that the projects will suffer. Example 6.1 below discusses the lack of qualified staff involved in coordinating and overseeing the U.S. reconstruction efforts in Iraq and describes some of the problems that resulted from that situation.

Example 6.1: Unqualified staff managing Iraq reconstruction projects

During the first several years of reconstruction activities in Iraq, the lack of sufficient numbers of knowledgeable staff presented a serious problem to the success of the reconstruction projects. The Special Inspector General for Iraq Reconstruction found that among the key human resource problems during the first two years were inadequately qualified personnel and short tours of duty among those with needed expertise. Many program and project contracting officers did not have construction backgrounds.[7]

In his book *Imperial Life in the Emerald City: Inside Iraq's Green Zone,* Rajiv Chandrasekaran reported that political connections played a predominant role in the hiring of senior advisors in the Coalition Provisional Authority (CPA), the U.S.-led governmental organization in charge of the occupation and reconstruction of Iraq from June 2003 until 2004. The qualifications and technical skills and experience of these people were often a secondary consideration at best.

Coupled with the lack of qualifications among CPA staff was the fact that there were simply too few staff available to properly monitor the thousands of reconstruction projects planned and ongoing in Iraq. Among the problems that directly resulted from this lack of adequate staffing were that the CPA's contract files were in "disarray." Some contracts were missing while others were stored on personal e-mail accounts, individual hard drives, and external storage devices.[8]

In August 2003, the CPA established a program management office with the authority to oversee the execution of more than 2,300 projects in Iraq that were funded by an $18.4 billion congressional appropriation, according to the special inspector general. But the new office was still not provided with sufficient staff to operate effectively. Also lacking sufficient management staff, as it turned out, were the Army Corps of Engineers and the U.S. Agency for International Development, to which the CPA had turned for help. The CPA therefore decided to rely on contractors both for the management and the execution of the reconstruction program.[9]

In November 2003, when the $18.4 billion appropriation was approved, the program management office was staffed by just three people. The creators of the management office estimated it would need a staff of 100 government personnel to adequately oversee the reconstruction program. But by August 2004, the program management office had only 50 of the 100 people the director had requested, according to the special inspector general. Seven contractors were hired to work with a core team of government staff to perform program and project management. Another 12 contractors were hired to undertake the project work.

As the example above shows, public sector project teams were incapable by themselves of managing the reconstruction effort in Iraq. Private sector contractors were needed to help them. As we will discuss below, the use of contractors for that purpose can cause a number of problems that public sector managers should be aware of. One of those problems is confusion over lines of managerial authority.

In the Iraq reconstruction case and in many other public sector project cases, the lack of sufficient numbers of qualified personnel on the management teams has been a result, in part, of the legacy of public sector downsizing that we discussed in Chapter 1. The CPA wasn't a case in which expert personnel were terminated. Sufficient numbers of them were simply not recruited. The CPA appears to have been created with a limited-government perspective in mind.

TIPS FOR SUCCESS:

- Creating a team responsibility chart can help project managers assign project responsibilities clearly and effectively.
- If contractor personnel are recruited to help public sector staff manage projects, their roles and responsibilities must be clearly defined.

The Need for Clear Lines of Authority and Communication

Once the project manager has assembled his or her team, it is important all of the members know what is expected of them. One way to do this is to spell out specific project responsibilities of each team member. Trevor Young suggests creating a project responsibility chart, which lists the key project stages in sequential order along with the names of the people responsible for ensuring that the work of each stage gets done.

At the project kickoff meeting, the key project stages or milestones may be very preliminary in concept. It may also be possible that some of the responsibilities of the team members will be decided as a result of brainstorming at that kickoff meeting itself. Project responsibilities usually get spelled out more clearly as the project's plans and specifications progress.

Figure 6.2 displays a chart that project managers can use to keep track of the responsibilities of team members.

Maintaining Clear Lines of Authority When Using Contractors

As noted, the growing insertion of contractors into management roles on public projects has had the potential to blur lines of authority and communication. In the Iraq reconstruction situation discussed in Example 6.1, a lack of clarity in project management responsibilities resulted from the assignment of project management roles to contractors. Part of the reason for the confusion was that there was a lack of

KEY STAGE RESPONSIBILITY CHART								Sheet of Sheets	

TITLE OF PROJECT:

PROJECT SPONSOR:

PROJECT MANAGER:

PROJECT CUSTOMER:

PROJECT NO:

Prepared by:

Date

Version No:

Approved Date:

Line No.	KEY STAGE CODE	DESCRIPTION	RESPONSIBLE	DURATION days	PLANNED START	PLANNED FINISH	ACTUAL START	ACTUAL FINISH	PREDECESSOR KEY STAGE CODE	COMMENT
1										
2										
3										
4										
5										
6										
7										
8										
9										
10										
11										
12										
13										
14										
15										
16										
17										
18										
19										
20										

Figure 6.2 Project responsibility chart. (From Trevor L. Young, *The Handbook of Project Management*, revised 2nd edition. London: Kogan 2007.)

detail about those responsibilities in the management contracts. Some contractors subsequently made decisions that they were barred by federal regulations from making and performed other "inherently governmental functions."[10] Federal regulations state that functions considered to be "inherently governmental" include, among others, determining federal program priorities for budget requests, determining what supplies or services are to be acquired by government, approving contractual documents, defining requirements, and ordering changes in contract performance or quantities.[11]

The Office of Management and Budget's Circular A-76 more broadly describes inherently governmental functions as those that are "so intimately related to the public interest as to mandate performance by government personnel." The circular states that public activities may be outsourced when the contractor does not have the authority to decide on the course of action, but is authorized only to develop options or implement a course of action, with agency oversight. Thus, federal rules and guidelines specify contractor-provided management roles as being advisory in nature. The public agency manager must be in a position to make the final decisions. When project management contractors do not have clear instructions about their roles and responsibilities in that regard, confusion and project inefficiencies are bound to result.

The use of contractors as project managers can also lead to a steady erosion of public sector management authority. As Example 6.2 shows, a program to shift project decision-making authority to contractors in the development of space-based satellite systems resulted in an unintended loss in project management capacity and a negation of anticipated project savings.

Example 6.2: Unintended consequences in using contractors to manage satellite development projects

In the late 1990s, the Defense Department shifted key decision-making responsibilities in military contracting onto contractors, according to the Government Accountability Office. The new approach—known as Total System Performance Responsibility, or TSPR—was intended to simplify cumbersome procurement processes and foster innovation and management expertise from the private sector. However, the DoD later found that this approach "magnified problems related to requirements creep and poor contractor performance."[12]

The use of TSPR resulted in unrealistic assumptions about cost and schedule in four of six satellite development programs analyzed by the GAO. TSPR was one of a handful of factors identified by the GAO as contributing to billions of dollars in underestimated costs for those programs for the period from fiscal years 2006 through 2011.

The GAO further noted that under TSPR, the government decided not to obtain certain project cost data from the contractors. In some cases, the contracts did not allow the government to obtain cost data, including contractor cost and performance reports, even though such data are critical in developing sound cost estimates and for maintaining adequate oversight.

The ultimate result of the TSPR initiative was that the government ended up having less oversight of satellite development programs and less information from which to manage the programs than had previously been the case, the GAO concluded. Specifically, the reduction in government oversight and involvement under the TSPR initiative led to major reductions in various government capabilities, including losses in cost-estimating and systems-engineering staff. Ultimately, the reduction in systems engineering staff resulted in cost growth as the programs involved experienced technical and quality problems that the government was no longer in a position to detect and prevent. The Air Force subsequently rejected TSPR as a recommended contracting approach.

In one case involving the National Polar-orbiting Operational Environmental Satellite System (NPOESS), lines of authority and responsibility were particularly blurred because three separate government agencies were involved in managing the program—the DoD, the Department of Commerce, and NASA. In addition, under a version of TSPR, those public agencies took a backseat to the contractor, which ran the project team meetings.

Contractors can often provide public sector project management teams with needed expertise, particularly in technical areas, and they are frequently the only resource available to public agencies to undertake the project construction or development work. What is left for government in many cases is project management. When contractors are hired to perform managerial duties, government can lose its capacity in that area as well. If contractors are needed for project and program management, it is important to have a clear plan that defines the contractors' responsibilities combined with clear lines of authority that specify that the public sector manager is in charge.

Taking charge of contract management does not necessarily mean, however, that within the public sector management team itself a strictly hierarchical system of authority must always prevail. As we first noted in Chapter 4, different managerial accountability sturctures exist in public agencies just as they do in private sector organizations. It is important in both public and private sector organizations that the project management team choose the appropriate system for the particular project they are managing.

Ensuring an Appropriate Managerial Accountability Structure

Just as there is a large variety of types of public projects and project managers, there is also more than one type of managerial accountability system or structure under which those managers operate. Project managers and their teams will behave differently depending on the type of system involved.

In his book *Images of Organization*, Gareth Morgan describes a continuum of "species" of private sector organizations, ranging from those with management systems that are bureaucratic in nature to those that are "organic." In organizations with bureaucratic or hierarchical systems, all decision making is centralized at the top and employees must follow strict rules and procedures in carrying out their jobs.

TIPS FOR SUCCESS:

■ Different accountability systems in public agencies result in differing levels of control exerted by project managers over their teams.
■ Accountability systems can range from hierarchical to flexible and "organic."
■ The level of managerial control over project teams should be appropriately aligned with institutional and other forces outside the agency.
■ Managers can overcome alignment problems by ensuring adequate and open lines of communication and by effectively communicating the project vision to their teams.

Organic organizations at the other end of the continuum include structures such as matrix organizations and "adhocracies" in which the managerial style can be less formal and more flexible and therefore more suitable for the performance of "complex and uncertain tasks in highly turbulent environments." In adhocracy organizations, project teams often come together and later regroup into other teams.[13] Moreover, roles or jobs within flexible teams can be broadly defined, according to Morgan, with individuals being trained in multiple skills "so that they are interchangeable and can function in a flexible organic way."[14]

Morgan notes that a project manager must ensure that his or her organization's managerial system is aligned with the environment in which the organization operates as well as with its strategic planning, available technology, and with its employee culture. For instance, if the organization operates in a turbulent economic environment that requires flexible decision making, yet top management maintains a strong, hierarchical level of control, inefficiencies and other problems are likely to result. On the other hand, problems will also develop if "holistic" flexibility is given to teams in organizations that are subject to complex rules or regulations and in which processes have been highly standardized. As Example 6.3 illustrates, the use of an inappropriate accountability system in managing a public project or program can have fatal consequences.

Example 6.3: Inappropriate accountability systems and the Challenger space shuttle tragedy

In their paper, *Accountability in the Public Sector: Lessons from the Challenger Tragedy,* Barbara Romzek and Melvin Dubnick discussed how a major factor contributing to the fatal explosion in January 1986 of the space shuttle Challenger was an inappropriate emphasis at the National Aeronautics and Space Administration (NASA) on bureaucratic and political accountability systems that were ill-suited to the shuttle's mission.[15]

The technical cause of the explosion of the Challenger was a failure of "O-ring" seals in the joint between the lower segments of the right solid rocket motor. Top managers at NASA were apparently unaware of the opposition of engineers at Morton Thiokol, the shuttle contractor, to the launch of the shuttle at temperatures below 53 degrees Fahrenheit. Romzek and Dubnick maintained that the reason the engineers' opposition was ultimately not heeded by NASA had to do with an emphasis on bureaucratic and political control at the agency that hadn't always been the case there. In the 1960s, they pointed out, a very different accountability system had prevailed at the agency. That original accountability system was characterized by managerial deference to the expertise of the agency's professional staff, who were primarily aeronautical engineers. That professional accountability system had grown out of a sense of national crisis and out of President Kennedy's mandate to land an American on the moon by the end of the 1960s.

Internally, NASA developed a matrix structure in the 1960s in which both managers and technicians were assigned to project teams based on the expertise they could offer to particular tasks. The technical experts at NASA were given broad discretion to make managerial decisions, such as whether and when to launch spacecraft. In the 1970s, however, the accountability system at NASA began to change. With the successful 1969 landing on the moon of Apollo 11, America had won the "space race," and political and budgetary support for the agency subsequently began to level off. By the mid-1970s, NASA's budget was cut in half in real dollars and the staff was cut by 40 percent from the days of the Apollo missions. The shuttle program was proposed and born in this new environment. To get the program funded, NASA needed to establish new political alliances with Congress, the White House, and the military. In addition, with the cutbacks in staff came an increased reliance on contractors to accomplish technical tasks. The agency's accountability systems began to shift from a professional to a bureaucratic and political orientation.

Romzek and Dubnick contended that the launch on January 28, 1986 of the Challenger occurred in this new bureaucratic and political environment. Coupled with this had been growing political pressures on NASA that translated into internal pressure to set an ambitious launch date. The media had been reporting on delays in shuttle launches, and the Reagan White House had set a priority on making the shuttle system a "fully operational" commercial enterprise with routine launches.

Among the direct results of these new political pressures on NASA were that reporting requirements for safety concerns were reduced and the authority for launch go-ahead and other technical decisions was shifted from engineers and experts to supervisory personnel. Romzek and Dubnick concluded that as a result of these shifting accountability systems and political pressures, decision makers at NASA relied on supervisors to make the decision to launch the Challenger rather than deferring to professional experts.

Other organizational management experts who have examined the Challenger case have blamed the failed decision making in that case on the related phenomenon of groupthink, the dysfunctional dynamic of cohesive management teams that we discussed above. Debra Nelson and James Campbell Quick noted that the final accident report in the Challenger tragedy blamed "the NASA culture that downplayed risk and suppressed dissent for the decision."[16]

In Example 6.3, both groupthink and the inappropriate emphasis on bureaucratic and political accountability at NASA appear to have contributed to the

Challenger disaster. One of the characteristics of both of these factors was a lack of deferral to experts and a lack of consideration of or knowledge of their recommendations. Presciently, Romzek and Dubnick suggested at the end of their 1987 article that a post-accident push at NASA for greater emphases on legal and bureaucratic accountability systems would increase the chances for other shuttle failures. In fact, in February 2003, the space shuttle Columbia disintegrated during reentry, resulting in the loss of the entire seven-person crew. One could argue that Romzek and Dubnick's conclusions about inappropriate accountability systems involving the Challenger disaster could well apply to the Columbia tragedy 17 years later. Indeed, the final report on the Columbia disaster concluded that many of the managerial failures that caused the Challenger disaster repeated themselves with Columbia.

The final report of the Columbia investigation found, for instance, that although engineers within NASA had continued to worry that an errant piece of foam insulation may have done serious damage to protective tiles on the shuttle's wing, their concerns did not reach the mission management team. The management team even quashed three attempts by engineers to seek help from outside agencies in taking photos of the shuttle with spy telescopes on satellites or on the ground. The final report noted that engineers on the debris assessment team did not pass along concerns to the management team because "they were separated from the decision-making process by distance and rank."[17]

Romzek and Dubnick concluded that while a return to a professional accountability system at NASA might avert future accidents, the reality of NASA's institutional context made it highly improbable that such a return would ever happen. The agency, they concluded, was likely to face increased environmental pressures calling for the adoption of further political, bureaucratic, and legal mechanisms. Such, they said, is the challenge confronting all American public administrators.

Romzek and Dubnick clearly believe that public agencies and their managers face daunting obstacles in ensuring the proper alignment of accountability systems with institutional and other forces. That may well be the case. But it would also seem that public sector managers can take certain steps to make sure that bureaucratic and political pathologies, such as the groupthink that caused the Challenger tragedy, do not impede their programs and projects. Those steps might include some of the recommendations we've already given in this chapter and elsewhere in this book. For instance, it is often very helpful to involve all members of the management team in the project planning process and brainstorm with team members with relevant experience about all aspects of that process, from developing plans and specifications to projecting benefits and costs. When secrecy prevails in project management teams or project managers consult only with favored associates or with no one at all, important information will quickly become blocked at the top management level and serious problems will likely result. Even if a project manager is not able to change or fine-tune the accountability system he or she is faced with on a project, a conscious effort to open lines of communication or keep them open may help avert many serious problems, such as the lack of information flow that helped to doom the Challenger and Columbia flights.

In a sense, the key to overcoming accountability problems for public sector project managers may lie in what we pointed out earlier as an important quality of leadership—the ability "to invite people to feel they have a stake in realizing the (project) vision."[18] By maintaining open lines of communication, project managers help ensure that all members on the team feel they do have such a stake. We will discuss this and other motivational techniques that project managers can use with their teams later in this chapter.

> **TIP FOR SUCCESS:**
>
> Project managers must ensure that team members are trained or at least briefed on legal requirements and ethical practices relevant to their project responsibilities.

Coaching the Team on Legal Requirements and Ethical Practices

As we noted in Chapter 1, public sector project managers face a unique set of ethical responsibilities because they must place the public interest first in managing their projects. They must also deal with a complex system of statutes and regulations that govern virtually all aspects of their projects—from selecting contractors and other agents to the environmental, health and safety, and other impacts of their projects. But the project managers can't be everywhere at once. Their teams must understand ethical and legal requirements as well.

William Sims Curry describes the actual experience of a novice public agency contracting professional, shortly after accepting his first contract management position. In this case, a prospective contractor attempted to ply the new contracting staffer with drinks and entertainment during an official visit by the government contract team to the contractor's facility. At one point, while driving to a "trendy local establishment," the new staffer was asked by a representative of the contractor "to name whatever entertainment he desired." Fortunately, despite the fact that the employee had not yet had any organizational training in ethics or avoidance of conflicts of interest, he recognized the offer as inappropriate. And despite the fact that more senior members of his organization appeared to be accepting favors beyond what he considered reasonable, he refused to accept any further corporate favors.[19]

Curry recommends that public agencies ensure that instruction in ethics and avoiding conflicts of interest are included in their new-hire training programs. On public projects, public sector managers may not often have the luxury of formal training for new recruits to their teams. Managers, however, can determine the level of ethics training or instruction that the team members do have and can include a discussion of ethics and conflict-of-interest laws and policies in the briefing on legal requirements, if necessary. Curry also recommends that public agencies examine their policies on acceptance of gifts from contractors. Similarly, agencies should promote periodic educational programs that inform all agency personnel that the acceptance of all-expense-paid trips by contractors or prospective contractors is contrary to agency policy.

Steven Cohen and William Eimicke maintain that in addition to the need for training of government employees involved in contracting and contract management, in particular, there is also a need for stronger laws to protect or even encourage public agency whistleblowers who are aware of and report corrupt practices.[20] It should go without saying—but often, unfortunately, needs to be said—that a public sector administrator or manager should not discourage or, even worse, discipline an employee or project team member who brings forward a report about possible corruption within the agency. On the contrary, a responsible and ethical public official will want to investigate the charges immediately and determine whether they have merit.

How a project manager responds to a whistleblower is part of the test of a project manager's leadership. It reflects the attitude the project manager brings to the entire enterprise. Is he or she interested in undertaking the project successfully and in the public interest; or is he or she more concerned with protecting the private interests of contractors or campaign contributors? In the following chapter, we will discuss some specific legal requirements and ethical issues involving the procurement of contractors and consultants.

TIPS FOR SUCCESS:

- Team motivation can be enhanced by positive feedback and regular and productive project meetings.
- An organizational culture of openness, transparency, and trust can motivate project teams to work efficiently and effectively.

Motivating the Project Team

Motivating the project management team and keeping the team members motivated throughout the project is partly the responsibility of the project manager and partly up to the team members themselves. External issues such as the type of managerial accountability system involved can also influence team motivation. In fact, much of the following discussion and recommendations on team motivation tie in closely with our previous discussion of appropriate accountability systems in project-based organizations.

In this author's own experience working in the public sector, a key source of motivation has been the openness of top project managers to ideas and input from below. There are a number of ways to accomplish this. J. Davidson Frame suggests that top managers provide positive feedback on performance and publicly acknowledge good performance. As previously noted, Frame has also suggested that holding productive meetings helps build team cohesion. Holding these meetings periodically is not only important in maintaining control over the project's cost, performance, and schedule, but it helps keep the project staff motivated throughout the project as well.

Further, it is important to include all team members in meetings in which their areas of expertise might be relevant. In an uncertain political and economic climate, in particular, many public sector employees feel insecure about their jobs. Once a periodic meeting schedule has been started, it is important to stick to the schedule, even when things are not going smoothly on the project or within the public agency itself. An entire project team, if not the entire staff of an agency, can lose morale quickly if once-periodic meetings with top managers are stopped whenever the going gets rough at the agency. It is important, of course, that these are real meetings in which substantive issues are discussed and frank give-and-take among the participants is encouraged.

In general, organizational experts appear to agree that a nurturing atmosphere created by a project manager or top managers in an agency combined with openness are the best motivators of staff to perform effectively. There are exceptions to this, though. Gareth Morgan describes a culture of fear and intimidation at ITT, under the "tough and uncompromising leadership" of Harold Geneen, which nevertheless proved highly successful in catapulting the company to heights of profitability and corporate dominance.[21] But while the atmosphere at ITT may have been intimidating under Geneen, Morgan describes him as a man who used a prosecutorial style to elicit necessary justifications for proposed options for action from his employees. He wanted to know what everyone had to say and whether their proposals would stand up under scrutiny, according to Morgan, and it was apparently not his intention to intimidate people for the purpose of silencing dissenting voices.

On the other hand, private and public sector scandals such as Enron and the Bay of Pigs provide case studies of intimidating organizational atmospheres that— like the Challenger and Columbia cases—resulted in the silencing of important sources of information.

Enron, for instance, reportedly had a corporate climate in which anyone who tried to challenge questionable accounting and financial practices of the company faced the prospect of being reassigned or losing a bonus. In a case study written about the firm, John Alan Cohan stated that Enron was "widely reputed to have a had 'go-go' culture in which senior officials cast aside traditional business controls…[T]op officers were unaware of financial details and cast a relaxed attitude about conflicts of interest among executives."[22] As Morgan and others have pointed out, a corporate culture established by those at the top is an important determiner of how lower-level employees will behave and of their sense of motivation.

In the Bay of Pigs fiasco, then President John F. Kennedy authorized an abortive and ill-fated invasion by Cuban exiles of a beachhead on Cuba in 1961 in hopes of toppling the communist regime led by Fidel Castro. Richard E. Neustadt and Ernest R. May conclude that the Bay of Pigs was perhaps "*the* classic case of presumptions unexamined" in American presidential history up to that time. The presumptions that resulted in the Bay of Pigs disaster persisted due to a lack of input from colleagues in the administration who could have questioned them. One of those presumptions that Kennedy and his advisers held was that there would be prompt uprisings against Castro once the exiles who were recruited for the invasion landed on the beach there and proclaimed a rebel government.

Neustadt and May maintain that there were high-level officials within the CIA who would have "scoffed" at the notion that the Cuban population would have welcomed the American-sponsored invasion. But, they said, Kennedy wasn't even aware that the organizers of the invasion had "walled themselves off from colleagues who might have challenged their presumptions." They add that most of those whose comment or advice Kennedy asked were "too inhibited to question his underlying presumptions or to spell out theirs."[23]

Cohan suggests that CEOs of corporations can have a big impact in promoting a culture of trust, transparency of communication, direct lines of communication, and honest and ethical behavior. It would seem from the Bay of Pigs example and many other similar cases throughout history, that those organizational qualities of trust, transparency, and openness of communication are just as important in the public sector. Cohan offers a number of suggestions for companies to help them avoid dysfunctional organizational cultures that can lead to Enron-style failures. Below is a selection of those recommendations that would appear to apply to public sector project management teams, and that would appear likely to help ensure team motivation throughout the project if implemented:

1. Employees should be encouraged to expose wrongdoing without fear of retribution.
2. A communication system needs to be in place that enables information to move upward without getting distorted.
3. Appropriate programs must be in place to inform employees of the need to avoid conflicts of interest and to comply with laws.
4. Employees with the proper skills and "emotional intelligence" should be recruited to the project team.

Regarding Item 4 above, we've discussed the need for hiring qualified employees on projects. A sense among project team members that their colleagues on the team are qualified and committed to the project is an important team motivator as well.

In sum, successful public sector project management teams are built and sustained according to a number of principles that apply in other sectors as well. Project managers must select the most qualified people they can to serve on their teams.

They must exercise positive leadership qualities to build cohesion among their team members, while avoiding the potential for groupthink to emerge. They must maintain open and clear lines of communication and authority within the project management team and extending to contractors and consultants working on the project. They must ensure that the team members are aware of applicable laws and regulations as well as ethical practices that pertain to the project; and they must try to ensure that they and their team are operating under an accountability system that is appropriate to the project. All of these factors are important in ensuring that the team is motivated to carry out its project-related duties efficiently and effectively.

Endnotes

1. See for example Young, Trevor L. 2007. *The Handbook of Project Management,* revised 2nd edition. London: Kogan Page Publishers. Also, Morgan, Gareth. 2006. *Images of Organization.* Thousand Oaks, CA: Sage Publications, Inc.
2. See for example Morgan; also Lewis, James P. 1998. *Team-Based Project Management.* New York: American Management Association.
3. See for example Bennis, Warren, and Joan Goldsmith. 2003. *Learning to Lead: A Workbook on Becoming a Leader.* Basic Books. Also, Lewis, James P. *Team-Based Project Management.* Bennis and Goldsmith draw a sharp distinction between managers and leaders in this regard. They contend, for instance, that managers are concerned with such things as hierarchical control and maintenance of the status quo, and they have a "short-range view," whereas leaders are innovative, inspire trust, and have a long-range perspective (8). It seems, however, that leadership and management could be viewed as being inseparable. Leadership could be seen as a key quality of being a good manager—a quality that enables the manager to sort out when to take the short-range or long-range view, when to exercise control or depend on trust, or when to maintain the status quo or to be innovative.
4. Frame, J. Davidson. 2002. *The New Project Management.* San Francisco: Jossey-Bass.
5. Lewis, James P. 1998.
6. Nelson, Debra L. and James Campbell Quick. 2009. *Organizational Behavior: Science, the Real World, and You,* 6th edition. Mason, OH: South-Western Cengage Learning.
7. Office of the Special Inspector General for Iraq Reconstruction. 2006. *Iraq Reconstruction: Lessons in Contracting and Procurement.*
8. Office of the Special Inspector General for Iraq Reconstruction. 2007. *Iraq Reconstruction: Lessons in Program and Project Management.*
9. Office of the Special Inspector General for Iraq Reconstruction. 2007.
10. Office of the Special Inspector General for Iraq Reconstruction. 2007. *Iraq Reconstruction: Lessons in Program and Project Management.*
11. Federal Acquisition Regulations (FAR 7.503).
12. United States Government Accountability Office. 2006. *Space Acquisitions: DoD Needs to Take More Action to Address Unrealistic Initial Cost Estimates of Space Systems.* GAO-07-96.
13. Morgan, Gareth. 2006.
14. Morgan, Gareth, 2006. P. 103.
15. Romzek, Barbara S., and Melvin J. Dubnick. 1987. Accountability in the Public Sector: Lessons from the Challenger Tragedy. *Public Administration Review* 47:3:227–238. Romzek and Dubnick contend that in dealing with institutional forces, public organizations adopt four basic types of accountability systems: bureaucratic (or hierarchical), legal, political,

and professional. Each of these systems results in a different set of relationships within the organizations themselves and between them and the surrounding institutional forces.

16. Nelson and Quick. P. 341.
17. Schwartz, John and Matthew L. Wald. 2003. Final Shuttle Report Cites 'Broken Safety Culture' at NASA. *New York Times*. August 26, 2003.
18. Bennis and Goldsmith. P. 151.
19. Curry, William. 2008. *Contracting for Services in State and Local Government Agencies*. Taylor & Francis.
20. Cohen, Steven and William Eimicke. 2008. *The Responsible Contract Manager: Protecting the Public Interest in an Outsourced World*. Washington, D.C.: Georgetown University Press.
21. Morgan, Gareth. 2006. P. 129.
22. Cohan, John Alan. 2002. "I Didn't Know" and "I Was Only Doing My Job": Has Corporate Governance Careened Out of Control? A Case Study of Enron's Information Myopia. *Journal of Business Ethics* 40: 275–299. P. 277.
23. Neustadt, Richard, E., and Ernest R. May. *Thinking in Time: The Uses of History for Decision Makers*. 1986 New York: The Free Press. P. 140.

Chapter 7

Selecting the Best Agents, Part 2:
Contractors and Consultants

As we've discussed in previous chapters, the continuing shift of public sector functions and responsibilities to nonprofit and private sector agents has brought about a new focus in the public sector on procuring and managing contractors and consultants.

In a sense, nonprofit and private sector contractors and consultants are hired to become part of the public sector managers' extended project team. But, as we noted in Chapter 2, the principal-agent problem applies in these relationships. The private sector and nonprofit-sector agents' interests do not always coincide with the public's interests. These agents also often do their work in locations that are remote from the public sector managers and they usually have more knowledge and expertise about the technical aspects of their project-related work than the managers have.

It is therefore more and more important that government hire the best people, organizations, and firms that it can find for this work. After that, it is necessary—as we discussed in Chapter 2—for the public sector manager and his or her management team to ensure that these nonprofit and private sector agents perform the work efficiently and effectively.

The purpose of this chapter is to examine the procurement process for contractors and consultants and how public sector managers and their teams can make the best use of this process. In Chapter 9, we will take up the issue of *managing* contractors and consultants as part of the broader question of how best to manage the execution of public projects.

Procuring Contractors and Consultants

Procuring contractors and consultants has become a growing area of study and debate in both the government and academic arenas. Questions of ethics and fairness are central to this process. And much of the debate has centered on the balance that must be struck between ethics and fairness, on the one hand, and the timely and efficient selection of competent contractors and consultants, on the other.

This debate over procurement has, in fact, been a central part of the debate over rules that we discussed in Chapter 1. There is no question that public sector managers must deal with an increasingly complex set of rules governing procurement. One of the key responsibilities that public sector managers have consists of hiring the best agents within the context and constraints of the procurement rules. The Government Accountability Office points out that

> the objective of a public procurement system is to deliver on a timely basis the best value product or service to the customer, while maintaining the public's trust and fulfilling public policy goals.[1]

This is an important responsibility and is in many ways a heavier responsibility than those that typically fall to private sector managers. As Steven Cohen and William Eimicke note, public agencies are held to different and higher standards than those applied to private organizations.[2] For that reason, it is particularly important that public sector managers procure contractors and consultants for the right reasons.

As many experts point out, public sector managers should hire contractors and consultants when they do not have the capacity in-house to undertake the work.[3] Very few public jurisdictions, for instance, have the internal staff and resources needed to undertake public construction projects. In most of those cases, there is no choice—the public agency must hire a designer and general contractor from the private sector. For other types of projects, the question whether to contract out may not be as clear-cut. In those instances, public sector managers should carefully weigh the costs and benefits of contracting out. They should not outsource simply for ideological or political reasons or, as Cohen and Eimicke put it, "as a means of off-loading management headaches."[4] Cohen and Eimicke add that government should not use private contractors to accomplish tasks it can do as well or better with its own employees.

Once a decision has been made to contract for services or supplies, public sector managers should consult with their legal advisors to ensure that their procurement plans comply with the applicable rules.

Public Sector Procurement Rules

The overriding purpose of public sector procurement laws and regulations is to ensure that there is open and fair competition in the acquisition of supplies and services from nonprofit and private sector agents. While these requirements vary from state to state, most states and the federal government allow public jurisdictions to choose between two general types of competitive solicitation processes— bids and Requests for Proposals (RFPs).

Bids, the more traditional public procurement process, are associated with strictly controlled procurement procedures. Bids must generally be based on complete plans and specifications and are opened publicly on the date of a specified deadline for the bid submissions. Public agencies must generally select the low-bidder who demonstrates responsiveness to the bid specifications and who meets a standard of competence and integrity.

RFPs generally allow public agencies to grant flexibility to proposers in developing plans and specifications for the project. The decision to award a contract is based on both the technical merit of the proposal and the price. Unlike bids, RFPs are not always opened publicly and generally allow the public agency to negotiate over the price and specifications with the selected proposer. There are a number of variations on the RFP theme, including Requests for Qualifications (RFQs), which are based largely on the qualifications of proposed contractors or consultants, and not on plans or specifications. In Massachusetts, for instance, RFQs must be used in the selection of architects for public building projects and must be used in conjunction with bids and RFPs for the selection of contractors in public building projects costing more than $10 million.[5]

Key Characteristics of a Successful Procurement System

The Government Accountability Office describes a successful procurement system as having the following characteristics:[6]

1. Transparency
2. Accountability
3. Integrity
4. Competition
5. Organizational alignment and leadership
6. Human capital management
7. Knowledge and information management

These characteristics are based on guiding principles established in the Federal Acquisition Regulation as well as in model procurement codes issued by the American Bar Association and the National Association of Procurement Officials. One additional characteristic of a successful procurement system that we would add to this list is due diligence on the part of the public sector management team in selecting the most qualified agents to provide supplies and services.

In the rest of this chapter, we'll look closely at each of these successful procurement system characteristics:

TIP FOR SUCCESS:

Transparency in contract procurement involves "clear and written policies and procedures that are understood by all sources," according to the GAO.

Successful Public Procurement Characteristic #1: Transparency

As we discussed in Chapter 2, problems in transparency often arise in the procurement process, particularly in situations in which exemptions are sought from procurement laws and in which policies and procedures are not well understood. One example of this has been a growing involvement in public agency procurements of noncompetitive contracting arrangements that are designed to allow the public jurisdictions to incur expenses "off-budget" or "off-balance-sheet." These arrangements, by their definition, often lack transparency. In many of these cases, including some "public-private partnership" arrangements discussed in Chapters 1 and 2, claims are made by the parties involved that the projects entail little or no financial risk to the public jurisdictions, when, in fact, they can prove quite expensive over the long run. Similarly, the public is often uninformed about the way contractors are procured in the arrangements.

In Example 2.1 in Chapter 2, we discussed high costs and other problems that arose in a long-term, public-private partnership involving the Cranston, Rhode Island, wastewater treatment system, in which an off-budget financing arrangement was used. Pamela Bloomfield similarly discusses a 1991 prison construction project in Plymouth, Massachusetts, in which Plymouth County officials persuaded the state Legislature to enact special legislation authorizing the county to enter into a long-term financing lease for a new correctional facility to house federal, state, and county prisoners. The legislation exempted all project-related expenditures from state bidding and oversight laws and gave wide latitude to the county to negotiate no-bid contracts relating to the project. Despite that, the state was still obligated to pay the entire cost of financing the facility, which totaled more than $303 million over the 30-year financing period. Among the results of this arrangement was a little-noticed obligation on the part of the state to pay more than $4 million in costs incurred several years before by the same development team for a failed proposal to the federal government for a federal detention facility. [7]

Bloomfield contends that the impetus behind exemptions to public procurement laws is often the philosophy that the process should not be hampered by regulations that allegedly make government less efficient than the private sector. She notes that the ironic consequence of this, however, is that "[c]ontracts, hailed as models of market discipline, are then awarded to well-connected companies on a sole-source basis, unencumbered by market forces."[8] When planners and promoters of public projects suggest that exemptions are needed from procurement laws to permit the use of novel financing arrangements, it may well be a sign that a lack of transparency and other problems will follow.

TIPS FOR SUCCESS:

■ Accountability in public procurement involves "clear lines of procurement responsibility, authority, and oversight," according to the GAO.
■ The GAO recommends that at the state and local levels, a chief procurement officer should have "full-time, sole, and direct responsibility" for procurement programs.

Successful Public Procurement Characteristic #2: Accountability

In the previous chapter, we discussed the necessity of clear lines of authority and clear understandings of responsibility within the project management team of their management roles. Here we argue that this clarity of roles and responsibilities must extend to the relationships between project managers and their consultants and contractors, whether they are involved in project management or any other project-related work.

One example of procurement responsibility, authority, and oversight at the federal level is the requirement we discussed in Chapter 4 that contract procurement and administration staffs maintain control over contract awards and change orders and that their duties be kept separate from the duties of their day-to-day project management staff. As John Cibinic, Ralph Nash, and James Nagle point out, even though contractors will often routinely deal with a wide range of project management staff on public projects, federal *contracting officers* (COs) have the sole authority to legally bind the government to contracts and contract modifications. They note, however, that the authority of COs is nevertheless often fragmented, causing difficult legal problems in the contract administration process.[9]

As it has in many other areas of project management, the U.S. experience in rebuilding Iraq's infrastructure provides a telling example of the impact of unclear lines of contract procurement authority, responsibility, and oversight and the resulting impact of these issues on accountability.

Example 7.1: Lack of accountability in contract procurement in Iraq

As of July 2004, when the U.S.-led Coalition Provisional Authority—which had managed the occupational government of Iraq during much of the first year after the invasion—was dissolved, the CPA's functions were split between the State Department and Defense Department. However, accountability problems that had plagued the CPA were not resolved.

The Office of the Special Inspector General noted that under the new split arrangement between State and Defense, a virtual alphabet soup of federal entities was given responsibilities for procurement, contract administration, and other reconstruction management activities. Those agencies included the U.S. Agency for International Development (US AID); the Iraq Reconstruction Management Office (IRMO), which was under the State Department; the Program Contracting Office (PCO), which was under the Defense Department; the Joint Contracting Command-Iraq (JCC-I) office, which was intended to streamline contracting procedures and processes; and the U.S. Army Corps of Engineer's Gulf Region Division (GRD).

The special inspector general concluded that

> the many layers of management, including the program management contractors, made it difficult to determine who had ultimate authority over money, people, and projects.[37] [See our discussion in Chapter 6 of the use of contractors to undertake project management.]

One example of this confusion concerned the rehabilitation of a steam plant in the City of Doura in Iraq. The special inspector general cited a State Department draft report, which pointed out a complex series of contract and subcontract relationships involved in the project. The relationships involved the PCO, US AID, and the Bechtel Corp., which was both the project manager for US AID and the primary contractor and subcontracted to Siemens and Emerson for generator and control work. Siemens, in turn, was also subcontracting to Babcock for boiler work. The Iraqi Ministry of Electricity was also involved as a project manager. The State Department draft report stated the following:

> When one contractor at Doura was asked who is accountable for all the pieces fitting together, he said he was only accountable for doing his part. The [Ministry of Electricity]…(does) not seem to want to accept responsibility for success. A better approach is to have one experienced design and project manager over the entire job that can integrate and direct all subcontract work.[10]

These accountability-related issues lingered in Iraq-related procurement for years. In a 2009 report that addressed Defense Department contract management issues in both Iraq and Afghanistan, the GAO concluded that program managers were "not empowered to make go or no-go decisions," had little control over funding, had little authority over staffing, and were frequently changed during a program's development. Consequently, the GAO stated, Defense Department officials

> are rarely held accountable for…poor outcomes, and the acquisition environment does not provide the appropriate incentives for contractors to stay within cost and schedule targets, making them strong enablers of the status quo.[11]

If program and project managers are put in a position in which they are not authorized to make key project-related decisions and have little authority over staffing, chaos is likely to be the result. This is not to argue that public sector managers must always exert centralized or bureaucratic authority over contractors. As we noted in the previous chapter, flexible or "organic" accountability relationships are possible within project-management teams, and they are possible in relationships with contractors as well. Robert D. Behn suggests, for instance, that government should take a cue from business, which, he says, frequently operates on the basis of "trust rather than contracts."[12] And Cohen and Eimicke maintain that the trend in government is toward a series of relationships with private and nonprofit-sector agents that do not necessarily involve contracts or traditional bureaucratic and legal control.[13]

Nevertheless, while the traditional bureaucratic model may be changing, flexible network-style arrangements do not necessarily mean lines of authority or responsibility are not well understood within those networks or that public sector managers no longer have authority to make decisions. Guy VanRensselaer, an Organizational Improvement Specialist for the City of Madison, Wisconsin, maintains that in information technology projects, for example, it is important to have a project "sponsor" on the public sector management team who has the authority to make key procurement decisions. "The sponsor should have the authority to make decisions on change orders and not simply be the conduit," VanRensselaer said in an interview. In this respect, the sponsor would have authority similar to a contract officer at the federal level.

When lines of authority break down or become blurred, the networks themselves are likely to break down. And with that breakdown often come ethical problems, as we discuss in the next section.

TIPS FOR SUCCESS:

- Integrity in public procurement, according to the GAO, leads to public confidence.
- Public confidence is "earned by avoiding any conflict of interest, maintaining impartiality, avoiding preferential treatment for any group or individual, and dealing fairly and in good faith with all parties."

Successful Public Procurement Characteristic #3: Integrity

In the previous chapter, we discussed the need for training and instruction of public sector project team members in ethics-related matters. This is particularly important with respect to the procurement process. It is never helpful to a project manager to have a bidding or RFP process tainted by charges of favoritism or unfairness. Not only can this produce damaging media headlines, but it may also lead to litigation from aggrieved contractors that can cripple projects and their schedules.

Cohen and Eimicke advise government officials to "bend over backwards to recuse themselves from any contract situation where…a conflict [of interest] is possible." Those public officials should, moreover, be "proactive" in thinking through past relationships and anticipating potential conflicts.[14] Cohen and Eimicke point out that many conflicts result in efforts to reward contractors who happen to be campaign contributors or to reward former government officials now working in the private or nonprofit firms that are seeking government contracts. Not only can these situations result in awards of contracts to unqualified firms, but they can interfere with the proper oversight and management of those firms once they get the contracts.

The reconstruction effort in Iraq provides a clear example of lax standards in procurement ethics and integrity. As of early 2009, federal investigators were examining allegations of bribery and kickbacks in the procurement and management of contractors in the reconstruction effort. *The New York Times* reported that the investigations were beginning to focus on high-level government officials, including the role of a company, variously known as American Logistics Services and Lee Dynamics-International, which had repeatedly won construction contracts for millions of dollars "despite a dismal track record."[15]

TIPS FOR SUCCESS:

Project managers and their teams should understand conflict-of-interest standards regarding procurement.

At the federal level:

- Government employees with a financial interest in an organization are prohibited from "participating personally and substantially" in any matter concerning that organization and the government (18 U.S.C, section 208). The term *financial interest* can range from ownership in property and interests in stocks or bonds, to conducting employment negotiations with contractors.
- Former federal employees are prohibited for life from representing anyone else before the government on a particular matter (such as a contract procurement) that the employee handled "personally and substantially" while a government official (18 U.S.C., section 207).
- Former senior-level federal employees are prohibited for one year from appearing before the employee's former agency regardless of prior involvement in the matter (18 U.S.C., section 207).

Obviously, public sector project managers and their team members must avoid the acceptance of bribes and gratuities in exchange for contract awards. Conflicts of interest can be a grayer area, and federal and state laws and regulations covering those matters are complex.

Sometimes, the conflicts of interest of which public officials are accused are clear-cut. Cibinic, Nash, and Nagle state that it would be an egregious violation of the conflict-of-interest provisions if a contractor selected for a government contract were to subsequently hire a government employee who worked on the procurement before the contract award was made. They note, for instance, the case of Darleen A. Druyun, the Principal Deputy Assistant Secretary of the Air Force for Acquisition, who pled guilty in 2004 to a violation of 18 U.S.C., section 208 when she met with an officer of Boeing to discuss future employment at the same time she was negotiating a major contract with that company.[16]

In many cases, however, potential conflicts of interest do not necessarily fall into such bright categories. Example 7.2 provides an illustration of one of many types of potential conflicts that may not violate state or federal laws, but which can nevertheless result in an appearance of favoritism and run counter to the GAO guideline for integrity in public procurement.

Example 7.2: Potential conflicts of interest in Port of Seattle contracts

In the construction of the Third Runway Project at the Seattle-Tacoma International Airport (first discussed in Examples 4.1 and 4.3 in Chapter 4), a consultant (identified as SK) was working as a construction manager for the Port of Seattle, according to the Washington State Auditor.[17] In that capacity, SK was overseeing a contract with a construction company (identified as AH) for which SK had previously worked for 25 years.

The audit stated that although SK did not have authority under the Port of Seattle policies to approve contractor payments or change orders, he routinely signed off on such transactions, recommending their approval. The auditor concluded that even if SK no longer had any direct financial interests in Construction Company AH, there remained the appearance of a conflict of interest "in that SK may be inclined to afford favorable treatment to his former employer and former co-workers."

In another case, the auditor stated that a consultant identified as SW, who was working for a consulting company (E), was also the senior manager for the Port of Seattle for a large program management service contract. Consultant SW served on a selection committee that awarded a separate $5.8 million contract for work related to a terminal expansion project at the airport. The contract was awarded to Company AI, which was also a subcontractor to Company E on the program management service contract.

The state auditor maintained that both SK, in the first example, and SW, in the second, were in positions to give favorable treatment to companies with which they or their companies had current relationships or former relationships. The Port of Seattle responded to the auditor's findings by stating that SK had no financial interest in his former employer and that SW lacked any financial interest or direct connection to the selected firm. The auditor responded in turn that conflicts of interest are not limited solely to situations in which there is a direct financial interest. "At minimum," the auditor stated, "the appearance of these clear conflict of interest situations furthers the negative reputation that POS (the Port of Seattle) has among others in the contractor community that some contractors receive favored treatment by POS."[18]

In these two instances, a "Special Investigative Committee," which was led by a former United States Attorney, sided with the Port of Seattle and concluded in December 2008 that these cases did *not* constitute perceived conflicts of interest. Neither consultant, the Committee concluded, was in a position to exert undue influence. In an interview, an author of the state audit report said he stood by his conclusion that there was an appearance of a conflict of interest in both situations.

Whether or not any laws were violated and regardless of whether direct financial interests were involved in the two cases in Example 7.2, top Port of Seattle officials did not appear to be adhering to Cohen and Eimicke's advice that they "bend over backwards" or think proactively to avoid potential conflicts. The auditors, moreover, cited the Federal Acquisition Regulation, which states, in part:

> Transactions relating to the expenditure of public funds require the highest degree of public trust and an impeccable standard of conduct. The general rule is to avoid strictly any conflict of interest *or even the appearance of a conflict of interest* in government-contractor relationships. (FAR 3.101-1) [emphasis added]

To avoid the potential for conflicts of interest at the Port of Seattle, the Washington State Auditor recommended, among other things, the appointment of a chief procurement officer at the agency, establishment of an independent contract administration function, and changes to the delegations of authority for approving construction management expenditures. The Port responded that it agreed this recommendation "has merit," and was exploring ways to implement it.

TIP FOR SUCCESS:

The GAO describes competitive characteristics of a successful public procurement system as involving "specifications that do not favor a single source and solicitations widely publicized to benefit from the efficiencies of the commercial marketplace."

Successful Public Procurement Characteristic #4: Competition

Competition is widely agreed to be one of the most effective ways of ensuring that the best contractors and consultants are hired to undertake public sector projects and programs and that the supplies and services they provide are cost-effective.

John Donahue maintains that public contracting tends to be successful only when the contracts are subject to competition. The prospect of losing a contract to a competitor can serve as a strong incentive to completing the contract tasks efficiently and effectively.[19] As William Sims Curry notes:

> Competition provides a significant incentive for contractors to deliver their services at competitive pricing, produce high-quality services and adhere to their schedule commitments.[20]

At the same time, there is often resistance within government agencies to competitive contracting. On the one hand, noncompetitive, or sole-source, contracting is sometimes necessary in emergency situations in which there might not be time to advertise and undertake a bid or RFP process. In addition, many analysts make the argument that high-quality contracting performance and other efficiencies are achieved when a government agency is able to develop a relationship with a contractor or small group of qualified contractors over a period of time. In those situations, they argue, requiring contractors to periodically compete to maintain their contracts can prevent the development of a mutually high level of trust and cooperation between them and the government.

This argument has led many government agencies to develop lists of preapproved or "prequalified" contractors as well as the development of Indefinite Delivery/Indefinite Quantity (IDIQ) contracts, which are also often signed with prequalified contractors. (See our discussion of IDIQ contracts in Chapter 4.) The danger occurs when these arrangements become either sole-source procurements or when a small group of contractors appears to be getting favored treatment from government agencies.

In a memorandum sent to all senior federal procurement executives in 2007, the administrator of the Office of Management and Budget suggested that IDIQ contracts, in particular, were being procured without fully competitive processes. The administrator's memo included an "Assessment of Competition Practices" attachment, which suggested, among other things, that the agencies ask themselves whether they were providing bidders with sufficient information as well as clear performance measures in the statements of work on which to base their bids, and whether "sufficient time [had been] built into the acquisition process to maximize competition."[21]

Curry maintains that contractors that have been engaged in sole-source procurements tend to propose higher pricing than they would in a competitive environment and tend to increase their pricing at excessive rates. In addition, he argues, sole source contractors have a tendency to relax their efforts to meet project schedule and quality standards. Those issues are often coupled with ethical lapses in noncompetitive procurements such as the payment of gratuities to limit or eliminate competition. Curry notes that this concern is the basis for competitive procurement requirements at all levels of government and in all states.

Federal law, for instance, requires that "all procurement transactions be conducted in a manner providing full and open competition" (49 USC Part 18, Subpart C, Section 18.36). Sole-source procurement is allowed under the federal statute under a restricted set of circumstances, including public emergencies and situations in which competition is deemed inadequate after the "solicitation of a number of sources." Sole-source procurement is also permitted if the item is available only from a single source and if the awarding agency authorizes it.

Many states restrict sole-source contracting above a certain dollar threshold. Curry sent a questionnaire to all states and to city and county governments serving state capitals to determine the threshold at which service contracts require competition or a sole-source justification. He received responses from 12 states and six local agencies. The responses indicated dollar thresholds requiring sole-source justifications ranged from a low of $1,000 to a high of $62,600.

Dollar thresholds and other requirements for competition are sometimes ignored or evaded by public agencies, however. In the Port of Seattle case, the Washington State auditor contended that while Washington State law requires (with some exceptions) full and open competition for the procurement of "contracts for work" in excess of $200,000, the Port of Seattle interpreted the requirement to pertain only to construction contracts and not to consulting or other services contracts associated with construction. Thus, according to the auditor, the Port believed it was allowed to award contracts for professional and other consulting services without competition, regardless of magnitude, unless those contracts were for architectural and engineering services. (Under Washington State law, architectural and engineering services must be procured with full and open competition, although price negotiations with the selected firm are allowed.)[22]

Moreover, according to the Washington State auditor, the Port of Seattle used a "variety of techniques and means" to evade its own dollar thresholds for competitive procurement of consulting services. Those Port procurement policies were listed as (1) allowing sole source contracts of up to $50,000, (2) requiring limited competition for contracts between $50,001 and $200,000, and (3) requiring full and open competition for contracts exceeding $200,000. In 262 cases evaluated by the auditor, the initial contract was awarded in one competition category; but later amendments to the contracts moved them into higher competition categories. While the Port's policies allowed contract amendments up to $30,000 above the threshold categories, the Port repeatedly used a "purchase-splitting process" to circumvent the spirit and intent of the threshold requirements, according to the auditor. For instance, one consultant (or companies with which he was affiliated) received $320,000 via four no-competition service agreements, the auditor found.

In these instances, the Special Investigative Committee that followed up the Washington State Auditor's report, corroborated the auditor's findings and concluded that the "widespread practice" of circumventing competition requirements in procuring consulting contracts at the Port violated Port policies and, in some circumstances, constituted fraud.[23]

As the Washington State auditor noted, in addition to resulting in higher costs for services and lower quality of those services, the circumvention of competition requirements "sends a message to the consultant and contractor community that the…procurement process is not a fair one. This results in even further limitations" on competition in the procurement of goods and services.[24] The United States Attorney in Seattle opened a criminal investigation of the Port in January 2008 in the wake of the audit findings.[25]

The perception among contractors of unfairness in a procurement process is evident in the comments of two of five contractors that had declined to bid on a roofing contract with the Port of Seattle. According to an internal Port e-mail included in documents accompanying the state audit, one of the contractors stated that it didn't submit a bid because the winning contractor had "a lock" on the procurement. A second contractor stated that it had attended a pre-bid site tour and that an employee of the bidder that later won the contract "had access keys and used them during the walk thru."[26] The allegation that the bidder that later won the contract had keys to the building site was disputed by a Port official in a separate e-mail. Nevertheless, the comments from the two contractors indicate that a perception existed that this contract procurement process was an unfair one; and that perception was apparently a factor in discouraging at least those two contractors from submitting bids for the job.

Barriers to Competition in Long-Term Contracting

Even if public sector managers are sincerely interested in encouraging competition in the procurement of contracted supplies and services, economic and financial barriers can make that goal difficult to achieve in some circumstances. One of those barriers is often associated with long-term contracts for the development of costly public facilities. If, as Pamela Bloomfield points out, these contracting arrangements involve a requirement that contractors provide substantial up-front financing (as we talked about earlier in this chapter) as well as construction services, only the largest companies with access to the private capital needed may be able to bid on the projects. In addition, the cost of developing proposals for complex, long-term contracts can be so high that many potential competitors may decide that preparing a proposal is not worth that cost.[27]

Example 7.3 provides an example of a complex public works project, first discussed in Chapter 4 (Example 4.4), in which economic and financial barriers associated with long-term contracting appear to have limited effective competition.

Example 7.3: Limits to effective competition in the Lynn water and sewer privatization project

The Lynn (Massachusetts) Water and Sewer Commission issued Requests for Proposals in 1999 for both a major sewer separation project in the city and a contract to design and build improvements to and operate the city's wastewater treatment plant. Under special legislation, which exempted both projects from the state's public works bidding law,[28] the Sewer Commission entered into 20-year Design-Build-Operate (DBO) contracts for both the treatment plant and the sewer separation project.

In both cases, barriers to robust competition were thrown up as a result of a number of factors having to do with the nature complexity of the procurement processes.

For instance, as discussed in Example 4.4 in Chapter 4, the RFP for the sewer separation project did not provide proposers with information about the existing conditions of the sewer system. As previously noted, this lack of specifications regarding the existing system made the prospect of submitting a price for under-taking the work a risky proposition. The RFP also left it to the proposers to develop their own specifications for the sewer separation project. As a result, the potentially high cost of the proposal preparation discouraged rather than promoted competi-tion, according to the inspector general. In the case of the wastewater treatment plant contract, the fact that U.S. Filter had a longstanding contractual relationship with the sewer commission may have deterred potential competitors as well.

The special legislation established an RFP process, which stipulated that an evaluation committee would evaluate and rate both technical and price propos-als for the contracts. The sewer commission received two proposals in response to the RFP. One proposal was submitted by a team consisting of the construction firm of Modern Continental Construction Co., Inc., and the engineering firm of Metcalf & Eddy. The other proposal was submitted by U.S. Filter, which had been operating the sewer commission's wastewater treatment plant under a separate contract since 1985.

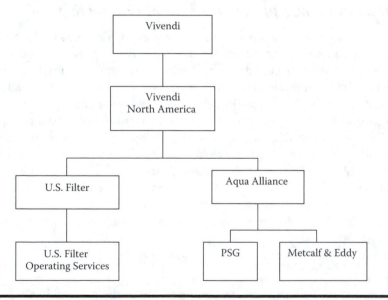

Figure 7.1 Organizational chart of entities bidding on the Lynn sewer and waste-water treatment projects: Vivendi Organizational Chart. (From Privatization of Wastewater Facilities in Lynn, Massachusetts. Massachusetts Office of the Inspector General. 2001.)

By the time the proposals were submitted in May 1999, U.S. Filter had been acquired by Vivendi, a multinational corporation. Metcalf & Eddy, the design firm that had teamed with Modern Continental, was a wholly owned subsidiary of Acqua Alliance, Inc., another company owned and controlled by Vivendi, according to the inspector general. Figure 7.1, based on an organizational chart submitted to the sewer commission by Metcalf & Eddy, shows the relationships among the bidding entities. The inspector general concluded that the fact that the two proposals for the sewer and wastewater treatment projects came from companies owned and controlled by the same corporation amounted to an absence of real competition in both procurements.

The lack of competition in both procurements resulted in contracts that lacked adequate performance guarantees and that were likely to result in higher costs to ratepayers than would shorter-term contracts procured under the state's public works bid law, according to the inspector general. In a postscript to this story, the sewer commission terminated its $48 million sewer separation contract with U.S. Filter in 2004 after discovering that the contractor's required $15 million letter of credit had expired in 2001.[29]

Example 7.3 is not intended here to flatly discourage public agencies from entering into complex or long-term contracting. The point of the example and our discussions in previous chapters as well about long-term contracts is to increase awareness among public sector managers of the potential risks of these arrangements and of their potential to discourage competition in the procurement of the contractors. We will discuss some additional financial risks of long-term contracts in the next chapter.

Proprietary Specifications

As we've noted above, federal law (and many state laws) require that public procurements be undertaken in a manner that provides for full and open competition. This is taken to mean that contract specifications, in particular, must be written so that they can be met by more than one supplier or manufacturer. One way in which true competition is sometimes avoided by public agencies is to list a brand name or single manufacturer in the specifications for a particular item.

At the federal level, the Federal Acquisition Regulation (FAR 10.002 and 36.202) states that proprietary or restrictive specifications must not be used unless it is "established conclusively that no substitute will serve the purpose."

Successful Public Procurement Characteristic #5: Organizational Alignment and Leadership

According to the GAO, this characteristic of successful public procurement involves the "appropriate placement of the acquisition [or procurement] function in the organization to cut across traditional organizational boundaries with stakeholders having clearly defined roles and responsibilities." For state and local governments to operate effectively, the GAO adds, "recommended practice is central leadership in the executive branch."

This successful procurement characteristic appears to be closely tied to successful procurement characteristic #2 concerning accountability and its requirement that there be "clear lines of procurement responsibility, authority, and oversight." One additional requirement here is that the acquisition function cut across "traditional organizational boundaries." As we discussed in Chapter 6, public sector project management teams are no longer always bound by traditional bureaucratic or organizational structures, but must properly align their organizational structure with the environment in which the organization operates as well as with its strategic planning, available technology, and with its employee culture.

Successful Public Procurement Characteristic #6: Human Capital Management

This successful procurement characteristic requires a "competent workforce responsive to mission requirements, with continued review and training to improve individual and system performance," according to the GAO.

In Chapter 6, we discussed the need for the selection of a competent public sector team that is qualified to successfully manage projects and procure contractors and consultants needed for that work.

> **TIP FOR SUCCESS:**
>
> Successful public procurement requires the use of "technologies and tools that help managers and staff make well-informed acquisitions decisions," according to the GAO.

Successful Public Procurement Characteristic #7: Knowledge and Information Management

There is no question but that the rise of Internet-based sites and sources of information on public contracting have changed the landscape of public procurement at all levels of government. At the federal level, the administrator of the Office of Management and Budget asked procurement executives in the 2007 memorandum discussed earlier whether they were:

1. Seeking information relevant to their procurements by publishing formal information requests in appropriate technical or scientific journals or business publications;
2. Using government and commercial databases to obtain information relative to their procurements; and

3. Participating in "interactive, on-line communication among industry, acquisition, personnel, and customers."[30]

The major advantage of Internet-based procurement resources appears to be the greater access to information that they promise to public managers and the time savings in the procurement process that they reportedly offer to both public sector managers and private sector contractors. The jury may still be out on whether these online processes help ensure high standards along other dimensions of procurement, such as transparency, accountability, integrity, and competition. To the extent that they make information more available to public managers and to the public itself through online databases, they do seem to have the potential to increase at least transparency in public procurement. On the other hand, the practice of putting most or all procurement-related information online may result in the long-term loss of a paper-based audit trail—an outcome that might actually decrease procurement-related accountability and transparency.

According to Lisa Cliff and Judy Steele, the Federal Business Opportunities Website at FedBizOpps (http://www.fedbizopps.gov or www.fbo.gov) has become "the single point of entry" for federal government procurement opportunities over $25,000. The system has eliminated the 15-day waiting period for posting in the Commerce Business Daily and greatly shortened acquisition lead-times. Cliff and Steele noted that more than 27,000 government buyers were registered to use FedBizOpps as of 2007, and more than 52,000 active synopses and solicitations were posted on the Website.[31] Cliff and Steele also pointed out that the Federal Funding and Accountability Transparency Act (P.L. 109-282) required the establishment of a free, public online database disclosing federal contract award information. This resulted in the establishment of a federal Website listing all contractors receiving federal funds at http://www.usaspending.gov/.

Among innovative procurement approaches cited in a 2006 GAO forum on federal acquisition challenges in the 21st century was the establishment of an "electronic marketplace" by the Naval Sea Systems Command. The Web-based process has vastly expedited the competitive award of the Command's contracts, according to comments at the forum. For example, a commenter at the GAO forum stated that a $150 million task order award, typically taking 6 to 12 months to be awarded, took 90 days under the online system; another $32 million financial management contract was solicited and awarded in 30 days.[32]

TIP FOR SUCCESS:

Project managers should consult with their legal staffs about requirements for evaluating contractors and consultants prior to selecting them for project work, and should ensure that relevant past performance information is available to them.

Successful Procurement Characteristic #8: Due Diligence in Selecting Contractors and Consultants

Even though a contractor may have submitted the lowest bid price and best technical proposal in a transparent, competitive, and ethically sound solicitation process, the result may well be disastrous if the contractor is not qualified to undertake the work. In selecting contractors and consultants, an additional critical safeguard for public agencies involves the exercise of due diligence in ensuring that those agents are qualified and are financially capable of carrying out the project work efficiently and effectively. The federal government and many states have varying due diligence requirements for public agencies. Those requirements often involve examining evaluations of previous projects done by bidders and checks of the bidders' financial conditions and records of previous contract terminations and litigation.

FAR 36.201 states that when contracts have ended, agencies must prepare evaluations of contractors' performance if the contract was over $550,000 in value or if it was over $10,000 and was terminated for default. In addition, past performance must be evaluated *in selecting* contractors for negotiated competitive procurements expected to exceed the "simplified acquisition threshold" of $100,000, unless the contracting officer documents the reason past performance is not an appropriate evaluation factor for the acquisition (FAR 15.304(c)(3)).[33] The evaluations should take into account, among other things, past performance information regarding predecessor companies, key personnel with relevant experience, and subcontractors that will perform major or critical aspects of the contract (FAR 15.305).

There are several Web-based databases that contain contractor performance reports, pertaining to different federal agencies. The Past Performance Information Retrieval System (PPIRS) (http://www.ppirs.gov/) is a central repository for those systems, according to a Small Business Administration guide.[34] The GAO, however, reviewed PPIRS data for fiscal years 2006 and 2007 and found that there was little systematic capture of past contractor performance information, such as contract terminations due to defaults or subcontract management.[35] The GAO also cited a lack of standardization in contractor performance ratings.[36]

For state and local project managers, there may be varying requirements for evaluating contractors and consultants prior to soliciting bids or signing contracts with them. Managers should consult with their legal staffs about those evaluation requirements and should ensure that information is available to them about past performance and other relevant factors about contractors, such as their financial conditions and records of litigation.

Selecting the Best Agents: Putting It All Together

At this point in the process of managing public projects, the manager and his or her team have come a long way. They have undertaken an extensive planning process involving many steps (some which may have been repeated several times), and they have undertaken a careful and competitive solicitation process for the best agents, both in-house and elsewhere, to undertake the project work.

But before anyone can put a shovel in the ground or start assembling a fleet of aircraft or develop a new generation of software to guide an orbiting telescope, agreements must be reached with those who will carry out that work. Those agreements must stipulate how the work is to be done and must sort out the risks involved, financial and otherwise, among the parties. In most instances, those agreements will take the form of contracts. In the next chapter, we will discuss critical aspects of the contract drafting process that will help public sector managers both protect the public interest in the course of their projects and ensure that the projects are completed successfully.

Endnotes

1. United States Government Accountability Office. 2007. *District of Columbia: Procurement System Needs Major Reform.* GAO-07-159.
2. Cohen, Steven and William Eimicke. 2008. *The Responsible Contract Manager: Protecting the Public Interest in an Outsourced World.* Washington, D.C.: Georgetown University Press. P. xii.
3. See for example Prager, Jonas. 1994. Contracting Out Government Services: Lessons from the Private Sector. *Public Administration Review* 54:2: 176–184. Prager maintains that "[c]ontracting out needs to be considered whenever the government entity cannot take advantage of the economies of scale and scope." P. 180.
4. Cohen and Eimicke. P. 30.
5. Commonwealth of Massachusetts, Office of the Inspector General. 2005. *Designing and Constructing Public Facilities: Legal Requirements, Recommended Practices, Sources of Assistance.* http://www.mass.gov/ig/publ/dcmanual.pdf
6. United States Government Accountability Office. 2007. GAO-07-159.
7. Bloomfield, Pamela. 2006. The Challenging Business of Long-Term Public-Private Partnerships: Reflections on Local Experience. *Public Administration Review* 66:3: 400–411. P. 401.
8. Bloomfield. P. 402.
9. Cibinic, John, Jr., Ralph C. Nash, Jr., and James F. Nagle. 2006. *Administration of Government Contracts,* 4th edition. CCH, Inc. P. 31.
10. Office of the Special Inspector General for Iraq Reconstruction. 2007. *Iraq Reconstruction: Lessons in Program and Project Management.* P. 86.
11. United States Government Accountability Office. 2009. *Defense Management: Actions Needed to Overcome Long-Standing Challenges with Weapon Systems Acquisition and Service Contract Management.* GAO-09-362T. Pp. 5 and 6.
12. Behn, Robert D. 2001. *Rethinking Democratic Accountability.* Washington, DC: Brookings Institution Press. P. 96.
13. Cohen and Eimicke. P. 42.
14. Cohen and Eimicke. P. 141
15. Glanz, James, C.J. Chivers, and William K. Rashbaum. 2009. Inquiry on Graft in Iraq Focuses on U.S. Officers. *New York Times.* February 15, 2009. http://www.nytimes.com/2009/02/15/world/middleeast/15iraq.html

16. See for example United States Department of Justice. Statement of Paul McNulty, Deputy Attorney General Before the Committee on Armed Services, United States Senate Concerning Boeing Company Global Settlement Agreement. August 1, 2006. http://www. globalsecurity.org/military/library/congress/2006_hr/060801-mcnulty.pdf; also, Wayne, Leslie. 2004. Air Force Asks for Broader Inquiry Into Charges of Favoritism in Boeing Contracts. *The New York Times*. October 12, 2004. http://query.nytimes.com/gst/fullpage. html?res=9F06EEDB113BF931A25753C1A9629C8B63&sec=&spon=&pagewanted=all; and Cibinic et al., P. 102.
17. Washington State Auditor. 2007. *Performance Audit Report: Port of Seattle Construction Management.*
18. Washington State Auditor. 2007. P. 136.
19. Donahue, John D. 1989. *The Privatization Decision: Public Ends, Private Means*. New York: Basic Books.
20. Curry, William. 2008. *Contracting for Services in State and Local Government Agencies*. Taylor & Francis.
21. Denett, Paul A., Administrator, Office of Management and Budget. "Enhancing Competition in Federal Acquisition." Memorandum for Chief Acquisition Officers and Senior Procurement Executives. May 31, 2007.
22. Washington State Auditor. 2007.
23. McKay, Mike, Krista Bush, John Keller et al. 2008. *Report of the Special Investigative Team* [Port of Seattle audit case]. December 3, 2008. McKay Chadwell, PLLC. P. 37.
24. Washington State Auditor. P. 66.
25. Brunner, Jim, and Bob Young. 2008. Possible Fraud at Port Focus of Criminal Probe. *Seattle Times*. January 8, 2008. http://seattletimes.nwsource.com/html/localnews/2004113088_port08m.html
26. Washington State Auditor. 2007. *Port of Seattle Audit Working Papers Concerning Main Terminal Roof Replacement.*
27. Bloomfield. P. 402.
28. The Massachusetts public works bidding law (M.G.L. chap. 30, section 39M) requires public agencies to select the most "eligible and responsible" bidder that submits the lowest bid for projects with expected costs of more than $10,000.
29. Bloomfield. P. 407.
30. These acquisition-related market research techniques are outlined in Federal Acquisition Regulation 10.002(b)(2).
31. Cliff, Lisa, and Judy Steele. 2007. Fulfilling the Promise of E-Gov Initiatives. *The Public Manager* 36.4, Winter 2007.
32. United States Government Accountability Office. 2006. *Comptroller General's Forum: Federal Acquisition Opportunities and Challenges in the 21st Century*. October 2006. GAO-07-45SP.
33. Effective January 29, 1999 the Director of Defense Procurement extended a class deviation to FAR 15.304(c)(3) and 42.1502(a). Under this deviation, all DoD contracting activities are required to prepare an evaluation of contractor performance for each contract expected to exceed $5 million for systems and operations support; $1 million for services, and information technology; and $100,000 for fuels and health care contracts.
34. United States Small Business Administration. Retrieval of Past Performance Evaluations guide. http://www.sba.gov/idc/groups/public/documents/co_denver/co_past_performance_eval. pdf
35. United States Government Accountability Office. 2009. *Federal Contractors: Better Performance Information Needed to Support Agency Contract Award Decisions*. GAO-09-374.
36. Some states, such as Massachusetts, may have more systematic contractor qualification and performance evaluation requirements than does the federal government. In Massachusetts,

for instance, the state Division of Capital Asset Management (DCAM) certifies contractors and subcontractors for public building construction projects over $100,000 in value. DCAM evaluates the contractors' past performance using contractor evaluations and numerical ratings provided by public and private owners of projects, which the contractors have completed in the last five years. General contractors bidding on public building contracts must also submit Update Statements showing current and recent projects, any significant changes in their financial position, and relevant litigation involving the bidder. In addition, contractors and subcontractors on building projects over $10 million in value must first be prequalified to bid, under a Request for Qualifications Process (Commonwealth of Massachusetts, Office of the Inspector General. 2005. *Designing and Constructing Public Facilities: Legal Requirements, Recommended Practices, Sources of Assistance.* http://www.mass.gov/ig/publ/dcmanual.pdf).

37. Office of the Special Inspector General for Iraq Reconstruction. 2007. *Iraq Reconstruction: Lessons in Program and Project Management.* P. 85.

Chapter 8

Enacting Advantageous Agreements

All principal-agent relationships, as John Pratt and Richard Zeckhauser would characterize them,[1] are based on formal or informal agreements that define those relationships. Agreements can exist on a large scale, such as a constitution, which defines the relationship between a people and its government; or on a much smaller scale, such as contracts between parties in business transactions or between contractors and public agencies. Project-related agreements also exist *within* public agencies among supervisors and subordinates whose jobs involve either managing projects or carrying out the project work. Those latter agreements may take the form of job or responsibility descriptions rather than contracts.

Because contracting between public agencies and private and nonprofit-sector agents has played such an increasingly large role in the undertaking of public projects, this chapter is devoted to the topic of drafting the contracts that are typically involved in those undertakings. These contracts are often between government agencies and engineers, architects, construction contractors, software developers, and many other types of consultants. While well-drafted contracts that protect the public interest are not sufficient to ensure that the public projects involved will be completed successfully, they are a necessary aspect of the process.

This chapter will discuss some of the key aspects and elements of public sector contracts and how those contracts can be drafted to ensure that the conditions necessary for successful projects are present. In all too many cases, poorly drafted contracts or contracts that are not advantageous to the public jurisdictions have doomed projects to failure and subjected taxpayers, ratepayers, and other segments of the public to high costs and poor quality or performance, sometimes for decades.

It is critically important that the public sector project manager gets it right at the contract drafting stage.

The Essential Elements of Contracts

William Sims Curry defines a contract as "an agreement that is legally enforceable and reflects the relationship between two or more parties for a specific time period." Such an agreement encompasses a promise by one of the parties to do something for the other party in exchange for something of value. Contracts, Curry adds, should be crafted to identify potential risks and describe how these risks are to be mitigated. All contracts must include an offer, acceptance, consideration (promises in the agreement that bind each party to the exchange of something of value), competent parties, and a legal purpose.[2]

Allocating Contract Risks

As Curry and others point out, much of the purpose of government contracting involves the allocation of risk.[3] In project management, risks, as we have discussed previously, are uncertainties that have the potential to affect the cost, schedule, and performance or quality of projects. In most cases, the impacts of these uncertainties are negative.

In signing contracts for major project work, it is important that the public sector manager (or agency head or contract officer) understands how risks are allocated among the contracting parties. As usual, the public interest is or should be paramount from public agency's point of view. Thus, it is in the contact drafting stage that public and private sector interests often come into the sharpest conflict. Contractors and consultants obviously have an incentive to draft or promote contract provisions that allocate as much of the risk as possible to the public agency.

This conflict in risk allocation becomes even more critical in signing long-term contracts because both parties have to live with the consequences of risk allocation decisions for decades, in some instances. The financial stakes are consequently much higher the longer the contract lasts. If a public agency signs a long-term contract that allocates all of the risk of future changes in law, for instance, to the public jurisdiction, the negative financial consequences to taxpayers or ratepayers can be lasting and significant.

The problem that many public sector managers face in many contract drafting and negotiation sessions, particularly at the local government level, is one of asymmetry of information and expertise. In dealing with plans, specifications, and financing for large and complex projects, the public sector management team may find itself outgunned by the private sector parties to the contract in terms of legal and technical expertise.[4] Under these circumstances, there is often a temptation to hire consultants to help in the contract drafting. But having hired consultants should not be taken as a reason for public sector managers to relax their guard, step back, and assume that the public interest will now be fully protected. In the final analysis, the public sector management team itself must ensure that the contract provisions are drafted in the public's best interest. This means ensuring an allocation of risk in the contract that is advantageous to the public agency without reducing the incentive to the contractor or consultant to perform its work efficiently and effectively.

Thus, while contracts should be advantageous to the public agency, those contracts should provide adequate protection to the contractor against risk as well. The Washington State Joint Legislative Audit and Review Committee points out contractually shifting risk to a contractor that is ill-suited to manage those risks can have unintended consequences.[5] The Future Imagery Architecture contract, which we discussed in Chapter 3 (Example 3.6), provides a vivid illustration of a contractor that was ill-suited to take on the considerable risks of combining an untried technology with an extremely tight budget and project schedule.

In the remainder of this chapter, we will look broadly at provisions in contracts that tend to have a significant effect on the level of risk those contracts pose to the public sector jurisdictions and at the consequent degree of advantageousness of those contracts to the public. Those aspects involve contract pricing structures, implied warranties, incentives that the contracts provide to the agents to carry out their work efficiently and effectively, express contract guarantees, and characteristics of contract scopes of work.

TIPS FOR SUCCESS:

Public sector project managers should be aware of the different risk allocations in different contract pricing structures. For instance, under:

- Firm-fixed-price contracts: The contractor bears most of the risk of cost increases.
- Cost-reimbursement contracts: The government accepts risks of increased costs.

The Contract Pricing Structure

Risks are broadly allocated by the type of pricing arrangement in the contract. For instance, in a cost-reimbursement pricing structure, the government accepts the risks of increased costs, delays, and nonperformance. If a "firm-fixed-price" for the work is agreed to at the start of the contract, the contractor bears the majority of these risks. The contract pricing structure, therefore, is a key determinant of the contract's risk allocation.

The following are some of the more common pricing structures in public sector contracting.

Firm-Fixed-Price Contracts

As noted, a firm-fixed-price contract involves a price for services that is agreed upon at the outset of the contract. The theory is that if the contractor's expenses turn out to be less than the fixed price, the contractor stands to make a profit. If those expenses turn out to be more than the contract price, the contractor must absorb the loss. There are no incentives in these contracts, however, to encourage contractors to exceed the minimal specifications in the contract or to achieve scheduled milestones or completion of the project before the contractual dates for those outcomes. But these contracts do provide a strong incentive to contractors to avoid cost overruns.

The Federal Acquisition Regulation states that firm-fixed-price contracts are recommended when there are "reasonably definite functional or detailed specifications" available for the contract work (FAR 16.202-2). Without reasonably definite specifications in a firm-fixed-price bid solicitation, contractors will find it more difficult to estimate a project's likely actual cost to them and will be less likely to bid on the project because of its potentially high risks to them. As a result, firm-firm-fixed price contracts—often also referred to as lump-sum contracts—are used most often in design-bid-build delivery approaches. The fixed price in those situations is the winning contractor's low bid, which is based on 100 percent complete plans and specifications.

Fixed-Price Incentive Contracts

Fixed-price incentive contracts are similar to firm-fixed-price contracts with the exception that these contracts include incentive payments to contractors for exceeding specifications or achieving milestones or completion before the contractual dates.

Under the Federal Acquisition Regulation, contract incentives are intended to establish reasonable and attainable performance targets and to motivate contractors to meet those targets and to discourage inefficiency and waste (FAR 16.401). At the federal level, there are two basic types of contract incentives—"incentive fees" and "award fees." The incentive fee is based on a formula determined at the inception of the contract. The incentive fee can apply to project costs, but may also apply to such things as technical characteristics and meeting the project schedule. The award fee is based on goals or criteria, which are sometimes subjective, rather than a formula.[6] The Government Accountability Office, for instance, suggests that award fees should be used to provide motivation to contractors in such areas as quality, timeliness, technical ingenuity, and cost-effective management.[7]

While contract incentives are intended to motivate contractors to achieve specific delivery targets or performance goals, they are not always managed properly, as we will discuss below.

Cost-Reimbursement Contracts

Unlike fixed-price contracts, cost-reimbursement (or cost-plus) contracts reimburse contractors for specific expenses that are deemed allowable by the public agency. As noted above, these contracts do not provide the contractor with the same incentive that fixed-price contracts do to control costs. Therefore, public agencies generally need to monitor the contractor's work and costs incurred under cost-reimbursement contracts especially carefully.

Cost-reimbursement contracts are generally considered to be more appropriate than fixed-price contracts when public agencies are not able to provide complete or detailed specifications for the work in the contract. The Federal Acquisition Regulation states that cost-reimbursement contracts are suitable when uncertainties inherent in the contract work do not permit costs to be estimated with the accuracy sufficient for using fixed-price contracts (FAR 16.301-2).

Given the risk inherent in cost-reimbursement contracts, Curry suggests that when those contracts are used, public agencies should first establish categories of costs that will or will not be reimbursed. At the federal level, the Federal Acquisition Regulation includes an extensive list of unallowable costs under cost reimbursement contracts, including costs for entertainment, fines or penalties, lobbying and political activity, public relations and advertising, alcoholic beverages, and losses on other contracts (FAR 31.201).

Cost-Plus-Fixed-Fee Contracts

This type of contract is intended to address the overspending incentive in cost-reimbursement contracts by limiting a contractor's profit to a fixed fee, regardless of the contractor's expenses.[8] The problem remains, however, that while the contractor's profit might be limited, there is still no incentive under this approach for the contractor to control its expenses for which it is reimbursed. This was allegedly the case on the Big Dig project in Boston in which the project management contract between the Massachusetts Turnpike Authority and the joint venture of Bechtel/Parsons Brinckerhoff was a cost-plus-fixed-fee arrangement. While Bechtel/Parsons' profit might have been limited under the contract, its compensation was not tied to deliverables or other measurable performance standards, according to the Massachusetts inspector general. As a result, project delays and construction contract changes only served to increase Bechtel/Parsons' compensation, the inspector general maintained.[9]

A variation on the cost-plus-fixed-fee approach is a Guaranteed-Maximum-Price (GMP) contract, which establishes a cap on the total contract price and usually obligates the project owner to pay actual costs plus a fee, up to the level of the GMP. The GMP offers protection to the public agency by providing it with the benefit of any realized savings if the contractor completes the work at less than the GMP.[10] Barbara Jackson maintains that GMP contracts "contain the best features of the lump sum and cost-plus-fee contracts" and have become popular in design-build project delivery in which contract pricing often occurs before designs and specifications are 100 percent complete. Jackson adds that owners and contractors often agree to split any project savings under GMP contracts.

Claude Lancome, executive vice president of Coast & Harbor Associates, Inc., an owner's project management firm in Massachusetts, maintains that many construction management at risk contracts fall under this GMP category as well. In those arrangements, as in design-build, the contractor is selected before the design or specifications are complete. Lancome said that in his experience, the GMP in CM at risk contracts is usually based on (1) the direct cost of the contractor's work (i.e., the amount paid to subcontractors including markups by the subcontractors); (2) the contractors "general conditions" costs, which include overhead; and (3) the contractor's fee, which can be either a fixed amount or a percentage of the total projected direct and general conditions costs.

But even GMP contracts may contain numerous provisions that allow the GMP to be exceeded, as we will discuss below. In some cases, the GMP itself may become relatively ineffective in limiting contract costs to the public agency.

Cost-Plus-Incentive-Fee and Cost-Plus-Award-Fee Contracts

As is the case with fixed-price-incentive contracts, cost-plus-incentive-fee contracts are intended to address the limitations of cost-plus and GMP contracts by directly addressing the issue of contract incentives. The incentive fees are intended to motivate contractors to complete the project work for less than an agreed-upon target cost or to meet the schedule. And as is the case with fixed-price contracts, award fees in cost-plus contracts can be used to achieve more subjective goals in areas such as quality, timeliness, technical ingenuity, and cost-effective management.

Getting the Incentives Right

As noted, the incentive fee and award fee provisions in contracts are intended to magnify or correct the impacts on risk allocation of basic contract pricing structures. A problem with incentive and award fees, however, is that they don't always work—or are not always used—as they were intended to by the drafters of the regulations that created them.

In 2005, the GAO found, for instance, that while the Defense Department was paying contractors millions of dollars in award and incentive fees, the Department was failing to ensure that the contractors met performance goals in the contracts. The GAO looked at a probability sample of 93 Defense Department weapons systems contracts out of a population of 570 in which award fees or incentive fees were paid between 1999 and 2003. The agency found that the Defense Department had provided an estimated $8 billion in award fees during that time, with most of the money paid regardless of whether the outcomes exceeded expectations or fell far short of them. About half of the 27 incentive-fee contracts that the GAO reviewed failed or were projected to fail to meet a key measure of program success—completing the project at or below the target price.[11] A follow-up study commissioned by the Defense Acquisition University, part of the Defense Department, noted that the GAO study set off "alarms" in procurement and contracting offices in the federal government and prodded Congress into requiring tighter controls over incentive contracts.[12]

There is a second potential problem with contract incentive awards. They can be used by contractors to game the process. Karen Richey, a senior cost analyst at GAO, explained that in many instances, contractors agree to unrealistically optimistic project cost and schedule estimates to ensure both that they will win contracts and that they will subsequently receive incentive fees for meeting the estimates. In those instances, the contractor may have an incentive to inflate the projected budget for the work scheduled to be completed at particular milestones. This practice, known as "front-loading," can make it appear in the early stages of a project as though a contractor is running under budget, when in fact the true costs of the project are being pushed out until later in the schedule. As Richey pointed out, contractors who front-load their scheduled budgets "make everything look good for as long as possible until everything hits the fan and by then it's then too late to fix it."

Similarly, Richey said, tying incentive fees to the achievement of unrealistically optimistic project schedules can create an incentive for contractors to cut corners in the quality of their work. She maintained that GAO considers it acceptable to base incentive or award fees on the achievement of schedule-based milestones if those milestones are set realistically. The corner-cutting often occurs when project schedules are overly optimistic and the incentive fees are tied to those unrealistic projections.

In its Cost Assessment Guide for capital programs and projects, the GAO advises that rather than basing award fees on meeting specific budgetary milestone numbers, they should be based on achieving "program outcomes," and for practices such as establishing realistic cost and schedule estimates and providing accurate and timely data. Richey maintained that basing an award fee on establishing realistic cost estimates, for instance, and not tying it to a specific budget number or date gives the contractor an incentive to complete the task without the need to cut corners. It also does not unnecessarily punish contractors when inevitable variances occur between the budgeted and actual values of the work at a given milestone.

As Adam Vodraska, an assistant general counsel at GAO, noted, contractors should be encouraged to report variances between budgeted and actual data relating to the project's cost and schedule. (We will discuss the monitoring technique of comparing budgeted to actual work, known as Earned Value Management, in the next chapter.) Providing an incentive payment for avoiding a variance or withholding it for encountering a variance is a "disincentive to honest reporting" by the contractor, Vodraska maintained.

Cost-Plus-a-Percentage-of-Cost Contracts

These contracts are unlawful at the federal level [10 U.S.C., section 2306(a); 41 U.S.C., section 254(b); and FAR 16.102(c)] and in a number of states. They provide reimbursement to the contractor for allowable costs plus a fee based on a predetermined percentage of those costs. These provisions provide a strong incentive to contractors to increase their costs. The higher their costs are, the higher is the percentage-based fee that is tacked on to their reimbursement.

In the Port of Seattle construction examples that we discussed in Example 4.3 in Chapter 4, the Washington State Auditor was critical of the Port's payment of hourly rates to consultants under one contract, which were based upon actual salary times a predetermined and agreed multiplier. The auditor contended this arrangement amounted to a cost-plus-percentage-of-cost arrangement "under which the contractor has no incentive to control costs and instead has an incentive to *increase* costs" (emphasis in the original).[13]

The Contract Pricing Structure and Project Planning

Whether or not incentives are used and whatever pricing structure is chosen, it is important that project risks be anticipated and properly controlled. As Example 8.1 illustrates, poor project planning negated the effectiveness of a GMP in containing the costs and risks of a large school construction project in Los Angeles.

Example 8.1: How a GMP was not a GMP in the Belmont Learning Complex project

The Belmont Learning Complex, which was at one time called the most expensive school in America, was originally conceived in 1985 as a middle school in Los Angeles. The design-build project scope expanded, however, into a planned senior high campus, shopping mall, and affordable housing complex before it was officially abandoned. Adding to the potential problems, the partially completed facility had been knowingly situated on a former oil field and industrial site that was allegedly saturated with hazardous chemical wastes.

In 2000, an article about the Belmont Learning Complex in *The Nation* contended that by the mid 1990s, the project had become "mired in controversy over 'waste, fraud and abuse' (as one state assemblyman put it), [and] lack of accountability..."[14] By the time construction was stopped, more than $123 million had already been spent on the school. It wasn't until 2008 that the school was finally completed and opened under a new name—the Edward R. Roybal

Learning Center. The total price tag had risen by then to more than $400 million, including a $17 million gas mitigation system.[15]

In its final report on the project, the Los Angeles district attorney pointed out that the contract between Los Angeles Unified School District (LAUSD) and Temple Beaudry Partners, the initial project developer, was a GMP contract with a maximum price of $85.9 million plus a fixed fee to the developer of $3.3 million and a completion guarantee fee of $1.6 million. There was also a provision in the contract for the school district and contractor to split any savings should the project be completed at less than the GMP. However, there were also numerous opportunities within the contract for costs to rise above the GMP. Significantly, according to the district attorney's report, environmental risks were allocated to the LAUSD under the contract, including delay costs associated with remediating environmental problems.[16] The *Nation* article added that the contract also indemnified the developers from any claims arising from those hazardous materials.[17]

The Los Angeles district attorney concluded in 2003 that there was insufficient evidence to bring criminal charges against any of the public or private sector parties involved in the project and that the site was not contaminated with hazardous wastes as defined in the state's hazardous waste control law. The district attorney even concluded that there were valid reasons for the LAUSD to take on the responsibility for environmental remediation in the contract. This, in effect, gave the LAUSD the ability to minimize remediation costs because the project developer would undoubtedly have negotiated a high contingency fee had it assumed that risk, according to the district attorney.

Nevertheless, the district attorney's report concluded that the LAUSD needed to develop "an improved school construction process which is open, thorough, efficient, and unquestionably honest." The complexity of the original project, with its shopping mall and housing component, created significant uncertainties in the design and consequently the project cost, the report found. In addition, the district attorney cautioned that the original design-build approach to the project increased the risk of cost increases to the school district because the prospective contractors did not bid on a single design, but instead each proposed "its own unique solution with its own unique price."[18]

Among the district attorney's recommendations were that that LAUSD development contracts employ "a much greater clarity of terms regarding contractor payment schedules, front-loading of profits, and related issues." The report also recommended new protocols limiting risks if the school district were to use the design-build approach again.

The Belmont Learning Complex example indicates that there are clearly factors other than the pricing structure in contracts that can override whatever risk protections might be built into those pricing structures. In this case, the uncertainty and complexity of the project's design, the expanding scope of that design, uncertainties in contractor payment schedules, and environmental remediation issues overrode the protection afforded by the GMP. The contract pricing structure alone can thus affect a project's risk allocation only to a certain degree. Many other factors, such as proper alignment of the pricing structure with project management approach, adequate planning, and specific contract provisions and incentives can be equally important the allocation of risk.

We will turn next to some of those other important contract provisions that have the potential to affect the public jurisdiction's risk in undertaking projects.

TIPS FOR SUCCESS:

- Public sector managers should pay careful attention to the potential risk of contract provisions involving differing site conditions, changes in law, contract term length, indemnification, termination, and other matters.
- Managers should seek a legal review of all contract provisions with regard to their risk allocation potential.

Contract Provisions and Project Risk

As we have seen, even though a contract may be considered to be a firm-fixed-price or a GMP contract, that does not make it risk-free to the public jurisdiction. A key reason for that is that most fixed price and GMP contracts contain provisions that provide exceptions to the fixed price or GMP, particularly for risks such as unforeseen conditions or changes in law. For instance, most public construction contracts contain a "differing site conditions" clause, which allows the contractor to recover additional costs incurred if the contractor encounters conditions at the project site that differ "materially" from the contract specifications or that couldn't be reasonably foreseen. Similar clauses may cover changes in laws or changes in circumstances that increase costs to the contractor after the contract is signed.

At the federal level, the Federal Acquisition Regulation requires that a differing site conditions clause be inserted in all fixed-price contracts above $100,000 (FAR 36.502).[19] In some states, the differing site conditions clause may be statutorily required to be placed (or is automatically inferred to be part of) public sector construction contracts.[20] In the private sector, the risk of differing site conditions can be allocated by contract to either party but often resides with the contractor based on a right to inspect the site and perform certain investigations before the contract is awarded, according to Steven F. Wojtasinski, a public contract attorney. In the public sector, however, the risk generally falls on the public agency to adjust the contract price upwards for differing site conditions. For that reason, public sector managers should do as much investigation as possible of the site conditions during the project planning stage. They should be wary of contract provisions inserted by contractors that provide for price increases for such things as changes in law or circumstances.

Other key provisions that are often found in public sector contracts and which can have major risk allocation implications for public agencies include the following:

1. Contract term lengths: We have pointed out above and in previous chapters that the length of a contract term can have significant risk allocation implications for the public jurisdiction. As we noted in Chapter 2, these risk factors are impossible to quantify accurately over long periods of time.
2. Terms of compensation: Contracts should describe the type of pricing structure involved (fixed-price or cost-reimbursement) and the schedule of payments (e.g., monthly, upon the completion of contract milestones, or upon completion of the contract). Under cost-reimbursement contracts, the contract should specify the requirements for documentation that must accompany the invoice for payment.[21]
3. Termination provisions: Contracts should have provisions that apply to both parties regarding termination of the contracts for default, cause, and convenience. Curry maintains that government agencies should always attempt to negotiate termination rights in a contract that are equal to the contractor's termination rights.
4. Automatic renewal provisions: These provisions provide for automatic renewal of contracts unless a termination letter is sent in advance of the contract termination date. Curry maintains that these provisions are rarely beneficial to the public contracting agency.
5. Key personnel provisions: If the qualifications of particular individuals working for the contractor are considered important to the public agency, the contract should specify those individuals and their roles and should require written approval from the agency for any substitutions.
6. Records inspection provisions: The contract should provide the public agency with access to and the right to inspect contractor records, particularly in cost-reimbursement arrangements.
7. Indemnification provisions: These provisions provide that one or either party holds the other harmless for negligent acts or omissions or willful misconduct in the performance of the contract. Public sector managers should make sure these provisions apply to both parties and do not solely indemnify the contractor and not the public agency.
8. Insurance provisions: Public sector managers should make sure that their contracts require contractors to maintain insurance against claims for injuries or damages to property that are at least equal to the contractors' own standard insurance coverage. Curry maintains that contractors have been known to propose insurance coverage in contracts with public agencies that provides less protection than their own standard coverage.

There are many other terms and provisions commonly found in public sector contracting that can have risk implications, and space prevents a discussion of all of them here. Curry collected a set of 47 such provisions discovered in a survey of state and local government contracting. Those provisions concern additional subjects such as the contractor's standard of care, contract amendments, inspection of the work and the project site, transferring or assigning the contract to another contractor (successors and assigns), and conditions for subcontracting, among others.

Example 8.2 illustrates how a failure to negotiate advantageous contract provisions in a public project can provide public jurisdictions with a disproportionate allocation of risk.

Example 8.2: Inappropriate allocation of risk in the NESWC contracts

The Northeast Solid Waste Committee (NESWC) resource recovery project, which we first discussed in Chapter 3 (Example 3.4), involved the signing in the 1980s of 23 separate 20-year contracts. The contracts were each enacted between individual municipalities in northeastern Massachusetts and Massachusetts REFUSETECH, Inc. (MRI), a subsidiary of Wheelabrator Technologies, Inc.

MRI was selected through a competitive process to design, build, and operate a resource recovery facility capable of incinerating the communities' municipal solid waste and producing electric power from steam generated in the combustion process. The $197 million facility, located in North Andover, Massachusetts, began operating in 1985. The NESWC municipalities have continued to pay a disposal fee to MRI and continue to receive a portion of the revenue generated by the sale of electricity produced by the facility as an offset to the fee. The revenues from the sale of electricity are tied to the price of oil.

Despite promises that the NESWC project would prove cost-effective to the communities, it had actually become so expensive to the communities by the late 1990s that the Massachusetts Inspector General's Office was asked by a caucus of state legislators representing the municipalities to investigate the project. By 1997, the communities were paying $95 per ton for waste disposal at the facility, nearly twice the current market price in the region. By 2005, when the contracts finally came to an end, the disposal fee had topped out at $145 per ton, according to Ray Santilli, assistant town manager of North Andover.

In a 1997 report, the Massachusetts inspector general determined that a critical reason for the sharply escalating municipal waste disposal rates lay in the nature of the contracts originally signed by the municipalities. The terms of those contracts or service agreements had been developed in negotiations between the state and MRI. As the inspector general noted:

> Although the service agreements developed by the Commonwealth and signed by the NESWC communities contain protections for both the bondholders (who financed the facility) and for MRI...these agreements provide the NESWC communities with almost no control over facility costs or protection from the financial risks of this public-private partnership.[22]

Among the contractual provisions that the inspector general identified as being unduly risky to the municipalities were the following:

- The disposal fee formula in the contracts required the communities to pay the debt service for the facility and an amount that MRI calculated to cover its operational costs and profit. At the end of the 20-year contract term, MRI would own the facility. In effect, as the inspector general pointed out, the contract required the communities to buy the facility for MRI and provide the company with a guaranteed income stream to operate it. This eliminated most of MRI's risk for the venture and placed the risk on the communities.

- The contracts required the NESWC communities to compensate MRI for any loss in profits resulting from unforeseen changes in circumstances. The company invoked this clause in 1989 when it sought a hike in the disposal fee because a downturn in the price of oil in the 1980s had lowered the company's profit from its share of electricity revenues. MRI claimed the decline in oil prices constituted an unforeseen circumstance. In 1992, an arbitration panel found in favor of MRI on this matter and awarded the company $3.4 million in the form of higher municipal disposal fees.
- The contracts required the communities to assume all risk of increased design, construction, operational, and financing costs of improvements to the NESWC facility required to comply with any change in environmental laws after 1979. In 1997, the communities were faced with the prospect of amortizing new air pollution controls at the facility, which were required by the state and by the 1990 amendments to the federal Clean Air Act. The improvements were projected at the time to cost $43 million.
- The contracts committed each community to pay MRI for a minimum number of tons of waste, regardless of whether or not the community actually produced that amount of waste. As a result of that "put-or-pay" clause, the municipalities were paying some $1.7 million a year for waste they weren't even sending to the resource recovery facility. The put-or-pay provision further proved to be a disincentive to recycling for the communities.[23]

The NEWSC project may be seen as an extreme example of one-sided contracting that is disadvantageous to public jurisdictions. Clearly, the state of Massachusetts, which had received assistance from a consultant in the negotiation of those contracts, did not take proper care to ensure that the contract risks were allocated equitably. As an update to this case, the contractual obligations of the municipalities in the NESWC project concluded in September 2005, according to Santilli, the assistant town manager of North Andover. At that time, most of the municipalities, including North Andover, entered into 1-year, 3-year, or 5-year individual agreements with Wheelabrator North Andover to continue to dispose of their trash at the North Andover facility. The per-ton disposal fees for the new agreements were substantially less under the new contracts than were the fees imposed on the NESWC communities during the latter years of that contractual relationship. None of the new individual agreements contained a put-or-pay or "guaranteed annual tonnage" provision for any community, according to Santilli. He said that North Andover's disposal fee under the new contract dropped from $145 to $71.50 per ton.

Implied Warranties and Duties

In addition to its allocation via contract provisions, risk is also allocated in contracts through implied warranties or duties, many of which are viewed as responsibilities of public agencies, and some of which are the responsibility of contractors. For instance, contracts at the federal level have been found to contain implied warranties that the project site will be accessible to the contractor, that utilities will be available, that the government has disclosed all information it possesses about the site, that its factual statements are correct, and that its cost estimates have been made with due care.[24]

There is also an implied warranty in federal public sector contracts that the specifications in the contracts are not defective or do not contain omissions (see the discussion on *Spearin v. United States* in Chapter 4) and that the specifications will not create unforeseen problems for the contractor. There are exceptions to this latter warranty, however. If the contractor prepared the specifications, the risk of extra costs falls on the contractor. Also, if the contractor has discretion in how to undertake the work, which is often the case with performance specifications, the contractor assumes the risk of extra costs as well.[25] This is not meant to imply, however, that public agencies should therefore allow contractors to prepare their own specifications in undertaking public projects. As we have previously discussed, public agencies assume other risks—that are potentially equal to or greater than the risk of preparing defective specifications—when they rely on contractors to develop their own plans and specifications for projects.

Under the Uniform Commercial Code, there are also implied warranties that apply to any product or goods produced by the contractor. One is an implied warranty of merchantability, which requires that the goods or products meet the standards of the trade. Another is an implied warranty of fitness for a particular purpose. That purpose is likely to have been made clear by the project owner in the specifications.

Express Contractual Guarantees and Warranties

In addition to implied warranty provisions, a project's level of risk to public jurisdictions can be significantly affected by guarantees and warranties that may be expressly required or negotiated in the contracts. In addition to cost guarantees, such as the GMP, these may involve guarantees that the contractor will meet certain performance standards for the project or face financial penalties if it fails to meet the standards. Such guarantees are particularly important in long-term contracts for which, as we have discussed, it is particularly difficult to project risks.

Example 8.3 describes the potential impact of a lack of critical contract guarantees in a long-term Design-Build-Operate contract signed in the Lynn, Massachusetts wastewater privatization project, which we previously discussed in Examples 4.4 and 7.3.

Example 8.3: Lack of contractual guarantees in the Lynn wastewater and sewer privatization project

Starting in the 1980s, the Lynn (Massachusetts) Water and Sewer Commission constructed a wastewater treatment plant and later began separating combined sewers throughout the city to correct a problem caused by the untreated discharge of wastewater into river and ocean waters during periods of heavy rain. The various projects were undertaken under a consent decree entered into with the federal Environmental Protection Agency, which had brought suit against the city in 1976 for violations of the Clean Water Act.

As noted in previous references to this case, the Commission issued an RFP for a long-term Design-Build-Operate (DBO) contract in 1999 for a major new sewer separation project in a portion of the city and a separate RFP for a contract to operate the city's wastewater treatment plant and to design and build improvements to the treatment facility. The Commission obtained special legislation, which exempted both procurements from the state's public works bidding law. The stated rationale for the legislative exemptions, which allowed the alternative DBO approaches to the projects, was that the proposers would bear the risk for meeting the project objectives. Those objectives were to reduce combined sewer overflows to comply with the Clean Water Act, according to the Massachusetts inspector general.

The inspector general noted that the then mayor of Lynn stated during a 1998 sewer commission meeting that each proposer responding to the sewer-separation RFP would be required to guarantee that its technical approach would meet EPA standards. However, the actual RFP contained vague language stating only that the contractor would perform the contract services "in accordance with certain guarantees of performance (if applicable to the technology proposed), applicable law, and industry standards."[26] The inspector general contended that this requirement "was essentially an invitation for proposers to determine the extent and nature of the performance guarantees" it would provide.[27]

The inspector general also listed a number of other provisions in the actual DBO sewer separation contract that it contended would absolve U.S. Filter from more responsibility than would a "typical, conventional construction contract." Among those provisions were:

- A provision specifying that U.S. Filter would be responsible for fixing its own defective sewer rehabilitation and sewer separation work only if the Sewer Commission discovered the defect within one or five years respectively following the completion of that phase of the project. Given that the contract called for the work to be performed over a nine-year period, the contract language excessively limited U.S. Filter's risk, the inspector general found.
- A provision limiting U.S. Filter's liability for failure to perform in conformance with the contract to the amount of the company's performance bond.
- A provision broadly waiving implied warranties involving the project work of merchantability, fitness for a particular purpose, and custom and usage "as to any of the Design/Build Work."
- A provision protecting U.S. Filter from "incidental, consequential or punitive damages," even if the Sewer Commission were able to prove that the company had engaged in material, false representations in the contract or had failed to perform its contractual obligations.

As for the wastewater treatment plant, the inspector general found that the separate, 20-year DBO contract contained a number of cost-adjustment provisions that were drafted in U.S. Filter's favor. One was a provision allowing U.S. Filter to increase its contract operations fee if the volume of water entering the facility ("flows") or water quality factors ("loadings") exceeded baseline parameters. There was no provision to reduce the cost to the sewer commission if flows were to decrease, even though the commission had projected that the planned sewer-separation work would reduce those flows.

The Lynn DBO contract example above highlights the need for a thorough legal review of all terms and provisions in public sector contracting, particularly with regard to the risk-allocation potential of these provisions. It is important to note that public managers should seek in-house legal advice, if possible, on these provisions before agreeing to them, even if the managers engage outside legal consultants and engineers to examine those risks. In the Lynn case, the inspector general found that the sewer commission spent millions of dollars on engineering and legal consultants and still ended up with DBO contracts that were not advantageous to it in terms of risk allocation.[28]

Breach-of-Contract Provisions

In addition to motivating the contractor to perform efficiently and effectively with appropriate pricing structures and positive contract incentives that are advantageous to the public agency, a contract may contain provisions to protect the agency against breaches of the contract. In some cases, for instance, liquidated damages provisions can be included in contracts. These provisions require a reimbursement by the *contractor* of costs incurred by the *public agency* should the contractor fail to complete its contractual obligations on time through its own fault. Another breach-of-contract provision is one that allows an owner to terminate a contract for default if the contractor fails to meet contractual obligations. In Chapter 9, we will discuss the importance of invoking such provisions when warranted to properly manage projects.

In addition to their dependence on the type of contract and its specific provisions and implied warranties, risk allocations depend on many other factors, such as the financial stability of the contractor and the project delivery approach. In the traditional design-bid-build construction approach, for example, the risk of design errors and omissions falls largely on the owner and designer. In the design-build approach, that risk falls on the joint design-contractor. Yet, as we discussed above and will discuss further in the section below, other risks are associated with project delivery approaches in which clear scopes of work or specifications have not been developed by the public agency.

Clear Scopes of Work

We noted in Chapter 4 that developing clear scopes of work is a critical aspect of project planning and that the components of these scopes of work, such as detailed plans and specifications, are often an integral part of the competitive solicitation process for public projects. The scope of work then becomes an integral part of the contract itself.

TIPS FOR SUCCESS:

■ The contract should include a scope of work that is clearly stated.
■ Public agencies should carefully review contractor-drafted scopes of work.

Chapter 4 discussed a number of examples of problems that occurred on public projects when scopes of work were vague and specifications were inadequate. The Belmont Learning Complex case in Example 8.1 in this chapter further illustrates how risks caused by a poorly developed scope of work can outweigh other contractual protections such as a GMP. While highly detailed specifications may not always be necessary or desirable in the drafting of competitive solicitation documents and contracts, it is always necessary that the scope of work be clearly understood by all parties.

Curry warns that public agency managers should give particularly close scrutiny to contracts in which the contractor has prepared the scope of work or other contract provisions, or has made modifications to documents prepared by the agency. We noted in Chapter 4 that contractors often prepare detailed scopes of work, including plans and specifications, in alternative project delivery approaches, such as design-build. Curry states that

> when the contractor prepares the scope-of-work and/or other contract provisions, or makes modifications to agency prepared documents, the contractual documents need to be carefully scrutinized. Contractor-prepared documents, or modifications to agency documents, are generally made to limit the contractor's risks. Oftentimes, such reductions in the risks to the contractor are limited to the point where the contractor's commitment is negligible. Department personnel…need to… determine whether a positive cost/benefit relationship still exists after the contractor's changes are incorporated into the contract.[29]

Similarly, as we discussed in previous chapters, contracts that transfer project oversight and other management responsibilities to contractors can prove unduly risky to public jurisdictions. Also risky are contracts whose scopes of work combine managerial and oversight functions with design and/or construction requirements.

In the Big Dig project in Boston, for example, the Massachusetts inspector general contended that under a project management contract with the Massachusetts Turnpike Authority, Bechtel/Parsons Brinckerhoff was responsible for both preparing and overseeing preliminary and some final design work; implementing value engineering reviews and other quality control measures; preparing construction bid packages and overseeing construction contracts; negotiating construction contract changes and claims; and performing general record-keeping activities, among other functions.[30] In effect, Bechtel/Parsons' scope of work under its contract was so inclusive that it raised a number of potential conflicts of interest for the contractor.

For instance, the contract required Bechtel/Parsons to oversee its own design work in some instances and to "reveal problems even when such problems are associated with (Bechtel/Parsons') own design work." The inspector general noted that it was aware of no evidence that Bechtel/Parsons had ever "acknowledged making a mistake that contributed to increased costs and schedule delays." The inspector general concluded that

> by contracting with [Bechtel/Parsons] to perform the full range of project management services and to oversee its own work, the Commonwealth has weakened its capacity to exert effective control over the cost and quality of the services [Bechtel/Parsons] provides.[31]

The field of public sector contracting is extremely complex, and we have been able only to provide a broad overview of it here. We hope the examples above are persuasive in demonstrating the need to pay close attention to contract structures and provisions and the impact they have on project risk allocation. In the final analysis, public agencies need experienced attorneys to draft their contracts. In the next chapter, we will examine how many of these contractual elements play out in the management of actual projects.

Endnotes

1. As noted in endnote 3 of Chapter 2, a "principal" and an "agent" are considered in this book, as Pratt and Zeckhauser express it, to be "parties bound together by an agreement that attempts to align *divergent motivations*." (Pratt. John W., and Richard J. Zeckhauser. 1991. *Principals and Agents: The Structure of Business*. Boston: Harvard Business School Press. P. ix.)
2. Curry, William. 2008. *Contracting for Services in State and Local Government Agencies*. Taylor & Francis. P. 5.
3. See for example Cibinic, John, Jr., Ralph C. Nash, Jr., and James F. Nagle. 2006. *Administration of Government Contracts,* 4th edition. CCH, Inc.
4. See for example Prager, Jonas. 1994. Contracting Out Government Services: Lessons from the Private Sector. *Public Administration Review* 54:2: 176–184; and Werkman, Janet, and David L. Westerling. 2000. Privatizing Municipal Water and Wastewater Systems: Promises and Pitfalls. *Public Works Management & Policy* 5:1:52–68.
5. Washington State, Joint Legislative Audit and Review Committee. 2005. *An Assessment of General Contractor/Construction Management Contracting Procedures*. http://www.leg.wa.gov/reports/05-9.pdf
6. Frame, J. Davidson 1994. *The New Project Management*. San Francisco: Jossey-Bass. Also see FAR 16.405-2.
7. United States Government Accountability Office. 2009. *GAO Cost Estimating and Assessment Guide: Best Practices for Developing and Managing Capital Program Costs*. GAO-09-3SP.
8. Frame, J. Davidson. 1994.

9. Commonwealth of Massachusetts, Office of the Inspector General, 2003. *Analysis of Bechtel/Parsons Brinckerhoff's Reply to* The Boston Globe's *Investigative News Series Concerning the Big Dig.* http://www.mass.gov/ig/publ/catglbrp.pdf

10. Jackson, Barbara J. 2004. *Construction Management Jump Start.* San Francisco: Sybex, Inc.

11. United States General Accounting Office. 2005. *Defense Acquisitions: DoD Has Paid Billions in Award and Incentive Fees Regardless of Acquisition Outcomes.* GAO-06-66.

12. Tremaine, Robert L. 2008. Incentive Contracts: The Attributes That Matter Most in Driving Favorable Outcomes. *Defense Acquisition Review Journal* 15.3 (Dec. 2008): 216–238.

13. Washington State Auditor. 2007. *Performance Audit Report: Port of Seattle Construction Management.* P. 77.

14. Anderson, Susan. The School That Wasn't. *The Nation.* June 5, 2000. http://www.thenation.com/doc/2000065/anderson.

15. Blume, Howard. 2008. Belmont school to reopen with new face, new name. *Lost Angeles Times.* August 10, 2008. http://articles.latimes.com/2008/aug/10/local/me-belmont10

16. Cooley, Steve. 2003. Final Investigative Report: Los Angeles Unified School District Belmont Learning Complex. Belmont Task Force, Los Angeles District Attorney's Office. March 2003. http://da.co.la.ca.us/pdf/BLC_Final_Report.pdf

17. See Anderson, Susan. June 5, 2000; also, Business Wire. *Belmont Firms File for Binding Arbitration.* April 19, 2000. The Gale Group, Inc. http://www.allbusiness.com/legal/labor-employment-law-alternative-dispute-resolution/6468009-1.html

18. Cooley. P. 215.

19. The Federal Acquisition Regulation also provides for a category of "fixed price contracts" that allow for adjustments to the fixed price for such things as unforeseeable increases in labor and materials costs.

20. See for example Massachusetts General Law Chapter 30, section 39N

21. Commonwealth of Massachusetts, Office of the Inspector General. 1997. *Massachusetts Certified Public Purchasing Official General Seminar handbook.*

22. Commonwealth of Massachusetts, Office of the Inspector General. 1997. *The North East Solid Waste Committee Project: Planning and Development of a Public-Private Partnership.* P. 2.

23. For a discussion of each of these disadvantageous contract provisions, see Commonwealth of Massachusetts, Office of the Inspector General. 1997.

24. Cibinic et al. 2006

25. Cibinic et al. 2006. P. 277

26. Commonwealth of Massachusetts, Office of the Inspector General. 2001. *Privatization of Wastewater Facilities in Lynn, Massachusetts.* P. 17.

27. Commonwealth of Massachusetts, Office of the Inspector General. 2001. P. 17.

28. According to the inspector general, the Lynn Sewer Commission signed a contract with Hawkins, Delafield & Wood (HDW), a New York–based law firm that was involved in consulting with several cities involved in long-term DBO contracts for wastewater treatment and sewer separation projects. In the Lynn Sewer Commission's case, the contract with HDW called for the commission to pay the law firm at a rate of $215 an hour, but contained no estimated total cost, maximum dollar amount, or schedule. HDW billed the Commission at an average rate of more than $40,000 per month for privatization assistance over a three-year period, for a total cost of more than $1.5 million. (Massachusetts Inspector General, 2001. P. 64).

29. Curry. 2008.

30. Commonwealth of Massachusetts, Office of the Inspector General. 2003.

31. Commonwealth of Massachusetts, Office of the Inspector General, 2003. P. 22

Chapter 9

Controlling Public Projects

The execution stage of the project is ready to begin. The planning, the selection of the project team and the contractors and consultants, and the drafting and signing of all or most of the contracts have largely been completed. Now comes the moment of truth. Will the project manager be able to keep things under control once the actual construction, production, or assembly starts? Will he or she be able to deliver the final product on time, within budget, and at the expected quality level?

From this point on, the project manager has three basic tasks, according to Trevor Young—measuring, evaluating, and correcting. Measuring involves determining the project's progress through formal and informal reporting. Evaluating involves determining the cause of deviations from the plan and how to react. And correcting involves taking actions to correct the situation.[1] The plan itself may have to be adjusted, as Paul Mlakar pointed out in Chapter 2.

In this chapter, we'll look at these three project control steps—measuring, evaluating, and correcting—and examine why a public sector manager's attention to each step is needed to keep the project under control during the execution stage.

Measuring Project Progress

Project managers measure progress during the execution or production stage by monitoring the ongoing work—a process that can range from visual inspections to examining contractor reports. In most instances, project monitoring involves measuring progress against the project's budget and schedule. And it involves checking whether the work conforms to the plans and specifications.

> **TIP FOR SUCCESS:**
>
> An active role by public sector managers in monitoring their projects during the execution or production stage is essential in ensuring the continuing success of those projects.

As we have previously noted, the need for monitoring is a consequence of the principal-agent problem. And as we discussed in Chapter 2, this is a major area of neglect in public sector contracting. Jonas Prager points to evidence ranging from a backlog of audits of Defense Department contracts to a general lack of resources for monitoring at the state and local levels of government in drawing the conclusion that monitoring is under-emphasized in the public sector.[2] Yet, monitoring is key to ensuring that a project's legal requirements are being complied with; that its specifications are being met; that the project's risks are under control; and that the project's cost and schedule objectives are being attained.

Robert Dolan, the mayor of Melrose, Massachusetts, maintains that successful project management during the execution stage requires active attention by the owner. Dolan took office in the midst of the controversial Mount Hood public works project in his city, which we discuss below in Example 9.1 and previously discussed in Chapter 3 (Example 3.5). He faced two major tasks almost simultaneously—the remediation of environmental problems caused by the Mount Hood project and the construction of a needed middle school in his city. Dolan oversaw the successful completion of both undertakings. The key in both cases, he said, was adequate project monitoring.

With respect to the middle school, Dolan said he personally visited the construction site every week to monitor progress. He also hired "the best (owner's) project manager in the state. I overpaid, but I knew I'd get it back." And he hired a lawyer to oversee construction issues. With respect to the public works project, he relied on a group of trusted advisors, including an architect who shut down his business for eight months to help. Dolan maintained that for mayors of small municipalities, in particular, proper management of public building and other construction projects can often become the key to their legacy. "You're building a part of you," he said. "You will forever be equated with that school you built."

During the construction of the Harvard Massachusetts library, which we discussed in Chapter 3 (Example 3.2), monitoring was taken seriously by the three citizen managers. They made a point of visiting the project site on a regular basis and attended the weekly construction meetings at the site with representatives of the general contractor, architect, and owner's project manager. When projects are complex, an owner's representative or owner's project manager can become increasingly important as an additional source of monitoring on behalf of the owner.[3]

Updating Project Records

When project monitoring is done, the results of measurements and observations must be recorded and the project records updated. In the Port of Seattle case, as we discussed in Example 4.1 in Chapter 4, the Washington State Auditor alleged a lack of adequate record-keeping procedures. If measurements of project progress and costs are not recorded and updated once the project execution stage has begun, managers will be confronted with situations in which key decisions are likely to be based on incomplete or outdated information.[4]

The consequence of the lack of a viable information management system becomes exponentially greater as the size and complexity of the project or program grows. As a participant at a 2006 forum on lessons learned from program and project management in Iraq noted, "[w]hen you lose track of a program, a big program like this with [2,300] projects, you never get it back."[5]

Example 9.1 provides an illustration of some of the consequences of the failure of a municipal government to maintain and update records and otherwise adequately monitor a public works project during its execution stage. (As noted above, these monitoring shortcomings refer to a period before Melrose Mayor Dolan assumed office and instituted changes in the management of this project.)

Example 9.1: Results of inadequate monitoring and oversight in the Mount Hood public works project in Melrose, Massachusetts

As part of the Mount Hood public works project, fill from underneath Boston Harbor began arriving at the Mount Hood Memorial Park and Golf Course in Melrose, Massachusetts, at a rate sometimes exceeding 180 truckloads per day. At the start of the fill deliveries in May 2000, Melrose officials intended to use the fill from the Big Dig project in Boston to construct ball fields in the park in their city and to upgrade the fairway of the golf course. Ultimately, more than 700,000 tons of fill were delivered to the park over a period of more than a year, from May 2000 until July 2001.

Under a July 2000 contract with the project contractor, Gator Development Company, Inc., (which was signed after the project had already started), the city of Melrose was required to hire a "Clerk of the Works/Environmental Monitor" to supervise the fill operations on a daily basis, report daily to the City Engineer, and submit biweekly status reports to the Melrose Conservation Commission. The Massachusetts inspector general found that the city initially hired a company, which was also managing the park and golf course, to provide the clerk-of-the-works services. However, after six months, the city Park Department terminated this clerk-of-the-works arrangement and for the next seven months, the city had no one assigned to supervise the fill deliveries until a new clerk of the works was hired in May 2001.[6] In addition:

- Although Gator Development was required under its contract to pay the city to receive the fill based on a price of 70 cents per ton, the Park Department did not collect or maintain shipping tickets corresponding to the fill deliveries, as required by the contract.

- The Park Department did not maintain its own logs or other records of fill deliveries until May 2001—almost the entire fill delivery period. As a result, the city underestimated the amount of revenue that was due from Gator Development by some $42,000, according to the inspector general.

The installation of the fairway drainpipe, which we first discussed in Example 3.5, took place when no clerk of the works was assigned to the project by the city. As a result, according to the inspector general, no city official was present at the site when the installed pipe failed and later had to be abandoned. As previously noted, the drainpipe failure contributed to flooding and silt deposits in surrounding wetlands, which later proved to be expensive for the city to remediate. Because the city had not been in a position to supervise the drainpipe installation, it had little information or documentation about the situation, other than what was provided by the fill delivery contractor. As a result, the city had no legal recourse to recover damages from the drainpipe installation contractor.

TIP FOR SUCCESS:

Key records that managers should consult during the project execution stage are those that allow comparisons of the rate of the contract's completion to the contractor's expenditure rate.

Project managers need information during the execution stage that can be used to periodically compare the planned and actual project costs and schedule and to accurately forecast the funds and the time needed to complete the project tasks.[7]

In some cases, such as the Mount Hood project discussed above, the project may generate revenues, which serve to offset costs. In those instances, managers must keep records that allow them to measure their net costs (revenues minus actual costs) and compare that net expenditure rate to the project's completion rate. In the Mount Hood case, this was not done, according to the Massachusetts inspector general; and, as a result, city officials had little idea what the project's true cost or schedule would ultimately be while the project was ongoing. It was only well into the project that city officials realized that the revenues received from the fill deliveries would not be sufficient to build the planned ball fields and upgrade the golf course fairway. For instance, the Park Commission sought bids for a baseball field at Mount Hood in June 2001, shortly before the fill deliveries ceased. The Commission never awarded a contract, however, because it lacked a source of funding for the ball field.[8]

At the federal level, cost and project schedule information is compiled by many agencies in "contract performance reports," which are the government's "primary source for program cost and schedule status," according to the Government Accountability Office.[9] The GAO suggests that reviewing contract performance report data on at least a monthly basis helps managers track program progress and risks.

Elements of contract performance reports include cost and schedule data for each element of a project's Work Breakdown Structure. In addition, these reports display cumulative, current, and forecasted cost and schedule data (usually in detail for the next six months). And the reports contain project staffing forecasts that can be correlated with the budget plan.

Analyzing the Project Data Using Earned Value Management

A second critical aspect of project monitoring, in addition to collecting data and maintaining adequate records, is to analyze the data from those records in the most effective way possible. This can be a problem at some levels of government in which there is little standardization in the use of project monitoring data. At the federal level, that standardization has been around for many years in the form of process known as Earned Value Analysis (EVA) or Earned Value Management (EVM). Federal agencies are required to use EVM to measure cost and schedule progress on major projects and programs.[10]

Under EVM, both the actual amount of work and the actual dollar value of the work that has been performed by the contractor are compared at specific points on the project schedule to the dollar value of the work that had been budgeted. Both the owner and contractor are encouraged to participate in EVM assessments.

TIP FOR SUCCESS:

Project monitoring systems that measure both cost and schedule data are superior to systems that measure only cost or schedule data alone.

Techniques such as EVM are more accurate than the often-used method of simply comparing the dollar amount actually spent at a specific point on the project schedule to the dollar amount budgeted. That measure only gives the contractor and public sector manager an idea whether the project is running under, at, or over budget at a given time. EVM allows managers to gauge whether the project is meeting both the budget and the schedule. For instance, a project might appear to be running under budget, but less than the scheduled amount of work may have been done as of that given time, leading to the likelihood that the project will not meet the scheduled completion date. Conversely, a project may appear to be running over budget, but more than the scheduled amount of work may have been done, leading to the likelihood that the project will ultimately be completed ahead of schedule and possibly under budget.

The Government Accountability Office notes that EVM is based on best management practices used in American industry since the early 1900s, when a form of the technique was used to assess industrial engineering performance in factories. In the 1960s, the Defense Department adopted EVM-based criteria to provide minimum standards for objective performance reporting for defense contractors. Today, EVM, which is based on guidelines developed by the American National Standards Institute (ANSI) and the Electronic Industry Alliance (EIA), comprises "common sense program management practices that would be required to successfully manage any program, regardless of size, cost or complexity."[11] The AINSI/EIA standards have been adopted by industry and by major U.S. government agencies, and by government agencies in Australia, Canada, Japan, Sweden, and the UK, according to the GAO.

EVM establishes a number of key measures, intended to gain a full picture of the status of the project at a given time in relation to budgeted schedule and cost. The GAO explains that the EVM process is tied to the project's Work Breakdown Structure (see our discussion of the WBS in Chapter 5) and is integrated into the project schedule and budget.

One of the key steps in the EVM process is to compute a "planned value" and an "earned value" for work to be done under the project. Those numbers are associated with the amount of work scheduled to be completed and actually completed at various project milestones. Often, those values are expressed in dollar terms.

Specific EVM measures include the following:

- **The Budgeted Cost of Work Scheduled (BCWS):** The BCWS is the planned or budgeted value of project work to be completed at given points on the schedule. Figure 9.1 shows the BCWS for selected elements of the Work Breakdown Structure of a hypothetical computer science building, four months into construction. It shows, for instance, that as of the end of the month of April, the cumulative value of the BCWS is projected to be $3.9 million.
- **The Budgeted Cost of Work Performed (BCWP):** The BCWP is the actual amount or "earned value" of the work that has been done at given schedule points. In Figure 9.1, the BCWP or earned value as of the end of April is $2.7 million. This variance indicates that $1.2 million worth of work is behind schedule. The BCWP is compared to the BCWS to determine the schedule variance.
- **The Actual Cost of Work Performed (ACWP):** The ACWP is the actual dollar value of the work that has been performed at given schedule points. In Figure 9.1, the ACWP at the end of April was $3.3 million, meaning the project is running $600,000 over budget for the amount of work actually performed. The cost variance is calculated by comparing the ACWP with the BCWP. These variances are red flags that should alert the owner that the project is not going to meet its estimated cost at completion (EAC).
- **The Budgeted Actual Cost (BAC) and the Estimated cost at Completion (EAC):** The BAC is the planned total project cost. The EAC is, as noted, the amount the project is projected to cost at completion, given what has transpired thus far. In the case depicted in Figure 9.1, the BAC is $15.5 million. As the graphs in Figure 9.2 indicate, as of the end of October, the EAC for this project is $17.6 million. Thus, the project is projected to have a final cost

In thousands

Legend: Task scheduled △   Task completed ▲

Task description	J	F	M	A	M	J	J	A	S	O	N	D	Budgeted	% Complete	Earned
Concrete	300 ▲	500 ▲	200	△ ▲									$1,000	100%	$1,000
Framing		500 ▲	1,000	500 △									2,000	60	1,200
Roofing			100 ▲	800	△ 600 △								1,500	30	500
Electrical					1,000	1,500	△ 1,500 △						4,000		
Communications							600	1,200	1,200	500 △			3,500		
Interior										800 △	1,200	1,500 △	3,500		
Monthly budget (BWCS)	$300	$1,000	$1,300	$1,300	$1,600	$1,500	$2,100	$1,200	$1,200	$1,300	$1,200	$1,500			
Cum BWCS	300	1,300	2,600	3,900	5,500	7,000	9,100	10,300	11,500	12,800	14,000	15,500			
Earned value (BCWP)	100	500	1,500	2,700											$2,700
Actual Cost (ACWP)	200	700	1,900	3,300											

Figure 9.1   Based on Monthly Program Assessment Using Earned Value Chart: GAO Cost Estimating an Assessment Guide, 2009.

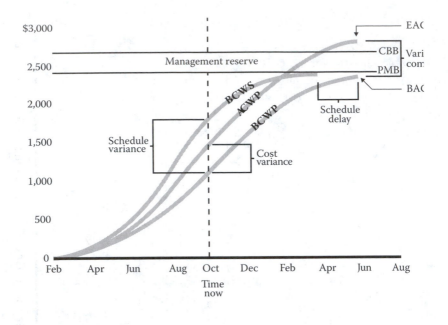

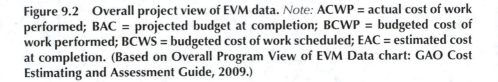

Figure 9.2 Overall project view of EVM data. *Note:* **ACWP = actual cost of work performed; BAC = projected budget at completion; BCWP = budgeted cost of work performed; BCWS = budgeted cost of work scheduled; EAC = estimated cost at completion. (Based on Overall Program View of EVM Data chart: GAO Cost Estimating and Assessment Guide, 2009.)**

overrun of $2.1 million. It is also projected to be completed about three and a half months behind the planned schedule. The management reserve of $1.4 million will not be enough to cover the projected cost overrun.[12]

The GAO contends that using an EVM system can give a project manager an early insight into a project's final cost and schedule outcome. The agency notes that a sample of more than 700 contracts showed that the final outcome was indicated by performance trends once the contracts were as little as 15 to 20 percent complete.[13]

It is important to remember that while different project and contracting approaches may require different levels of monitoring, all projects require at least some monitoring by public sector managers. Even in a fixed-price contract, a public sector manager does not want to be surprised by major variances between planned and actual data regarding the cost and schedule. As we noted in the previous chapter, variances between planned and actual cost and schedule numbers occur in all projects, and contractors should be encouraged to report them.

Evaluating and Correcting Project Problems

When measurements and analysis of that data indicate that variances have occurred on the project between projected and actual schedule and cost or between the plans and specifications and the actual work performed, it is evidence, as we previously stated, that certain project-related risks have been realized.

In many cases, the corrections that must be made involve trade-offs between the project cost, scope, and schedule. For instance, one common correction that managers make when delays appear to threaten the ability to reach the project's completion date is to "crash the schedule." This practice involves accelerating scheduled activities on the project without changing the scope of work. The trade-off in that case is that the cost of the project increases because additional resources (e.g., crew sizes or work hours per crew) are needed if the scope is to be maintained. Another approach is to reduce the project scope. The trade-off here lies in the potentially reduced quality or performance of the project.

The theory underlying this book is that projects will be less likely to experience major variances between planned and actual results and a consequent need for trade-offs among the cost, schedule, and scope if the public sector project manager follows the strategic management framework we've outlined so far (see Chapter 2 for a discussion of the framework itself). However, once problems arise in the course of project execution, managers need to react systematically to them. Trevor Young suggests that managers should analyze those problems in terms of four areas of focus:

1. What areas of the project are affected?
2. What are the consequences if the problem is not resolved?
3. What actions are proposed to resolve the problem, and what are the cost and resource implications of those actions?
4. What is the current rating of the problem (are its potential consequences major, significant, or limited)?[14]

These four areas of focus might actually be considered a first step in managing problems that arise in projects. In fact, they all appear to fit within the first step of the Plan-Do-Study-Act cycle, a contribution of the influential Total Quality Management (TQM) movement for improving business management.

As is the case with overall project development, the first step in managing the execution phase of a project under the Plan-Do-Study-Act cycle is to develop a plan for what needs to be done when problems arise. Step 2 is to implement the plan. Step 3 is to study the results. Depending upon the results, Step 4 can involve adopting the new procedure or changing the plan.[15] Young's four areas of focus on project execution problems can be seen as part of developing a plan to deal with each problem.

> **TIP FOR SUCCESS:**
>
> A systematic process is best for dealing with problems that arise during the project execution stage. One process, known as the Plan-Do-Study-Act cycle, involves
>
> 1. Developing a plan to deal with the problem;
> 2. Implementing the plan;
> 3. Studying the results; and either
> 4. Adopting the new procedure or changing the plan.

Focusing on Quality in Projects

Thus far, we have largely concentrated on dealing with cost and schedule problems that arise during the project execution stage. Those two areas of cost and schedule do, in fact, constitute the primary sources of concern for many project managers. But, as we alluded to above, a focus on just those two issues can come at the expense of the project's scope and its quality, in particular.

> **TIP FOR SUCCESS:**
>
> An emphasis on quality assurance and control in undertaking projects can reduce costs and help reach schedule goals.

We noted in Chapter 1 that project managers sometimes place more emphasis on meeting schedule and cost goals than on meeting the scope and quality standards of their projects. W. Edwards Deming, one of the architects of TQM, maintained at the outset of his book, *Out of the Crisis,* that quality should actually be first on the manager's priority list, and that when quality is maintained or improved, cost and schedule issues, which he refers to as productivity, will improve as well. It is "folklore," he argues, that higher quality results in lower productivity. In fact, the opposite is true because when quality improves, less rework is needed and the result is lower costs as well as other economic benefits.[16]

The Project Management Institute adds that it is a mistake to sacrifice quality to meet a project's schedule because of the likelihood that errors will go undetected.[17] Yet, the propensity to rush quality inspections, in particular, to meet the schedule is a common one and is aptly illustrated in Example 9.2 about the sinking of the U.S. submarine *Thresher.*

Example 9.2: What Sank the *Thresher*?

On April 10, 1963, the nuclear-powered submarine *Thresher* sank 220 miles off the coast of Cape Cod with 129 men aboard. There were no survivors.

In a comprehensive article about the sinking, author Dean Golembeski pointed out that due in part to political pressure to deploy new weapons systems quickly in response to the Soviet threat at that time, design, testing, and quality standards had been relaxed in the rush to launch the *Thresher*.[18] The *Thresher* sank during a test dive after a pipe burst in the hull of the vessel, setting off a chain of events that sent the sub plunging to ocean depths that collapsed and split apart the hull. The court of inquiry found that during the final overhaul of the *Thresher* at the Portsmouth Naval Shipyard about a year before the sub sank, 14 percent of the sub's soldered pipe joints had failed ultrasonic tests. Despite these results, the court found that Portsmouth "did not aggressively pursue the ultrasonic inspection of…(pipe) joints" in the *Thresher* even though the rejection rate "was a clear indicator that additional action was required."[19] The court of inquiry further found that serious failures of similar pipe joints had been found in five other submarines prior to the launching of the *Thresher*, yet that information wasn't shared or acted upon.

In his article, Golembeski stated that during a subsequent investigation by the congressional Atomic Energy Committee of the sinking of the submarine, the president of the court of inquiry testified that the shipyard had been trying to meet a deadline for completing the *Thresher*'s overhaul. The president of the court of inquiry stated that

> to have gone further with the testing [of the pipe joints] would have required unlagging of piping and delaying the ship and running up the cost of the overhaul and, you know, the many attendant things when you delay the ship.[20]

Also testifying before the congressional committee was Adm. Hyman G. Rickover, the father of the nuclear Navy, who maintained that he had brought concerns about equipment and materials standards and quality to his superiors before the sinking, but that those superiors believed implementing tougher standards would have added to the costs of submarines. Yet, argued Rickover:

> If you have good procedures, good specifications, and good people you will save money…If you buy one really good suit, it is better than two cheap suits. It is that sort of saving.[21]

Rickover's argument in Example 9.2 is largely the same one Deming and others have made that the adoption of management processes that help improve quality will result in less project rework and consequential delays and cost overruns. An emphasis on quality may also avert potential tragedy, as the case of the *Thresher* demonstrates.

In comments to *CommonWealth* magazine in Massachusetts about the Big Dig project in Boston, three prominent project officials similarly maintained that the project's emphasis on meeting cost and schedule at the expense of quality was misguided and ineffective. James Rooney, who was assistant project director of the Big Dig for the Massachusetts Turnpike Authority in the mid 1990s, contended that

Bechtel/Parsons Brinckerhoff, the state's construction manager for the project, sacrificed the completeness of the project design to try to maintain the project schedule. The practice, he said, was "like giving out a book of change-order coupons with the bid documents."[22]

Andrew Natsios, who took over management of the Big Dig for the Massachusetts Turnpike Authority in 2000, after massive cost overruns were disclosed, argued that because of mounting pressure to control costs, both public and private sector managers of the project de-emphasized both oversight and quality control over time, with disastrous consequences.[23] And Fred Salvucci, who was Massachusetts transportation secretary in the 1970s and later in the 1980s, told the magazine that he thought the concurrent Boston Harbor cleanup project was more successful than the Big Dig because the managers of the Boston Harbor project "weren't looking to cut quality as a means of cutting costs."[24]

Project quality is often considered as two separate concepts—Quality Assurance and Quality Control. Quality Assurance involves procedures and policies that lead to high project quality, while Quality Control primarily deals with conformance to plans and specifications. Barbara Jackson further breaks these concepts down as follows:

Quality Assurance processes: These involve the hiring of high-quality personnel; having a commitment to employee training; establishing strict rules to promote safety; prequalification of contractors and subcontractors; and providing incentives for employee excellence.

Quality Control is ensured by: the submittal by the contractor to the architect or designer of documentation or samples to verify that materials and equipment comply with plans and specifications; the use of "mock-ups" (small models using specified materials) and shop drawings in construction projects; the use of materials that have been approved by organizations such as the American Society for Testing and Materials and Underwriters Laboratories, Inc.; and a commitment to ongoing testing and inspection of the project work as it progresses. [25]

Jackson suggests, as one example of an important quality control measure, that the project owner ensure that each delivery of materials and equipment to a project site be checked to make sure it is in accordance with the purchase order and specifications. If the materials are not as specified, they should not even be unloaded from the delivery truck. This quality control measure was not used by the City of Melrose in the Mount Hood case, discussed in Example 9.1. As noted, no one inspected the trucks coming to the project site with fill in that case—an omission that left the city vulnerable to risks of contaminated materials among other problems.

Controlling Cost Growth and Cost Overruns

The previous discussion of project quality is not meant to imply that a vigorous effort to control project costs and meet scheduled milestones is not necessary or important. All three elements—cost, schedule, and scope—must be balanced in successful project management.

Public sector project managers must, in fact, be vigilant about two major cost issues—cost overruns and cost growth. William Sims Curry draws a distinction between the two. Cost growth, he notes, occurs when a change is made in the scope of work of a project that results in an amendment to the contract, which increases the contract cost.[26] A public agency may seek the change in the scope of work when it makes a decision to add features or equipment to a building that were not in the contract plans or specifications. A change in scope may also result when a contractor invokes contractual provisions, such as the differing site conditions clause, that allow it to increase its charges. The increased costs associated with changes in scope are normally paid by the project owner after the contractor has submitted a change order. Change orders are amendments to the contract that are agreed to by both parties and are normally approved only after a cost estimation process has been undertaken and the project manager or contract officer determines that sufficient funds are available to make the change.

A subset of cost-growth is sometimes referred to as "scope creep"—a situation in which changes are made to the project scope without undertaking a formal change order process. John Baniszewski at NASA has described scope creep as

> gradual growth to the work done under a contract, resulting from well-meaning people deciding that certain work not originally anticipated under the original contract needs to be done.[27]

Baniszewski adds that scope creep is bad because it usually occurs without the knowledge of senior-level project managers and "doesn't become apparent until it has grown very big." "Thorough and integrated cost and scheduled performance analysis" is needed to prevent it, he notes.

Cost overruns occur when contractors are unable to complete their work at the contractually budgeted price. Because cost overruns occur without an associated change in scope or change order, the financial risk of cost overruns tends to fall primarily on the contractor in fixed-price contracts and on the project owner in cost-reimbursements contracts.

Cost (and schedule) overruns can often be dealt with and corrected via the Plan-Do-Study-Act process that we described above. If the analysis of the project data show that the contractor is overrunning the budget, for instance, decisions can be made to alter the schedule or scope, as described. Cost growth, however, involves an agreement by the project owner and contractor to add to the project scope. The change-order process itself is the corrective action. Nevertheless, the change order process can be among the most difficult and uncertain issues that the project management team encounters.

Barry LePatner maintains that the uncertainty of the change order process "is the single biggest contributor to fixed-price construction contracts not being as

> **TIP FOR SUCCESS:**
>
> Project managers must be vigilant about change orders submitted by contractors. They should make sure:
>
> ■ The contract specifies the pricing for all change-order work.
> ■ The contractor documents all costs associated with change orders when submitting change-order requests.

'fixed' as they initially appear."[28] The uncertainty often arises when the project specifications are open to interpretation, as we discussed in Chapter 4. As we have also discussed, there are many ways in which the responsibility for cost growth on a project can be placed on the owner, particularly if the contractor is able to persuade the owner that it has encountered unforeseen conditions or that there are omissions or errors in the plans or specifications.

LePatner adds that the contractor's big advantage when submitting change orders is that because it already has the job, it can now operate in a competition-free environment. That monopolistic nature of the contractor's relationship with the owner once it has won the contract gives the contractor an incentive to bid low on both public and private sector projects and later recoup its own losses and even make a large profit via the change-order process. The owner, who has less knowledge and information about the true cost of the work involved, often has little leverage to question the contractor's judgment. As LePatner explains:

> The companies that do the best financially are often not those that build the best, but those that are the best at bidding strategically to win the job for the right to subsequently induce owners to pay more than the amount specified in the base contract.[29]

For reasons such as those, project owners must be particularly vigilant about change orders. Despite their built-in disadvantages that LePatner noted, public sector project managers do have a number of steps they can take to help level the playing field. First, as we stated in the previous chapter, the contract itself should specify the pricing requirements for change orders, including administrative markups. The contract should also, as pointed out, require the contractor to provide full documentation for all of the change-order work done and the associated charges. Further, as we have previously discussed, sufficiently detailed plans and specifications can provide the owner with leverage over a contractor that claims omissions in the plans. And, if the cost of a major change order appears excessive, the Massachusetts Inspector General's Office suggests that owners consider the feasibility of bidding the additional work or undertaking the additional work separately after the construction project has been completed.[30]

James Rooney, who, as executive director of the Massachusetts Convention Center Authority (after his involvement with the Big Dig), oversaw the construction of the $850 million Boston Exhibition and Convention Center, maintains that it is possible to be firm with contractors and win at least some of the battles over change orders. He said, for instance, that the superintendent of the construction management firm that built the convention center had a habit of taking risks to maintain the project schedule, including putting up drywall before the building was fully closed in. When it did indeed rain, Rooney said he forced the company to replace the drywall at the contractor's own cost. He said he also forced the company at its own cost to replace some 4,000 square feet of glass that appeared to have blemishes.

In addition, Rooney filed suit against the project architect for having specified the wrong-sized piping for the building's hot and chilled water system, among other problems. The case went to a jury and Rooney and the architect settled for $24 million.[31]

Enforcing Agreements

In addition to monitoring project progress, making needed corrections, and carefully reviewing change orders, managers can keep projects under control by enforcing contract provisions when necessary that protect the public jurisdiction's interests. If, for instance, the contractor fails to meet contractually required project milestones, the project manager may need to enforce a liquidated damages provision, if it exists in the contract.

Public sector project managers obviously want to maintain a positive relationship with their contractors and consultants, and a "partnering" arrangement (which we discussed in Chapter 2) is clearly ideal. But, as the Boston Convention Center and the Melrose middle school examples that we discussed above show, there are times when project managers have to show firmness in their control of their projects. This often means they have to be ready and willing to enforce project-related contractual agreements. When they fail to do so, not only do public sector managers leave themselves vulnerable to delays and overcharges, but their inaction sends a message to contractors that they will not be penalized for that poor performance.

Example 9.3 discusses a public agency's failure to exercise and enforce key contract penalty provisions and the consequent weakening of its bargaining position with project contractors and consultants.

Example 9.3: A failure to enforce contract penalty provisions in the University of Massachusetts Computer Science Center project

Following the construction of a computer science building at the University of Massachusetts at Amherst (which we previously discussed in Examples 4.6 and

5.1), the state's public construction management agency—the Division of Capital Asset Management (DCAM)—offered to settle a $2.7 million claim filed by the general contractor for $1.4 million. The claim was based on a 10-month delay in the actual completion date of the project from the contractual completion date.

Suffolk Building Corporation, the general contractor, contended that the delay was the fault of DCAM and the University of Massachusetts (the user agency of the building) because of their alleged inability to agree on key aspects of the project design. The Massachusetts inspector general, however, maintained, after a detailed review of the project, that the delay was largely caused by factors under Suffolk's control. In its report, the inspector general also concluded that the contractor's $2.7 million claim had been inflated by charges for damages not permitted under Suffolk's contract with DCAM, by overstated indirect costs, and by charges for undocumented design services that could not be verified.

In particular, the inspector general noted that while the contract contained a number of provisions that could have protected the state's interests in the project, DCAM's settlement recommendation made no reference to those provisions. For instance, the contract explicitly limited the circumstances under which delay damages could be applied. According to the inspector general, had DCAM invoked this contract provision, it could have foreclosed Suffolk's ability to recover damages on that portion of its claim.

In addition, Suffolk failed to comply with a contract requirement that it submit daily records of labor and materials to preserve its right to submit a claim for work done on the building's underground steam line. DCAM did not enforce that contract requirement.

Finally, DCAM's top management rejected the recommendation of a resident engineer in the agency that $202,000 be deducted from payments to Suffolk in liquidated damages for having failed to complete the project by the contract deadline. The contract specified a rate of $1,000 per day in liquidated damages for failure to meet the deadline. However, DCAM's top managers not only declined to deduct liquidated damages from the payments to Suffolk, according to the inspector general, they apparently failed to consider the imposition of those damages in making the $1.4 million offer to settle Suffolk's claim.[32]

The Computer Science building example above is not unusual. In what seems a remarkably similar set of circumstances, the Port of Seattle failed to enforce contractual provisions with several contractors, including one hired to upgrade the Seattle-Tacoma International Airport's central mechanical plant in 2001, according to the Washington State Auditor. Among the contractual provisions that the Port did not enforce was one authorizing the withholding of progress payments if the contractor failed to provide required monthly project schedule updates. The Port also failed to enforce a liquidated damages provision in that contract even though the contractor had failed to meet both interim project milestones and the final completion date. The auditor concluded that the Port's failure to enforce those and other provisions left it at a disadvantage in negotiations over a $1.9 million delay claim later submitted by the contractor. In the mechanical plant contract alone, the Port approved 22 change orders that boosted the initial $6.6

million contract by more than 21 percent. That project also experienced a 74 percent schedule overrun, according to the auditor.[33]

Partnering and Change Orders

As we have discussed, "partnering" is a growing practice in project management under which the public sector management team and the contractors and consultants involved in the project pledge to maintain a nonadversarial relationship characterized by trust and conflict resolution. It does not work in every case, hence the need for contracts and a willingness by the owners to enforce them. But in situations in which a spirit of trust does exist, even the change-order process does not need to be an adversarial one. In the Harvard, Massachusetts, library case, Peter Jackson, one of the three citizen managers, maintained that because a spirit of partnering existed among the parties, the managers were able to expedite the change-order process—a development that helped get the project completed on schedule and within budget.

Jackson, a former project manager with the U.S. Army Corps of Engineers, said he was given discretion by the library building committee to approve change orders in consultation with the architect and owner's project manager. The process was done via e-mail and later recorded on change-order forms provided by the American Institute of Architects. "I'd get an e-mail," Jackson said, referring to a request from the contractor for an increase in the contract price to cover additional work. "I'd double-check with the architect and the owner's project manager and ask for a price check. If both agreed, I'd confirm with the (two other citizen) managers. And 15 to 20 minutes later, I'd e-mail a confirmation to the contractor." Often, subcontractors were on site, ready to do the work without delay, saving time and labor cost, Jackson said.

A final change order log for the library project shows that 128 change orders were approved on the project, totaling $289,355, and boosting the contract price of $6,100,000 by 4.75 percent. The final construction cost of $6,389,000 was within the project's 5 percent contingency reserve.

Keeping Stakeholders Informed of the Project's Progress

Public sector managers have one other major obligation in addition to monitoring the progress of their projects and evaluating and correcting problems as they arise. They must keep key project stakeholders informed of the status of the projects, particularly of the cost and schedule projections and the major problems that arise. The stakeholders range from upper management within the public agencies in charge of the projects to legislative funding committees to members of the general public itself. Those stakeholders in upper management should receive the most frequent and detailed status reports. But other stakeholders should be kept informed as well, though usually on a more informal basis.

The managers of the Harvard public library project made a concerted effort to keep the public informed of the ongoing construction progress of the library. Roy Moffa, one of the three managers, noted that the three hosted tours of the building during the construction phase to anyone who wanted one. They also sent a bimonthly newsletter to all town residents with information about the project's progress from the planning stage, starting in 2002, until the library was completed in 2007.

This commitment to transparency is not always kept, particularly when bad news is involved. On the Big Dig project in Boston, project managers used "a largely semantic series of exclusions, deductions, and accounting assumptions" to cover up $6 billion in cost overruns, according to the Massachusetts inspector general. The inspector general also alleged that Big Dig officials in two successive state administrations submitted inaccurate disclosure documents about the project's cost for bond issues between 1996 and 1999.[34]

A federal agency similarly provided misleading information on the cost to complete the Basrah Children's Hospital in Iraq, which we first discussed in the introduction to this book. According to the Special Inspector General for Iraq Reconstruction, the U.S. Agency for International Development (USAID) reported to Congress in April 2006 that there were no problems with the project schedule even though the agency had been briefed a month earlier by the project contractor that the project was 273 days behind schedule. In addition, USAID continued to report the project cost as $50 million, even though the contractor, Bechtel National, Inc. was estimating the cost at $98 million by April 2006.[35]

While there is a natural temptation to cover up bad news, the danger in the practice is obvious. Nothing depresses public confidence in a public project faster than headlines that cost and schedule problems have been covered up. From that point on, these problems generally start to compound themselves.

In the following, and final, chapter of this book, we will continue our discussion of project control issues; but our focus will be on project closeout and long-term operational and maintenance issues. Although his or her project may be nearing substantial completion, the public sector project manager's work is far from over.

Endnotes

1. Young, Trevor L. 2007. *The Handbook of Project Management*, revised 2nd edition. London: Kogan Page Publishers. P. 191. See also, Lewis, James P. 2007. *Fundamentals of Project Management*, 3rd edition. New York: American Management Association.
2. Prager, Jonas. 1994. Contracting Out Government Services: Lessons from the Private Sector. *Public Administration Review* 54:2: 176–184.
3. See, for example, LePatner, Barry B. 2007. *Broken Buildings, Busted Budgets: How to Fix America's Trillion-Dollar Construction Industry.* Chicago: The University of Chicago Press. P. 172.

4. Washington State Auditor. 2007. *Performance Audit Report: Port of Seattle Construction Management.* P. 151.
5. Office of the Special Inspector General for Iraq Reconstruction. 2007. *Iraq Reconstruction: Lessons in Program and Project Management.* P. 61.
6. Commonwealth of Massachusetts, Office of the Inspector General. 2002. *Review of the Mount Hood Public Works Project in Melrose.*
7. Curry, William. 2008. *Contracting for Services in State and Local Government Agencies.* Taylor & Francis.
8. Commonwealth of Massachusetts, Office of the Inspector General. 2002.
9. United States Government Accountability Office. 2009. *GAO Cost Estimating and Assessment Guide: Best Practices for Developing and Managing Capital Program Costs.* GAO-09-3SP. P. 249.
10. Office of Management and Budget. 2006. *Capital Programming Guide.* Supplement to Circular A-11, Part 7. The OMB Capital Programming Guide requires that "all major acquisitions with development effort are to include the requirement that contractors use an EVM system that meets the ANSI (American National Standards Institute) guidelines (ANSI/EIA-748-A)."
11. United States Government Accountability Office. 2009. P. 204.
12. For descriptions of EVM or EVA (earned value analysis) in a private sector context, see, for example, Young, Trevor, L. 2007; Jackson, Barbara J. 2004. *Construction Management Jump Start.* San Francisco: Sybex, Inc.; Project Management Institute. 2004. *A Guide to the Project Management Body of Knowledge,* 3rd edition. Newtown Square, PA: Project Management Institute; Frame, J. Davidson. 1994. *The New Project Management.* San Francisco: Jossey-Bass; Lewis, James P. 2007. *Fundamentals of Project Management,* 3rd edition. New York: American Management Association; and Ritz, George J. 1994. *Total Construction Project Management.* McGraw-Hill.
13. United States Government Accountability Office. 2009. P. 206.
14. Young, Trevor L. 2007.
15. American Society for Quality. 1999. *The Certified Quality Manager Handbook.* Milwaukee: ASQ Quality Press. P. 310.
16. Deming, W. Edwards. 1986. *Out of the Crisis.* Cambridge: MIT Press. P. 1.
17. Project Management Institute. 2004. P. 180.
18. Golembeski, Dean J. 1997. What Sank the *Thresher? Invention & Technology.* Summer 1997.
19. Golembeski, Dean J. 1997. P. 29.
20. Golembeski, Dean J. 1997. P. 29.
21. Golembeski, Dean J. 1997. P. 31.
22. *CommonWealth* magazine. 2006. *Learning from the Big Dig: What lessons can be drawn from an engineering triumph now marked by Tragedy? We asked eight expert observers for answers.* Fall 2006. P. 61.
23. *CommonWealth* magazine. 2006.
24. *CommonWealth* magazine. 2006. *Second-Guesswork: Fred Salvucci Insists That the Big Dig Was the Right Project, Just Not Done Right.* Fall 2006. P. 68.
25. Jackson, Barbara J. 2004.
26. Curry, William. 2008. *Contracting for Services in State and Local Government Agencies.* Taylor & Francis.
27. Baniszewski, John. *Government Contracting: A Project Manager's Perspective.* PowerPoint presentation. U.S. Department of Energy. Available online at http://management.energy.gov/documents/ProjectManagementContractingOfficers.pdf
28. LePatner, Barry B. 2007. P. 19.

29. LePatner, Barry B. 2007. P. 27.
30. Commonwealth of Massachusetts, Office of the Inspector General. 2005. *Designing and Constructing Public Facilities: Legal Requirements, Recommended Practices, Sources of Assistance.* http://www.mass.gov/ig/publ/dcmanual.pdf.
31. Talcott, Shasha. 2006. Convention Center Gets $24 Million Settlement: Project Design Team Faced Suit over Roof, Heat and Cooling Woes. *Boston Globe.* July 22, 2006. http://www.hotel-online.com/News/PR2006_3rd/Jul06_BostonCC.html
32. Commonwealth of Massachusetts, Office of the Inspector General, 2001. *A Report on the Design and Construction of the University of Massachusetts Computer Science Center.*
33. Washington State Auditor, 2007.
34. Palmer, Thomas C. Cerasoli Charges Big Dig Coverup. *Boston Globe.* March 21, 2001. http://boston.com/globe/metro/packages/bechtel/archives/032101.htm
35. Office of the Special Inspector General for Iraq Reconstruction. 2006. *Review of the U.S. Agency for International Development's Management of the Basrah Children's Hospital Project.* SIGIR-06-026.

Chapter 10

Project Closeout and Beyond

As the project execution stage nears its end, a new and exciting period begins for the project management team. The final product is nearly ready for unveiling to the public. The ribbon-cutting ceremony is near at hand. But the team cannot afford to take its eye off the ball and let up on the measuring, evaluating, and correcting process.

Barbara Jackson points out that the project closeout period can be one of stress and anxiety as both the project management team and the contractor sprint to the finish line—often a grand opening or deadline set far in advance for use or occupancy. As Jackson notes, "[t]he school buses will be arriving with children whether the contractor is ready or not."[1]

The first major milestone in the closeout phase is the project's "substantial completion." Substantial completion generally means that the work is sufficiently complete so that the owner can put the product to its intended use, and only minor items are left unresolved. Substantial completion is often certified by the architect or designer.

Barry Bramble and Michael Callahan explain that upon substantial completion of a construction project, the liquidated damages period ends and the owner or user agency has the right to occupy the facility and becomes responsible for operation and maintenance of the equipment. If the contract provided for progress payments with some of those amounts retained by the owner, substantial completion usually involves the payment to the contractor of most of the "retainage." If the owner determines there has been defective work, damages can now be deducted from the final payment; but the owner may have to prove the work was defectiveif the matter goes to litigation.[2] Substantial completion also marks the start of express and implied warranties that apply to the contractor.

Final Steps in the Closeout Process

In construction projects, the substantial completion milestone is usually followed by completion of the "punch list," which comprises the minor items that must be resolved before the final contract payment is made. Punch-list items are often noted during a final walk-through by the owner, designer, and contractor. The final contract payment, including payment of the final retainage amount, is usually made upon completion of the punch list.

> **TIP FOR SUCCESS:**
>
> In construction projects, public sector managers should attend the final punch-list walk-through. Completion of the punch-list items can make a substantial difference to users of the new facility.

Additional closeout steps can include issuance by building officials of a certificate of occupancy in building construction projects, testing of equipment and systems, and training the owner's personnel in the operational and maintenance of systems and equipment.

Evaluating the Contractor

Once the final payment has been made, the public sector manager should evaluate the contractor's performance in terms of cost, quality, and schedule. William Sims Curry suggests that contractor performance reports include a recommendation whether to award a similar contract to the same contractor in the future, with a written reason for that recommendation.[3]

As we noted in Chapter 7, federal regulations require federal agencies to prepare evaluations of contractors' performance for contracts over $550,000 in value or for contracts over $10,000, which were terminated for default. Some states, such as Massachusetts, require project evaluations as part of the eligibility or prequalification process involved in bidding on construction projects.

At the federal level, projects of all types are often subject to longer-term evaluations that are done six months to a year after the completion of the projects, programs, or systems. The evaluations include "post-implementation reviews" and "post-occupancy evaluations," according to the Office of Management and Budget. Both of these types of evaluations are meant to assess the efficiency and effectiveness of a project or program investment and whether the investment supports the agency's mission and long-term strategic goals.[4]

Publicizing the Completed Project

We have noted the importance of keeping stakeholders informed of the project's progress during the planning and execution stages. They should also be informed, of course, that the project has been completed. In the Harvard library case, the project managers invited the entire town to a grand opening event, which included speeches outside the new building by those involved in the financing, design, and construction of the library, and by local politicians. The highlight was an invitation for everyone to see the new building for themselves. The front doors were opened and people were invited inside to wander around wherever they wanted. It was a day of considerable pride and excitement for young and old alike.

Publicizing a completed project is a very variable undertaking for the simple reason that public projects themselves are so variable. What works for a new town library will not work for a new navigational satellite system. But at the very least, news about newly completed projects can be disseminated via press releases, calls to radio and television news stations, postings on Websites, and even posts on agency blogsites.

Announcements of newly completed projects also must be tailored to fit particular groups of stakeholders. Detailed budget and schedule numbers must be provided to top administrators of the project owner or user agency and possibly to oversight and funding agencies and relevant legislative committees—potentially the same people and organizations that received the initial feasibility study for the project, which we discussed in Chapter 3. Those detailed numbers are not likely to be provided to the general public. But other information, particularly about the benefits of completed projects, should certainly be given to the public. If, in fact, the project ran over the budget and schedule, that situation may have become well known to the public long before the project was completed. As we noted in the previous chapter, it is important in those cases that public sector managers be truthful about the project's financial situation and not try to cover up bad news. At the same time, placing the focus on the fact that the project has finally been completed and that it will provide public benefits can only help in that situation.

The Project or Program Operational Stage

For many projects, operational issues extend well beyond the completion of the execution or production stage. In design-build-operate (DBO) projects, in particular, the public sector project manager or owner may stay engaged with a contractor for many years as the contractor takes over operation of a facility that it previously designed and constructed. As was the case with the design and construction phase, it is a mistake for public sector managers to consider that they no longer have a role to play during the operational phase of such projects. Active monitoring of the contractor's operational activities remains important throughout the life-cycle of many of those projects.

TIP FOR SUCCESS:

Active monitoring of a project's costs and quality during its operational stage can be just as important as active monitoring during its construction or production stage.

During the operational stage of many projects, the public agency continues to pay the contractor. Moreover, as we have previously noted, long-term DBO contracts, in particular, may contain risks of price increases to public jurisdictions that cannot be accurately quantified at the start of the contract term.

But a contract need not be a long-term one to require active monitoring of operational risks. In Example 10.1, we discuss consequences of inadequate record-keeping during both a project's construction and operational stages. The case concerns the construction and operation of the Millennium Dome in Britain. While this project-based context is slightly different from the American-oriented public sector projects we have discussed so far in this book, the consequences of inadequate monitoring are certainly the same.

Example 10.1: Consequences of inadequate operations monitoring in the Millennium Dome project in the UK

In 1997, the Millennium Commission, a public entity in the United Kingdom, approved a grant from England's national lottery of up to £449 million to the New Millennium Experience Company to build and operate the Millennium Dome in Greenwich, and to organize events to celebrate the year 2000. The idea was to create something on the scale of the Great Exhibition of 1851 or the Festival of Britain of 1951. The New Millennium Company itself is characterized as a "nondepartmental public body."[5]

The completed Millennium Dome has a circumference of one kilometer and includes a central arena in which live Millennium shows were staged throughout the year 2000, in addition to 14 interlinked "zones," each with a different theme, and an auditorium capable of seating 5,000 people. The Dome was completed on schedule in December 1999.

The project, however, did not end with completion of the Dome. The project's total projected cost of £758 million included an operational phase that involved the staging of the celebratory events. The Dome was projected to attract 12 million paying visitors. A contingency reserve of £88 million was built into the total projected cost, and a separate negative contingency amount of £45 million was subtracted from the projection of the revenue that the Dome was expected to attract. But by the end of September 2000, the Dome had attracted only 3.8 million paying visitors and 900,000 nonpaying visitors. Starting in January 2000, the Commission was forced to provide four additional public funding grants totaling £179 million to the New Millennium Company to keep the project going, bringing total public funding to £628 million.

Among the causes of the project's financial problems, according to the British National Audit Office, were the following:

- An over-projection of visitors
- An over-projection of revenue from corporate sponsors
- A lack of a plan on how to respond if visitor income fell
- A lack of operational staff expertise
- Overly complex organizational arrangements and lines of accountability

In particular, the New Millennium Company's own auditors noted that cash-flow forecasts for the project were based on the approved budget for the project rather than a "realistic assessment of actual income and expenditure through to completion."[6] Moreover, there was no central tracking system for project invoices, and the New Millennium Company was unable to report the project's financial position accurately to those with oversight of the project.

In other words, project managers did not accurately assess the project's costs and revenues during and after construction of the Dome. They did not have procedures in place to conduct adequate monitoring during both the construction and operational stages of the project. One result was that unexpected liabilities totaling more than £5 million in constructing the Dome only came to light between March and July 2000, well after the Dome had been opened for visitors and exhibitions, according to the National Audit Office.

Encountering unexpected costs during a project's production and operations stages is usually a sign of the realization of normal project risks. If, however, as was the case with the Millennium Dome project, managers do not have a reliable means of tracking those costs as they arise, they will quickly find themselves in a position in which it is too late to respond when risks do develop into problems.

In the Millennium Dome case, the lack of continuing project monitoring coupled with a lack of contingency planning left the public-agency managers with few financial choices other than seeking additional public funding to keep the project afloat. The National Audit Office report pointed out that project managers were concerned about the potential trade-off in reducing the scope of the program activities to reduce costs in the face of declining revenues. The concern was that reduced program activities could serve to depress public interest in the project and revenues might decline even further. While these were no doubt legitimate concerns, the managers' failure to adequately monitor the revenues and expenses as they occurred appear to have made those revenue projections a guessing game.

Maintaining Public Projects over the Long Term

Aside from managing the project planning, execution, and operational issues we've discussed throughout this book, managers of almost all public projects involving the creation of tangible assets must be concerned with the long-term maintenance of those assets. That this is a major area of neglect is evident in the ongoing debate and concern over the state of this country's infrastructure, both public and private.

A growing number of observers contend that both government and the private sector rely on an aging public infrastructure and do not take effective steps to repair or replace it. The American Society of Civil Engineers had assigned an overall grade of D to the state of the nation's infrastructure as of the summer of 2009 (www.infrastructurereportcard.org). As architecture scholar Sarah Williams Goldhagen pointed out regarding the state of America's infrastructure:

> Bridges, utilities, and flood-prevention systems, whether publicly or privately owned, are grossly neglected. Suburbs are sprawling like unchecked chickweed. Cars are stuck in ever-mounting hours of traffic. Cities are bleeding people. School buildings are overpopulated and crumbling. Waters are polluted. Shipping ports are decrepit.[7]

William F. Marcuson added that

> Americans need to understand when they vote down a tax increase on gas, they are truly sentencing themselves to even more time in traffic, less time with their families, and greater risk for tragedies like the I-35W bridge collapse in Minneapolis in August 2007.[8]

TIP FOR SUCCESS:

Planning for, adequately financing, and undertaking long-term maintenance of public assets will prevent the need for repairs that are likely to cost many times as much as the maintenance costs themselves.

David Westerling and Steve Poftak have noted the application of DeSitter's "Law of Fives," which projects that if long-term maintenance is not performed on a public asset, repairs equaling five times the maintenance costs are eventually required. Discussing the situation in Massachusetts, they pointed out that since asset deterioration occurs gradually, there is a tendency in government to defer preventative maintenance. One reason for this is that maintenance is treated in most public agency budgets as a discretionary expense—one which takes away from spending on programs in the agency's operational budget. This, combined with a "diffusion of responsibility and outright inability to monitor asset condition," results in a "massive and growing maintenance backlog."[9]

Goldhagen has identified a number of political reasons for the American neglect of its assets and infrastructure, but perhaps her key explanation is that since the Reagan administration, the federal government has shifted much of its responsibility for maintenance and upgrades to state and local governments. Partly as a result of that, the maintenance and upgrading of the nation's infrastructure is increasingly falling into private hands, she contended. Many of these public-private partnerships have resulted in excessive payments to developers and in the development of so-called public spaces that are inaccessible to the public or ill maintained. Goldhagan believes this infrastructure privatization spells "social disaster" in the short term and "economic disaster" in the long term. She argued:

> Infrastructure is the classic public good that the free market does not and cannot provide. On the scale that is necessary, only the federal government can make the difference.[10]

Example 10.2 discusses some of the consequences of deferred maintenance on a landmark structure in Boston, the Longfellow Bridge, and how systematic, ongoing maintenance of this public asset would have probably saved millions of taxpayer dollars in the long run.

Example 10.2: Consequences of deferred maintenance on the Longfellow Bridge

The Longfellow Bridge, which connects the cities of Cambridge and Boston over the Charles River, was constructed in 1907 out of granite and steel. It is characterized by intricate stonework and ornamental towers that rival the great bridges of Europe. Westerling and Poftak noted that mortared granite piers supporting the bridge are connected by 11 steel arches, which support a concrete deck. The total cost to build the bridge in 1907 was $2.6 million, which equates to $137.8 million in 2007 dollars. As of 2007, the Longfellow Bridge was carrying over 49,500 vehicles per day in addition to an estimated 97,000 daily riders of the Massachusetts Bay Transportation Authority subway transit system.[11]

According to Westerling and Poftak, the bridge underwent only two repair projects in its hundred-year lifetime—the first in 1959 and the second in 2002. The 1959 project included some structural repairs and replacements, while the 2002 project involved repairs to the steel structure as well as sidewalk and street light safety repairs. About $160,000 was spent on graffiti removal.

In 2006, a state inspection report described some of the original deck sections of the bridge as being in "serious condition with large rust holes." There were numerous other problems noted in the inspection:

- The steel superstructure's stringers and floor beams were in poor condition with "heavy rusting and section loss."
- The superstructure's curved arch ribs had heavy rusting throughout.
- The substructure's pier walls displayed a variety of cracked and deteriorated mortar joints. Four of the piers had vertical cracks extending down through four courses of granite block.
- The bridge's four distinctive ornamental towers had settled, were starting to lean, and had developed cracks.

While these various structural problems did not constitute an immediate danger to public safety, Westerling and Poftak stated that such a danger was considered to be likely if action was not taken to repair the bridge within the next few years.

Estimates in 2007 of the cost to make repairs to the bridge ranged as high as $200 million. Westerling and Poftak calculated that had the state spent an amount equal to 1 percent of the bridge's capital cost during each year of its life on maintenance, the total cost as of 2007 to restore the bridge to good condition could have been reduced by more than $80 million.

The Longfellow Bridge provides a clear illustration of the need for public managers to take a long-term view of the projects they undertake. Goldhagen, for instance, expressed full support for the Obama administration's $850 billion economic stimulus package, which was introduced in 2009 and designed to fund projects to repair and upgrade the nation's infrastructure. But she cautioned that the long-range planning of those infrastructure projects should not be neglected "in the short-term interest of creating jobs."

Goldhagen has made a number of recommendations for better maintenance of public and private assets, including the establishment of a National Infrastructure Agency, which would plan, fund, and coordinate infrastructure maintenance and improvement over the long term. It would seem that such an agency might also provide guidance to states and municipalities on cost estimation and other project management practices. At the federal level, agencies such as the Defense Contract Management Agency and the Defense Contract Audit Agency help the Defense Department undertake a wide range of program and project management activities, including project cost analyses.

A National Infrastructure Agency or perhaps a National Capital Management Agency might help governments at the federal, state, and municipal levels both plan public projects more rationally and manage their long-term preservation. Such an agency might help governments establish what Nicholas Kulish refers to as a national vision about how to upgrade the nation's physical plant and avoid the undertaking of dubious public projects. Kulish cites the example of the notorious "Bridge to Nowhere" that dogged Republican vice presidential candidate Sarah Palin in the 2008 presidential campaign, adding that all too often, "[m]oney gets doled out in earmarks that are stuck into budget bills by congressmen looking to win favor back home."[12]

Goldhagen and others, such as Kulish, also recommend that Congress establish a federal line-item capital budget for infrastructure maintenance, as most other developed countries have done. At the state and local levels, Goldhagen contends, officials should "demand federal assistance to address their infrastructural needs." Municipal officials should "find the legal and political mechanisms (such as metropolitan district authorities of broad scope) that would allow them to work in concert with, rather than in competition with, their counterparts in neighboring communities."[13]

Westerling and Poftak recommend enacting capital maintenance reserve funds on the state level and suggest that states provide funding to oversee and monitor asset maintenance. They note that Massachusetts, for instance, does not have one system to adequately inventory assets, assess their condition, or estimate the cost of deferred maintenance. They also recommend the creation of state infrastructure banks to help fund transportation projects through a combination of federal funds, state appropriations, and bond proceeds (see our discussion in Chapter 1 on public project financing mechanisms).

Westerling and Poftak also recommend a move away from a straight-line method of depreciating public assets in favor of one which requires public agencies to have an asset management system and regular reporting on maintenance efforts. This so-called "modified method" of depreciating assets is permissible under Government Accounting Standards Board standards (GASB Statement 34). Westerling explained in an e-mail interview that under the modified accounting method, public agencies must perform an annual assessment of each of their assets—a practice that provides a better understanding of those assets and their condition. Under the straight-line depreciation method, all assets fall off the agency's books after 40 years.

Finally, Goldhagen has called for leadership in addressing our infrastructure needs. "How did Boston's Central Artery project happen?" she asked. "Fred Salvucci, then transportation secretary of Massachusetts, lived and breathed that project for nearly two decades, persuading local government officials, state authorities, federal representatives, and community boards that he was right." The lack of such leadership today explains why the "pathetically ill-conceived" design for the Rose Fitzgerald Kennedy Greenway on the reclaimed Central Artery land has been "hung out to dry," she maintained.[14]

Goldhagen, Kulish, and others have argued that effectively planned and controlled infrastructure projects are needed to respond to the needs and demands of the 21st century. Global warming is just one example of those demands. If, said Kulish, global warming will indeed result in ever rising sea levels and more powerful storms, "the United States is going to have to learn how to build, and, more importantly, how to build right."[15]

Conclusion

Using examples from federal, state, and local governmental experience, we have attempted in this book to impart some practical lessons and recommendations to public managers on bringing their projects to successful conclusions. The key lessons are that managers must:

- View public projects from a comprehensive and long-range perspective as solutions to public problems.
- Systematically and strategically plan those projects from a wide variety of perspectives, including legal requirements, stakeholders' views, cost, schedule, and risk.
- Develop clear project scopes of work as part of the planning process.
- Ensure that effective internal controls are present to prevent fraud, waste, and abuse.

- Select qualified people to serve on the project management team and ensure that the managerial accountability structure of the team is appropriate to the type of project being undertaken.
- Select contractors and consultants through transparent, accountable, and competitive processes that ensure that the best and most qualified people will undertake the project work.
- Draft contracts for the project work that equitably distribute the risks between the public jurisdiction and private agents.
- Stay involved in monitoring the progress of the projects regarding cost, schedule, and quality, and continue that involvement, if applicable, through the project's operational stage.
- Ensure that sufficient funding and attention are paid to the long-term maintenance of assets created by public projects.

Public sector project managers do not face an easy task. Failure in managing public projects is often remembered long after the managers have left their public positions. And given the exodus of talented people from government in recent years combined with the sense of disdain for public service that many politicians tend to impart, it is sometimes a wonder that people are willing and able to undertake public projects at all. Yet public projects are critical to the economic health of a nation as well as a source of lasting and important benefits to its people.

It is unfortunate that public projects seem to go wrong so much of the time. Yet in many cases, it seems that the problems could have been preventable. It is our hope that this book will provide critical tools to public managers to ensure that the usual problems that plague public projects are indeed prevented and that the projects that are undertaken are both beneficial and successfully completed and maintained.

Endnotes

1. Jackson, Barbara J. 2004. *Construction Management Jump Start.* San Francisco: Sybex, Inc. P. 124.
2. Bramble, Barry B., and Michael T. Callahan. 1999. *Construction Delay Claims,* 3rd edition. Aspen Law Publishers Online.
3. Curry, William. 2008. *Contracting for Services in State and Local Government Agencies.* Taylor & Francis.
4. Office of Management and Budget. 2006. *Capital Programming Guide.* Supplement to Circular A-11, Part 7.
5. Bourn, Sir John. Comptroller and Auditor General, British National Audit Office. 2000. *The Millennium Dome.* November 9, 2000. http://www.nao.org.uk/system_pages/idoc.ashx?docid=ff541347-f82b-4dad-8175-9ce8fb4a02e3&version=-1.
6. Bourn, Sir John. 2000. P. 45.

7. Goldhagen, Sarah Williams. 2007. American Collapse: is it already too late for America's infrastructure? *The New Republic.* August 27, 2007. Updated December 25, 2008. http://www.tnr.com/politics/story.html?id=9ead077c-1299-4f58-82d5-f3a91bfe19c4

8. Marcuson, William F. 2008. Fixing America's Crumbling Infrastructure: A Call to Action for All. *Public Works Management & Policy.* 12: 473–475.

9. Westerling, David, and Steve Poftak. 2007. *Our Legacy of Neglect: The Longfellow Bridge and the Cost of Deferred Maintenance.* Pioneer Institute White Paper, No. 40.

10. Goldhagen, Sarah Williams. 2007.

11. Westerling, David, and Steve Poftak. 2007.

12. Kulish, Nicholas. 2006. Things Fall Apart: Fixing America's Crumbling Infrastructure, *New York Times.* August 23, 2006. http://select.nytimes.com/2006/08/23/opinion/23talking-points.html?_r=1

13. Goldhagen, Sarah Williams. 2007.

14. Goldhagen, Sarah Williams. 2007.

15. Kulish, Nicholas. 2006.

Appendix 1

Discussion Examples Used in This Book

Chapters						
Introducing project management and introducing a strategic framework (Chapters 1 and 2)	Preliminary project planning (Chapter 3)	Intermediate project planning (Chapter 4)	Final project planning (Chapter 5)	Selecting the project management team and the best contractors and consultants (Chapters 6 and 7)	Enactment of advantageous agreements (Chapter 8)	Controlling the project execution (Chapter 9), and project closeout and beyond (Chapter 10)
Examples						
1.1 Managerial pushback in the design and construction of the University of Massachusetts Computer Science Center	3.1 Lack of timely post-war project planning in Iraq	4.1 Failings in internal control procedures in Port of Seattle construction contracts	5.1 Underestimating the design-build schedule for the University of Massachusetts Computer Science Center Project	6.1 Unqualified staff managing Iraq construction projects	8.1 How a GMP was not a GMP in the Belmont Learning Complex project	9.1 Results of inadequate monitoring and oversight of the Mount Hood public works project
2.1 Nontraditional financing in the Cranston, RI, wastewater treatment project	3.2 Correctly identifying the problem: the Town of Harvard library project	4.2 Contract administration and project management on the Boston Harbor and Big Dig projects	5.2 Estimating software technology costs in satellite systems	6.2 Unintended consequences in using contractors to manage satellite development projects	8.2 Inappropriate allocation of risk in the NESWC contracts	9.2 What sank the *Thresher?*

3.3 Incorrectly identifying post-war problems in Iraq	3.4 Faulty presumptions and the NESWC project	3.5 Noncompliance with rules in the Mount Hood public works project	3.6 Optimistic cost projections in the Future Imagery Architecture project
4.3 Vague technical specifications lead to major contract cost increases at the Port of Seattle	4.4 Unclear specifications in the Lynn water and sewer privatization project	4.5 KBR IDIQ contracts are subject to cost overruns in Iraq	4.6 Risks imposed by a performance specification in the University of Massachusetts Computer Science Center project
5.3 Failure to obtain budget authorization for a scope expansion of the L.A. District Courthouse construction project	5.4 Using key planning steps in successfully managing a public sector software technology project		
6.3 Inappropriate accountability systems and the Challenger Space Shuttle disaster	7.1 Lack of accountability in contract procurement in Iraq	7.2 Potential conflicts of interest in Port of Seattle contracts	7.3 Limits to effective competition in the Lynn water and sewer privatization project
8.3 Lack of contractual guarantees in the Lynn water and sewer privatization project			
9.3 A failure to enforce contract penalty provisions in the University of Massachusetts Computer Science Center project	10.1 Consequences of inadequate operations monitoring in the Millennium Dome project	10.2 Consequences of deferred maintenance on the Longfellow Bridge	

Appendix 2

Master List of Tips for Success for Public Sector Project Managers

1. Project Planning: Getting the Concept Right

A. Correctly identifying the problem

> **TIP FOR SUCCESS:**
>
> In planning a public project, a manager must frame the problem or problems correctly that the project is meant to solve. This involves correctly identifying the goals the project is meant to achieve and the obstacles in the way of achieving them.

B. Questioning presumptions

TIP FOR SUCCESS:

Project managers should ask Neustadt and May's two questions about the options they are considering for public projects:

1. What are the presumptions behind the pros and cons for the options we're considering?
2. What experience, if any, validates those presumptions?

C. Understanding the project context and stakeholders

TIP FOR SUCCESS:

A key part of the planning process is understanding who the project stakeholders are and how to structure a positive relationship with them.

D. Developing realistic preliminary project cost and risk estimates

TIP FOR SUCCESS:

Using analogy-based or parametric cost estimating techniques are relatively simple ways at the outset of projects to derive unbiased estimates of their likely costs.

2. Developing and Refining Project Planning (internal controls and project specifications)

A. *Establishing the right project internal control structure*

TIP FOR SUCCESS:

GAO's key aspects of internal control are:

- Create a working environment that stresses ethics and competence
- Identify all project risks
- Establish controls over management procedures
- Establish controls over information systems
- Ensure a management system that allows for a free flow of information
- Monitor the internal control system periodically

B. *Two important project control activities*

TIP FOR SUCCESS:

Public-sector project managers should:

- Maintain adequate and proper project documentation
- Keep contract administration duties separate from day-to-day project management duties

C. *Developing clear project specifications*

TIPS FOR SUCCESS:

- Specifications define the project.
- Specifications should be clear and precise.

D. *Specifications and alternative project delivery methods*

TIP FOR SUCCESS:

Construction projects using delivery methods in which the design and specifications are not complete can pose an increased risk of cost increases.

E. *Performance versus design specifications*

TIP FOR SUCCESS:

A mix of performance and design specifications is often used in complex public projects. Disputes can arise if performance specifications, in particular, are unclear.

3. Finalizing Project Planning (schedule and cost estimation)

A. *Developing the project schedule*

TIPS FOR SUCCESS:

- The project schedule becomes more fully developed as the project design is refined.
- The public-sector project manager should develop a "macro-schedule" that stresses strategic goals and objectives.
- The contractor's schedule covers all construction or project work activities.

B. Scheduling the project work

TIPS FOR SUCCESS:

Effective project scheduling involves:

1. Developing a project Work Breakdown Structure to determine all work activities.
2. Developing a logic diagram to determine activity durations.
3. Determining the schedule's "critical path."

C. Refining the cost estimate

TIPS FOR SUCCESS:

- The degree of refinement of project cost projections depends on the level of completeness of the plans and specifications.
- Just as each element of the Work Breakdown Schedule is used to develop the project schedule, each element of the WBS is used to compute a project cost estimate.

D. Refining risk assessments

TIPS FOR SUCCESS:

- In assessing project risks, the project management team should brainstorm over everything that might possibly go wrong on the project.
- Sensitivity and uncertainty analyses can help cost estimators establish a range of probabilities for the project's potential cost, based on known risks.

E. Developing realistic presumptions behind cost and risk estimates

TIPS FOR SUCCESS:

- The project management team should continually question presumptions that underlie risk and cost estimates.
- Realistic cost estimates, budgets, and affordability assessments are key to preventing a vicious cycle leading to schedule delays and cost overruns.
- Project stakeholders should be kept informed of project risks and changes in assumptions underlying project costs.

4. Building the Project Team

A. Establishing a committed and cohesive team

TIPS FOR SUCCESS:

Project managers can establish team cohesion and commitment by:

- Communicating clearly with the team members at the outset about the nature and importance of the project.
- Establishing open lines of communication throughout the project.
- Addressing the dual-loyalty problem in matrix organizations.
- Holding regular and productive meetings with the staff.

B. Ensuring the team personnel are qualified

TIPS FOR SUCCESS:

- Public sector project managers must recruit qualified personnel to their management teams and should *not* make hiring decisions based on political connections or friendships.
- Project management teams must have sufficient numbers of staff to manage projects effectively.

C. *The need for clear lines of authority and communication*

TIPS FOR SUCCESS:

■ Creating a team responsibility chart can help project managers assign project responsibilities clearly and effectively.
■ If contractor personnel are recruited to help public sector staff manage projects, their roles and responsibilities must be clearly defined.

D. *Ensuring an appropriate managerial accountability system*

TIPS FOR SUCCESS:

■ Different accountability systems in public agencies result in differing levels of control exerted by project managers over their teams.
■ Accountability systems can range from hierarchical to flexible and "organic."
■ The level of managerial control over project teams should be appropriately aligned with institutional and other forces outside the agency.
■ Managers can overcome alignment problems by ensuring adequate and open lines of communication and by effectively communicating the project vision to their teams.

E. *Coaching the project team on legal requirements and ethical practices*

TIP FOR SUCCESS:

Project managers must ensure that team members are trained or at least briefed on legal requirements and ethical practices relevant to their project responsibilities.

F. Motivating the project team

TIPS FOR SUCCESS:

- Team motivation can be enhanced by positive feedback and regular and productive project meetings.
- An organizational culture of openness, transparency, and trust can motivate project teams to work efficiently and effectively.

5. Procuring Contractors and Consultants

A. Successful public procurement characteristic: Transparency

TIP FOR SUCCESS:

Transparency in contract procurement involves "clear and written policies and procedures that are understood by all sources," according to the GAO.

B. Successful public procurement characteristic: Accountability

TIPS FOR SUCCESS:

- Accountability in public procurement involves "clear lines of procurement responsibility, authority, and oversight," according to the GAO.
- The GAO recommends that at the state and local levels, a chief procurement officer should have "full-time, sole, and direct responsibility" for procurement programs.

C. *Successful public procurement characteristic: Integrity*

TIPS FOR SUCCESS:

- Integrity in public procurement, according to the GAO, leads to public confidence.
- Public confidence is "earned by avoiding any conflict of interest, maintaining impartiality, avoiding preferential treatment for any group or individual, and dealing fairly and in good faith with all parties."

D. *Successful public procurement characteristic: Competition*

TIP FOR SUCCESS:

The GAO describes competitive characteristics of a successful public procurement system as involving "specifications that do not favor a single source and solicitations widely publicized to benefit from the efficiencies of the commercial marketplace."

E. *Successful public procurement characteristic: Knowledge and information management*

TIP FOR SUCCESS:

Successful public procurement requires the use of "technologies and tools that help managers and staff make well-informed acquisitions decisions," according to the GAO.

F. Successful procurement characteristic: Due diligence in selecting contractors and consultants

TIP FOR SUCCESS:

Project managers should consult with their legal staffs about requirements for evaluating contractors and consultants prior to selecting them for project work, and should ensure that relevant past performance information is available to them.

6. Enacting Advantageous Agreements

A. The contract pricing structure

TIPS FOR SUCCESS:

Public sector project managers should be aware of the different risk allocations in different contract pricing structures. For instance, under:

- Firm-fixed-price contracts: The contractor bears most of the risk of cost increases.
- Cost-reimbursement contracts: The government accepts risks of increased costs.

B. Contract provisions and project risk

TIPS FOR SUCCESS:

- Public sector managers should pay careful attention to the potential risk of contract provisions involving differing site conditions, changes in law, contract term length, indemnification, termination, and other matters.
- Managers should seek a legal review of all contract provisions with regard to their risk allocation potential.

C. Clear scopes of work

TIPS FOR SUCCESS:

- The contract should include a scope of work that is clearly stated.
- Public agencies should carefully review contractor-drafted scopes of work.

7. Controlling Public Projects

A. Measuring project progress

TIP FOR SUCCESS:

An active role by public sector managers in monitoring their projects during the execution or production stage is essential in ensuring the continuing success of those projects.

B. Updating project records

TIP FOR SUCCESS:

Key records that managers should consult during the project execution stage are those that allow comparisons of the rate of the contract's completion to the contractor's expenditure rate.

C. Analyzing the project data

TIP FOR SUCCESS:

Project monitoring systems that measure both cost and schedule data are superior to systems that measure only cost or schedule data alone.

D. Evaluating and correcting project problems

TIP FOR SUCCESS:

A systematic process is best for dealing with problems that arise during the project execution stage. One process, known as the Plan-Do-Study-Act cycle, involves:

1. Developing a plan to deal with the problem;
2. Implementing the plan;
3. Studying the results; and either
4. Adopting the new procedure or changing the plan.

E. Focusing on quality in projects

TIP FOR SUCCESS:

An emphasis on quality assurance and control in undertaking projects can reduce costs and help reach schedule goals.

F. Controlling cost growth and cost overruns

TIPS FOR SUCCESS:

Project managers must be vigilant about change orders submitted by contractors. They should make sure:

- The contract specifies the pricing for all change-order work.
- The contractor documents all costs associated with change orders when submitting change-order requests.

8. Project Closeout and Beyond

A. *Final steps in the closeout process*

TIP FOR SUCCESS:

In construction projects, public sector managers should attend the final punch-list walk-through. Completion of the punch-list items can make a substantial difference to users of the new facility.

B. *The project or program operational stage*

TIP FOR SUCCESS:

Active monitoring of a project's costs and quality during its operational stage can be just as important as active monitoring during its construction or production stage.

C. *Maintaining public projects over the long term*

TIP FOR SUCCESS:

Planning for, adequately financing, and undertaking long-term maintenance of public assets will prevent the need for repairs that are likely to cost many times as much as the maintenance costs themselves.

Appendix 3

Websites of Interest to Public Sector Project Managers

American Academy of Certified Public Managers

http://www.cpmacademy.org/

A professional association of public sector managers. To be eligible for membership, an individual must have earned the designation of Certified Public Manager (CPM) through a management program accredited by the National Certified Public Manager Consortium.

The American Association of State Highway and Transportation Officials (AASHTO)

http://www.transportation.org/

A nonprofit organization representing highway and transportation departments in the United States.

American Management Association

http://www.amanet.org/

A professional association that offers seminars, Webcasts and podcasts, conferences, business books, and research on business management.

American National Standards Institute (ANSI)

http://www.ansi.org/

A nonprofit organization that oversees the creation, promulgation, and use of standards and guidelines in fields including construction equipment, project management, energy distribution, acoustical devices, and many more.

American Public Works Association

http://www.apwa.net/

An international educational and professional association of public agencies, private sector companies, and individuals "dedicated to providing high quality public works goods and services."

American Society for Quality

http://www.asq.org/

A professional association that advances quality improvement to improve business results.

The Association for the Advancement of Cost Engineering (AACE International)

http://www.aacei.org/

A professional society for cost estimators, cost engineers, schedulers project managers, and project control specialists.

Building Design and Construction

http://www.bdcnetwork.com/

Website and monthly journal with news about the design and construction industry.

Committee of Sponsoring Organizations of the Treadway Commission (COSO)

http://www.coso.org/
Private sector organization providing guidance on organizational governance, business ethics, internal control, risk management, fraud, and financial reporting.

Construction Management Association of America

http://cmaanet.org/AR_Federal_Agent.php
A professional organization dedicated to the interests of professional construction and program management.

The Construction Specifications Institute

http://www.csinet.org/s_csi/index.asp
A national organization dedicated to creating standards and formats to improve construction plans and specifications and project delivery.

Defense Contract Audit Agency

http://www.dcaa.mil/
A federal agency that performs all contract audits for the Department of Defense and provides accounting and contract advisory services to DoD agencies responsible for procurement and contract administration.

Defense Contract Management Agency

http://www.dcma.mil/
A federal agency that helps Department of Defense agencies procure supplies and services, and write and manage contracts.

Federal Acquisition Institute

http://www.fai.gov/index.asp
Provides training and research in support of the federal procurement workforce.

Federal Acquisition Regulation Homepage

http://www.arnet.gov/far/
  Website providing access to, and information about, the Federal Acquisition Regulation.

Federal Business Opportunities

https://www.fbo.gov/index?cck=1&au=&ck=
  A federal Website marketplace for government purchases of supplies and services.

International Cost Engineering Council

http://www.icoste.org/index.htm
  An international professional organization promoting the science and art of cost engineering and project management.

The International Council on Systems Engineering

http://www.incose.org/
  A professional organization dedicated to advancing the practice of systems engineering in industry, academia, and government.

The International Journal of Project Management

http://www.elsevier.com/wps/find/journaldescription.cws_home/30435/description#description

The National Center for Public Productivity

http://andromeda.rutgers.edu/~ncpp/ncpp.html
  A research and public service organization devoted to improving productivity in the public sector. The Center publishes the journal *Public Performance and Management Review.*

The National Certified Public Manager Consortium

http://www.txstate.edu/cpmconsortium/
  Provides and monitors accreditation standards for Certified Public Managers.

Past Performance Information Retrieval System

https://www.ppirs.gov/
  A central repository for evaluations of performance of federal government contractors.

Project Management Institute

http://www.pmi.org/Pages/default.aspx
  A leading membership association for the project management profession. Primarily private sector oriented.

The Public Manager

http://www.thepublicmanager.org/
  A quarterly journal published by The Bureaucrat, Inc., a not-for-profit organization devoted to furthering knowledge and best practice at all levels of government.

Public Works Management and Policy

http://pwm.sagepub.com/
  A quarterly journal dedicated to the infrastructure profession.

R.S. Means

http://www.rsmeans.com/about/index.asp
  A private organization that provides building construction cost information to project owners, architects, engineers, and contractors.

The Society of Cost Estimating and Analysis

http://www.sceaonline.net/
A professional association dedicated to improving cost estimation in government and industry.

The United States Government Accountability Office

http://www.gao.gov/
A nonpartisan congressional agency that investigates how the federal government spends public funds.

The University of Wisconsin Certified Public Manager Program

http://www.dcs.wisc.edu/pda/cpm/current.htm

References

Altshuler, Alan, and David Luberoff. 2003. *Mega-Projects*. Washington, DC: Brookings Institution Press.

American Society for Quality. 1999. *The Certified Quality Manager Handbook*. Milwaukee: ASQ Quality Press.

Anderson, Susan. The School That Wasn't. *The Nation*. June 5, 2000. http://www.thenation.com/doc/2000065/anderson

Anechiarico, Frank, and James B. Jacobs. 1996. *The Pursuit of Absolute Integrity: How Corruption Control Makes Government Ineffective*. Chicago: University of Chicago Press.

Argyris, Chris. 1990. *Overcoming Organizational Defenses: Facilitating Organizational Learning*. Englewood Cliffs, NJ: Prentice Hall.

Ashkenas, R.N., et al. 2002. *The Boundaryless Organization: Breaking the Chains of Organization Structure*. San Francisco: Jossey-Bass.

Associated Press. 2001. South Boston Convention Center Faces Huge Cost Overruns. *Portsmouth (NH) Herald. Seacoast Online*. January 9, 2001. http://archive.seacoastonline.com/2001news/1_9_sb2.htm

Associated Press. 2008. Delays in Bidding May Jeopardize $35 Billion Pentagon Contract. *Boston Globe*. August 27, 2008. http://www.boston.com/business/articles/2008/08/27/delays_in_bidding_may_jeopardize_35b_pentagon_contract?mode=PF

Auditing Standards Board. American Institute of Certified Public Accountants. *Statement on Auditing Standards No. 99: Consideration of Fraud in a Financial Statement Audit*. http://www.aicpa.org/download/members/div/auditstd/AU-00316.PDF

Auger, Deborah A. 1999. Privatization, Contracting, and the States: Lessons from State Government Experience. *Public Productivity and Management Review*. 22:4:435–454.

Austin, Robert D. 1996. *Measuring and Managing Performance in Organizations*. New York: Dorset House Publishing.

Baniszewski, John. *Government Contracting: A Project Manager's Perspective*. PowerPoint presentation. U.S. Department of Energy. Available online at http://management.energy.gov/documents/ProjectManagementContractingOfficers.pdf

Behn, Robert D. 2001. *Rethinking Democratic Accountability*. Washington, DC: Brookings Institution Press.

Bennis, Warren, and Joan Goldsmith. 2003. *Learning to Lead: A Workbook on Becoming a Leader*. New York: Basic Books.

Bloomfield, Pamela. 2006. The Challenging Business of Long-Term Public-Private Partnerships: Reflections on Local Experience. *Public Administration Review* 66:3: 400–411.

Blume, Howard. 2008. Belmont school to reopen with new face, new name. *Los Angeles Times.* August 10, 2008. http://articles.latimes.com/2008/aug/10/local/me-belmont10

Bourn, Sir John. Comptroller and Auditor General, British National Audit Office. 2000. *The Millennium Dome.* November 9, 2000. http://www.nao.org.uk/system_pages/idoc.ashx?docid=ff541347-f82b-4dad-8175-9ce8fb4a02e3&version=-1

Bowman, J.S. (ed.). 1994. *Ethical Frontiers in Public Management: Seeking New Strategies for Resolving Ethical Dilemmas.* San Francisco: Jossey-Bass.

Bramble, Barry B., and Michael T. Callahan. 1999. *Construction Delay Claims,* 3rd edition. Aspen Law Publishers Online.

Bremer, L. Paul. 2006. *My Year in Iraq: The Struggle to Build a Future of Hope.* New York: Threshold Editions.

Brunner, Jim and Bob Young. 2008. Possible Fraud at Port Focus of Criminal Probe. *Seattle Times.* January 8, 2008. http://seattletimes.nwsource.com/html/localnews/2004113088_port08m.html

Bryane, Michael. 2003. Implementing Ethics Programs: The Role of Public Sector Project Design and Process Management. *International Journal of Politics and Ethics* 2:4.

Bryson, John M. 2004. *Strategic Planning for Public and Nonprofit Organizations,* 3rd edition. San Francisco: Jossey-Bass.

Burke, Rory. 2003. *Project Management Planning and Control Techniques*, 4th edition. UK: Burke Publishing.

Burman, Allan V. 2008. *Post Award Contract Management: Who's Minding the Store?* IBM Center for the Business of Government. http://www.businessofgovernment.org/pdfs/PostAwardContractManagement.pdf

Business Wire. *Belmont Firms File for Binding Arbitration.* April 19, 2000. The Gale Group, Inc. http://www.allbusiness.com/legal/labor-employment-law-alternative-dispute-resolution/6468009-1.html

Chandrasekaran, Rajiv. 2006. *Imperial Life in the Emerald City: Inside Iraq's Green Zone.* New York: Vintage Books.

Cibinic, John, Jr., Ralph C. Nash, Jr., and James F. Nagle. 2006. *Administration of Government Contracts,* 4th edition. Chicago: CCH, Inc.

City of Cranston, Rhode Island. Online information document. Available at http://www.cranstonri.com/pdf/fins_with_seal.pdf

Cliff, Lisa and Judy Steele. 2007. Fulfilling the Promise of E-Gov Initiatives. *The Public Manager* 36.4. Winter 2007.

Cohan, John Alan. 2002. "I Didn't Know" and "I Was Only Doing My Job": Has Corporate Governance Careened Out of Control? A Case Study of Enron's Information Myopia. *Journal of Business Ethics* 40: 275–299.

Cohen, Steven and William Eimicke. 2008. *The Responsible Contract Manager: Protecting the Public Interest in an Outsourced World.* Washington, DC: Georgetown University Press.

CommonWealth (magazine). 2006. *Learning from the Big Dig: What lessons can be drawn from an engineering triumph now marked by tragedy? We asked eight expert observers for answers.* Fall 2006.

CommonWealth (magazine). 2006. *Second-guesswork: Fred Salvucci insists that the Big Dig was the right project, just not done right.* Fall 2006.

Commonwealth of Massachusetts, Division of Capital Asset Management. Guidelines for the Preparation of Studies for Building Projects for Commonwealth of Massachusetts State Agencies, Building Authorities, Counties. Revision October 2000. http://www.mass.gov/cam/dlforms/STUguide.pdf

Commonwealth of Massachusetts, Division of Capital Asset Management. *Owners' Project Manager Guidelines.* December 2004. http://www.mass.gov/cam/Creform/Own_PM_Guide.pdf

Commonwealth of Massachusetts Division of Capital Asset Management. 2005. *Frequently Asked Questions Regarding the New Public Construction Reform Law,* April 21. http://www.mass.gov/cam/Creform/CRLFAQS.pdf

Commonwealth of Massachusetts, Office of the Inspector General. 1997. *The North East Solid Waste Committee Project: Planning and Development of a Public-Private Partnership.*

Commonwealth of Massachusetts, Office of the Inspector General. 1997. *Massachusetts Certified Public Purchasing Official General Seminar handbook.*

Commonwealth of Massachusetts, Office of the Inspector General. 1999. *A Management Review of Commonwealth Charter Schools.*

Commonwealth of Massachusetts, Office of the Inspector General. 2000. *Sabis International Charter School: Management Issues and Recommendations.*

Commonwealth of Massachusetts, Office of the Inspector General. 2001. *Privatization of Wastewater Facilities in Lynn, Massachusetts.*

Commonwealth of Massachusetts, Office of the Inspector General. 2001. *A Report on the Design and Construction of the University of Massachusetts Computer Science Center.*

Commonwealth of Massachusetts, Office of the Inspector General. 2002. *Review of the Mount Hood Public Works Project in Melrose.*

Commonwealth of Massachusetts, Office of the Inspector General. 2003. *Analysis of Bechtel/Parsons Brinckerhoff's Reply to* The Boston Globe's *Investigative News Series Concerning the Big Dig.* http://www.mass.gov/ig/publ/catglbrp.pdf

Commonwealth of Massachusetts, Office of the Inspector General. 2005. *Designing and Constructing Public Facilities: Legal Requirements, Recommended Practices, Sources of Assistance.* http://www.mass.gov/ig/publ/dcmanual.pdf

Construction Specifications Institute. *MasterFormat: 2004 Edition Numbers and Titles.* http://www.csinet.org/s_csi/docs/9400/9361.pdf

Cooley, Steve. 2003. Final Investigative Report: Los Angeles Unified School District Belmont Learning Complex. Belmont Task Force, Los Angeles District Attorney's Office. March 2003. http://da.co.la.ca.us/pdf/BLC_Final_Report.pdf

Curry, William. 2008. *Contracting for Services in State and Local Government Agencies.* Boca Raton, FL. Taylor & Francis.

Deming, W. Edwards. 1986. *Out of the Crisis.* Cambridge: MIT Press.

Denett, Paul A., Administrator, Office of Management and Budget. "Enhancing Competition in Federal Acquisition." Memorandum for Chief Acquisition Officers and Senior Procurement Executives. May 31, 2007.

Department of Defense. *Integrated Master Plan and Integrated Master Schedule Preparation and Use Guide.* October 21, 2005.

Dodd, Michael and J. Duncan Findlay, Editors. 2006. *State-by-State Guide to Construction Contracts and Claims.* New York: Aspen Publishers.

Donahue, John D. 1989. *The Privatization Decision: Public Ends, Private Means.* New York: Basic Books.

Edkins, Andrew J., and Hedley J. Smyth. Contractual Management in PPP Projects: Evaluation of Legal Versus Relational Contracting for Service Delivery. *Journal of Professional Issues in Engineering Education and Practice.* January 2006.

Farrell, Steven et al. *Recommended Practices for Hiring Owner's Project Managers: A Guide for Municipal Construction Projects, Edition 1.* Massachusetts Municipal Association and

AGC of Massachusetts. http://www.agcmass.org/uploadedFiles/Library/OPM%20 11-13-062.pdf

Federal Construction Council, Consulting Committee on Cost Engineering. 1993. *Experiences of Federal Agencies with the Design-Build Approach to Construction.* National Academy Press, Washington, DC.

Florida State University. *Leadership for Florida's Future: The Florida Certified Public Manager Program.* Program Guide/Handbook. June 2006.

Flyvbjerg, Bent. 2005. Policy and Planning for Large Infrastructure Projects: Problems, Causes, Cures. World Bank Policy Research Working Paper No. 3781.

Flyvbjerg, Bent, Mette Holm, and Soren Buhl. Summer 2002. Underestimating Costs in Public Works Projects: Error or Lie? *Journal of the American Planning Association.* http://pqasb.pqarchiver.com/planning/access/128776261.html?dids=128776261:128 776261:128776261:128776261&FMT=ABS&FMTS=ABS:FT:TG:PAGE&type=cu rrent&date=Summer+2002&author=Bent+Flyvbjerg&pub=American+Planning+Ass ociation.+Journal+of+the+American+Planning+Association&edition=&startpage=27 9&desc=Underestimating+costs+in+public+works+projects%3A++Error+or+lie%3F

Food and Water Watch. 2009. *Money Down the Drain: How Private Control of Water Wastes Public Resources.* http://www.scribd.com/doc/12765412/Money-Down-the-Drain

Forrer, John, James Edwin Kee, and Zhibin Zhang. 2002. Private Finance Initiative: A Better Public-Private Partnership? *Public Manager* 31(2): 43–47.

Fox, Charles J. 1996. Reinventing Government as Postmodern Symbolic Politics. *Public Administration Review* 56:3:256–262.

Frame, J. Davidson. 1994. *The New Project Management.* San Francisco: Jossey-Bass.

FRONTLINE. 2006. *The Lost Year in Iraq: Key Controversies and Missteps of the Postwar Period.* http://www.pbs.org/wgbh/pages/frontline/yeariniraq/analysis/fuel.html

Garafalo, Charles. 1999. *Ethics in the Public Service: The Moral Mind at Work.* Washington, DC: Georgetown University Press.

Garrett, Gregory A., and Rene G. Rendon. 2007. *U.S. Military Program Management: Lessons Learned and Best Practices.* Vienna, VA: Management Concepts, Inc.

Gavin, Robert. 2008. Nine Deaths at Perini Jobs Stir Questions. *Boston Globe.* September 10, 2008.

Gay, Sean. 2008. Commentary: Examining Fraud and Public Contracting. *Daily Journal of Commerce.* AllBusiness.com, Inc. June 20, 2008. Available online at http://www.allbusiness.com/company-activities-management/contracts-bids/11464093-1.html

Geiger, Dale R. 2001. Avoiding Pitfalls in Managerial Costing Implementation. *Journal of Government Financial Management* 50:1:27–34.

Giglio, Joseph M., and Charles Chieppo. 2008. Privatization That Protects Taxpayer Interests. *Boston Globe.* September 10, 2008.

Gilmour, Robert S., and Laura S. Jensen. 1998. Reinventing Government Accountability: Public Functions, Privatization, and the Meaning of State Action, *Public Administration Review* 58(3): 247–258.

Glanz, James, C.J. Chivers, and William K. Rashbaum. 2009. Inquiry on Graft in Iraq Focuses on U.S. Officers. *New York Times.* February 15, 2009. http://www.nytimes.com/2009/02/15/world/middleeast/15iraq.html

Gleick, Peter H., Gary Wolff, Elizabeth L. Chalecki, and Rachel Reyes. 2002. *The New Economy of Water: The Risks and Benefits of Globalization and Privatization of Fresh Water.* Oakland, CA: Pacific Institute for Studies in Development. http://www.pacinst.org/reports/new_economy_of_water/new_economy_of_water.pdf

Goldhagen, Sarah Williams. 2007. American Collapse: Is it already too late for America's infrastructure? *The New Republic.* August 27, 2007. Updated December 25, 2008. http://www.tnr.com/politics/story.html?id=9ead077c-1299-4f58-82d5-f3a91bfe19c4

Goldstein, Mark L. 1992. *America's Hollow Government: How Washington Has Failed the People.* Homewood, IL: Business One Irwin

Golembeski, Dean J. 1997. What Sank the *Thresher? Invention & Technology.* Summer 1997.

Goodsell, Charles T. 2004. *The Case for Bureaucracy: A Public Administration Polemic.* Washington, DC: CQ Press

Graham, Robert J., and Randall L. Englund. 1997. *Creating an Environment for Successful Projects.* San Francisco: Jossey-Bass.

The Guardian. July 7, 2005. *So, Mr. Bremer, where did all the money go?* http://www.guardian.co.uk/world/2005/jul/07/iraq.features11

Hall, Elaine M. *Managing Risk: Methods for Software Systems Development.* Boston: Addison Wesley.

Heisse, John R. (ed.) 1997. *The Design/Build Process: A Guide to Licensing and Procurement Requirements in the Fifty States and Canada.* American Bar Association.

Horman, Michael J., and Russell Kenley. 2005. Quantifying Levels of Wasted Time in Construction with Meta-Analysis. *Journal of Construction Engineering and Management* 131(1): 52–61.

Hulett, David T. *Schedule Risk Analysis Simplified.* Hulett & Associates. Website article available at http://www.projectrisk.com/Welcome/Schedule_Risk_Analysis_Simplif/schedule_risk_analysis_simplif.html.

Hulett, David T. *Advanced Quantitative Schedule Risk Analysis.* Hulett & Associates. Website article available at http://www.projectrisk.com/Welcome/White_Papers/1SchedRiskAnal.pdf

Jackson, Barbara J. 2004. *Construction Management Jump Start.* San Francisco: Sybex, Inc.

Kamarc, Elaine. 2007. *The End of Government…As We Know It: Making Public Policy Work.* Boulder, CO: Lynne Rienner Publishers, Inc.

Kassel, David S. 2008. Performance, Accountability, and the Debate over Rules. *Public Administration Review* 68:2: 241–252.

Kearns, Kevin P. 1996. *Managing for Accountability: Preserving the Public Trust in Public and Nonprofit Organizations.* San Francisco: Jossey-Bass, Inc.

Kelman, Steven. 1990. *Procurement and Public Management: The Fear of Discretion and the Quality of Government Performance.* Washington, DC: AEI Press.

Kepner-Tregoe. *Reducing Project Complexity.* Kepner-Tregoe, Inc. Website article available at http://www.kepner-tregoe.com/NewsArtPub/PubOverview-Position.cfm#

Kettl, Donald F. 1993. *Sharing Power: Public Governance and Private Markets.* Washington, DC: Brookings Institution Press.

Klein, Naomi. 2007. *The Shock Doctrine: The Rise of Disaster Capitalism.* New York: Metropolitan Books.

Kuehn, Ursula. 2006. *Integrated Cost and Schedule Control in Project Management.* West Sussex, UK: Kogan Page Publishers.

Kulish, Nicholas. 2006. Things Fall Apart: Fixing America's Crumbling Infrastructure. *New York Times* August 23, 2006. http://select.nytimes.com/2006/08/23/opinion/23talking-points.html?_r=1

LaBrosse, Michelle. 2007. Project Management: Best Practices for the Public Sector (Column). *The Public Manager* 36:2:25

LePatner, Barry B. 2007. *Broken Buildings, Busted Budgets: How to Fix America's Trillion-Dollar Construction Industry.* Chicago: The University of Chicago Press.

Lewis, James P. 1998. *Team-Based Project Management.* New York: American Management Association.

Lewis, James P. 2007. *Fundamentals of Project Management,* 3rd edition. New York: American Management Association.

Lewis, Raphael, and Sean P. Murphy. Easy Pass: Why Bechtel Never Paid for Its Big Dig Mistakes. *Boston Globe.* February 9, 10, 11, 2003. http://www.boston.com/globe/metro/packages/bechtel/

Little, Richard G. 1999. Educating the Infrastructure Professional: A New Curriculum for a New Discipline. *Public Works Management & Policy* 4:2: 93–99.

Lockyer, Keith. 1992. *Critical Path Analysis and Other Project Management Techniques.* Trans-Atlantic Publications.

Loulakis, Michael C. (ed.) 2003 *Design-Build for the Public Sector.* Aspen.

March, James, and Herbert Simon. 1993. *Organizations,* 2nd edition. Cambridge: Blackwell Publishers.

Marcuson, William F. 2008. Fixing America's Crumbling Infrastructure: A Call to Action for All. *Public Works Management & Policy,* 12: 473–475.

Massachusetts Water Resources Authority. *The Boston Harbor Project: An Environmental Success Story.* Website information on the Boston Harbor cleanup project. http://www.mwra.com/01news/2008/bhpenvironentalsuccess/bhpenvsuccess.htm

McKay, Mike, Krista Bush, John Keller et al. 2008. *Report of The Special Investigative Team* [Port of Seattle audit case]. December 3, 2008. McKay Chadwell, PLLC.

Miller, John B. 2000. *Principles of Public and Private Infrastructure Delivery.* Cambridge, MA: Massachusetts Institute of Technology

Moe, Ronald C., and Robert S. Gilmour. 1995. Rediscovering Principles of Public Administration: The Neglected Foundation of Public Law, *Public Administration Review* 55(2): 135–146.

Moore, Adrian. 2000. Long-Term Partnerships in Water and Sewer Utilities: Economic, Political, and Policy Implications: *Journal of Contemporary Water Research and Education* 117: 21–26.

Morgan, Gareth. 2006. *Images of Organization.* Thousand Oaks, CA: Sage Publications, Inc.

Murphy, Sean P. Big Dig's Red Ink Engulfs State. *The Boston Globe.* July 17, 2008 http://www.boston.com/news/traffic/bigdig/articles/2008/07/17/big_digs_red_ink_engulfs_state?mode=PF

National Transportation Safety Board. 2007. *Ceiling Collapse in the Interstate 90 Connector Tunnel, Boston, MA July 10, 2006: Accident Report.* NTSB/HAR- 07/02 PB2007-916203.

Neustadt, Richard, E., and Ernest R. May. 1986. *Thinking in Time: The Uses of History for Decision Makers.* New York: The Free Press.

Office of Management and Budget. 2006. *Capital Programming Guide.* Supplement to Circular A-11, Part 7.

Office of Management and Budget. *Circular A-76. Performance of Commercial Activities.*

Office of Management and Budget. *Circular A-123. Management's Responsibility for Internal Control.*

Office of Management and Budget. *Circular A-136. Financial Reporting Requirements.*

Office of the Special Inspector General for Iraq Reconstruction. 2006. *Review of the U.S. Agency for International Development's Management of the Basrah Children's Hospital Project.* SIGIR-06-026.

Office of the Special Inspector General for Iraq Reconstruction. 2006. *Iraq Reconstruction: Lessons in Contracting and Procurement.*

Office of the Special Inspector General for Iraq Reconstruction. 2006. *Review of the Use of Definitization Requirements for Contracts Supporting Reconstruction in Iraq.* SIGIR-06-019.

Office of the Special Inspector General for Iraq Reconstruction. 2007. *Iraq Reconstruction: Lessons in Program and Project Management.*

Osborne, David, and Ted Gaebler. 1992. *Reinventing Government: How the Entrepreneurial is Transforming the Public Sector.* Reading, MA: Addison-Wesley.

Ouchi, W.A. 1981. *Theory Z: How American Business Can Meet the Japanese Challenge.* Reading, MA: Addison-Wesley.

Pacific Consulting Group. Report for the City of Seattle on SFMS Redevelopment Project. June 1997.

Palmer, Thomas C. 2001. Cerasoli Charges Big Dig Coverup. *Boston Globe.* March 21, 2001. http://boston.com/globe/metro/packages/bechtel/archives/032101.htm

Peters, Thomas J., and Robert H. Waterman. 2004. *In Search of Excellence: Lessons from America's Best-Run Companies.* New York: HarperCollins Publishers.

Piotrowski, S., and Rosenbloom, D. Nonmission-Based Values in Results-Oriented Public Management: The Case of Freedom of Information. *Public Administration Review* 62:6: 643–657.

Powers, E. Michael. 2006. New Marching Orders: Military contractors faced a host of new procurement and delivery changes as bases prepare for worldwide troop deployment. *Constructor Magazine.* November/December 2006. McGraw-Hill Construction. http://constructor.construction.com/coverstories/archives/2006-11.asp

Prager, Jonas. 1994. Contracting Out Government Services: Lessons from the Private Sector. *Public Administration Review* 54:2: 176–184.

Pratt, John W., and Richard J. Zeckhauser. 1991. *Principals and Agents: The Structure of Business.* Boston: Harvard Business School Press.

Primack, Phil. Meeting market. *CommonWealth* magazine. Fall 2008.

Project Management Institute. 2004. *A Guide to the Project Management Body of Knowledge,* 3rd edition. Newtown Square, PA: Project Management Institute.

Project on Government Oversight. 2003. *Iraq Reconstruction Contracting Abuses.* October 27, 2003 Press Release http://www.commondreams.org/news2003/1027-07.htm

RAND Corporation. 2008. *After Saddam: Prewar Planning and the Occupation of Iraq.*

Rehfuss, John A. 1989. *Contracting Out in Government.* San Francisco: Jossey-Bass Publishers.

Ritz, George J. 1994. *Total Construction Project Management.* New York: McGraw-Hill.

Romzek, Barbara S., and Jocelyn M. Johnston. 2005. State Social Services Contracting: Exploring the Determinants of Effective Contract Accountability, *Public Administration Review* 65(4): 436–449.

Romzek, Barbara S., and Melvin J. Dubnick. 1987. Accountability in the Public Sector: Lessons from the Challenger Tragedy. *Public Administration Review* 47:3:227–238.

Rowe, Sandra. 2007. *Project Management for Small Projects.* West Sussex, UK: Kogan Page Publishers.

Rubin, Debra K. 2008. Bechtel, PB and Subs Sign $458-million Big-Dig Settlement. *ENR.Com.* January 23, 2008. http://enr.construction.com/news/finance/archives/080123c.asp

Savas, E.S. 2000. *Privatization and Public-Private Partnerships.* New York: Chatham House.

Schwartz, John and Matthew L. Wald. 2003. Final Shuttle Report Cites 'Broken Safety Culture' at NASA. *New York Times.* August 26, 2003.

Snyder, Cynthia. 2007. *Introduction to IT Project Management.* West Sussex, UK: Kogan Page Publishers.

Stamford Encyclopedia of Philosophy. *Contemporary Approaches to the Social Contract.* http://plato.stanford.edu/entries/contractarianism-contemporary/

State of Minnesota, Office of the Legislative Auditor. Greater Minnesota Corporation: Structure and Accountability. Summary. March 1991. http://www.auditor.leg.state.mn.us/Ped/1991/pe9105.htm

Talcott, Shasha. 2006. Convention Center Gets $24 Million Settlement: Project Design Team Faced Suit Over Roof, Heat and Cooling Woes. *Boston Globe.* July 22, 2006. http://www.hotel-online.com/News/PR2006_3rd/Jul06_BostonCC.html

Taubman, Philip. 2007. In Death of Spy Satellite Program: Lofty Plans and Unrealistic Bids. *New York Times.* November 11, 2007. http://www.nytimes.com/2007/11/11/washington/11satellite.html?hp#step1

Terry, Larry D. 2005. The Thinning of Administrative Institutions in the Hollow State. *Administration & Society* 37:4: 426–444.

Transit Cooperative Research Program. 2003. *Financing Capital Investment: A Primer for the Transit Practitioner.* Washington, DC.: Transportation Research Board. http://onlinepubs.trb.org/onlinepubs/tcrp/tcrp_rpt_89a.pdf

Tremaine, Robert L. 2008. Incentive Contracts: The Attributes That Matter Most in Driving Favorable Outcomes. *Defense Acquisition Review Journal* 15.3 (Dec. 2008): 216–238.

United States Court of Federal Claims. *Travelers Casualty and Surety of America v. The United States.* No. 02-584C & 03-1548C (Filed November 22, 2006).

United States Department of Justice. *Statement of Paul McNulty, Deputy Attorney General Before the Committee on Armed Services, United States Senate Concerning Boeing Company Global Settlement Agreement.* August 1, 2006. http://www.globalsecurity.org/military/library/congress/2006_hr/060801-mcnulty.pdf

United States General Accounting Office. 1999. *Standards for Internal Control in the Federal Government.* GAO/AIMD-00-21.3.1

United States General Accounting Office. *Internal Control Management and Evaluation Tool.* August 2001. GAO-01-1008G

United States General Accounting Office. 1997. *Privatization: Lessons Learned by State and Local Governments.* GAO-97-48.

United States General Accounting Office. 2003. *Federal Procurement: Spending and Workforce Trends.* GAO-03-443.

United States General Accounting Office. 2005. *Defense Acquisitions: DoD Has Paid Billions in Award and Incentive Fees Regardless of Acquisition Outcomes.* GAO-06-66.

United States Government Accountability Office. 2006. *Space Acquisitions: DoD Needs to Take More Action to Address Unrealistic Initial Cost Estimates of Space Systems.* GAO-07-96.

United States Government Accountability Office. 2006. *Comptroller General's Forum: Federal Acquisition Opportunities and Challenges in the 21st Century.* October 2006. GAO-07-45SP.

United States Government Accountability Office. 2007. *District of Columbia: Procurement System Needs Major Reform.* GAO-07-159.

United States Government Accountability Office. *Government Auditing Standards: July 2007 Revision.* GAO-07-731G.

United States Government Accountability Office. 2008. *Highway Public-Private Partnerships: More Rigorous Up-Front Analysis Could Better Secure Potential Benefits and Protect the Public Interest.* GAO-08-44.

United States Government Accountability Office. March 2008. *Stabilizing and Rebuilding Iraq, Actions Needed to Address Inadequate Accountability over U.S. Efforts and Investments.* Statement of David M. Walker. GAO-08-568T.

United States Government Accountability Office. June 2008. *Securing, Stabilizing, and Rebuilding Iraq: Progress Report.* GAO-08-837

United States Government Accountability Office. 2008. *Federal Courthouse Construction: Estimated Costs to House the L.A. District Court Have Tripled and There is No Consensus on How to Proceed.* GAO-08-889.

United States Government Accountability Office. 2009. *Defense Management: Actions Needed to Overcome Long-standing Challenges with Weapon Systems Acquisition and Service Contract Management.* GAO-09-362T.

United States Government Accountability Office. 2009. *GAO Cost Estimating and Assessment Guide: Best Practices for Developing and Managing Capital Program Costs.* GAO-09-3SP.

United States Government Accountability Office. 2009. *Federal Contractors: Better Performance Information Needed to Support Agency Contract Award Decisions.* GAO-09-374.

United States House of Representatives. Committee on Government Reform. June 27, 2005. *Halliburton's Questioned and Unsupported Costs in Iraq Exceed $1.4 billion.*

United States House of Representatives, Committee on Oversight and Government Reform. February 15, 2007. *Hearing on Iraq Reconstruction: An Overview. Preliminary Transcript.* http://oversight.house.gov/documents/20071114145606.pdf

United States Small Business Administration. Retrieval of Past Performance Evaluations guide. http://www.sba.gov/idc/groups/public/documents/co_denver/co_past_performance_eval.pdf

United States Supreme Court. *United States v. Spearin* (248 U.S. 132, 1918).

Washington State Auditor. 2007. *Performance Audit Report: Port of Seattle Construction Management.*

Washington State Auditor. 2007. *Port of Seattle audit working papers concerning main terminal roof replacement.*

Washington State, Joint Legislative Audit and Review Committee. 2005. *An Assessment of General Contractor/Construction Management Contracting Procedures.*

Wayne, Leslie. 2004. Air Force Asks for Broader Inquiry into Charges of Favoritism in Boeing Contracts. *The New York Times.* October 12, 2004. http://query.nytimes.com/gst/fullpage.html?res=9F06EEDB113BF931A25753C1A9629C8B63&sec=&spon=&pagewanted=all

Werkman, Janet, and David L. Westerling. 2000. Privatizing Municipal Water and Wastewater Systems: Promises and Pitfalls. *Public Works Management & Policy* 5:1:52–68.

Werkman, Janet, and Lisa Price. *Bid Protests under M.G.L. c. 30B: The Uniform Procurement Act.* Massachusetts Office of the Inspector General. http://www.mass.gov/ig/publ/c30bprot.htm.

Westerling, David, and Steve Poftak. 2007. *Our Legacy of Neglect: The Longfellow Bridge and the Cost of Deferred Maintenance.* Pioneer Institute White Paper, No. 40.

Wilson, James Q. 2000. *Bureaucracy: What Government Agencies Do and Why They Do It.* New York: Basic Books.

Wright, Donald P., and Timothy R. Reese. June 2008. *On Point II: Transition to the New Campaign: The United States Army in Operation Iraqi Freedom, May 2003-January 2005.* Fort Leavenworth, KS: Combat Studies Institute Press.

Yiftachel, Oren. 1998. Planning and Social Control: Exploring the Dark Side. *Journal of Planning Literature* 12:4:395–406.

Young, Ralph R. 2006. *Project Requirements: A Guide to Best Practices.* Vienna, VA: Management Concepts, Inc.

Young, Trevor L. 2007. *The Handbook of Project Management,* revised 2nd edition. London: Kogan Page Publishers.

Zepezauer, Mark, and Arthur Naimen. 1996. *Take the Rich off Welfare.* Odonian Press.

Index